IN THE RIVER THEY SWIM

To Kirk —
my first mentor
in economic
development.

Michael Fairbanks

IN THE RIVER
THEY SWIM

· · ·

ESSAYS FROM AROUND THE WORLD ON
ENTERPRISE SOLUTIONS TO POVERTY

· · ·

Edited by Michael Fairbanks, Marcela Escobari-Rose,
Malik Fal, and Elizabeth Hooper

With a Foreword by Dr. Rick Warren
Author of the global bestseller,
The Purpose Driven Life

TEMPLETON PRESS
WEST CONSHOHOCKEN, PENNSYLVANIA

Templeton Press
300 Conshohocken State Road, Suite 550
West Conshohocken, PA 19428
www.templetonpress.org

Designed and typeset by Gopa and Ted2, Inc.

Library of Congress Cataloging-in-Publication Data
In the river they swim : essays from around the world on enterprise
solutions to poverty / edited by Michael Fairbanks ... [et al.]; with a
foreword by Rick Warren.
p. cm.
Includes index.
ISBN-13: 978-1-59947-251-5 (hardbound : alk. paper)
ISBN-10: 1-59947-251-1 (hardbound : alk. paper) 1. Poverty—
Prevention. 2. Economic development—Social aspects.
3. Entrepreneurship—Social aspects. 4. Social responsibility of
business. 5. Servant leadership. I. Fairbanks, Michael, 1957-
II. Title: Enterprise solutions to poverty.

HC79.P6147 2008
339.4'6—dc22

2008040114
Printed in the United States of America

09 10 11 12 13 14   10 9 8 7 6 5 4 3 2 1

This book is dedicated to Sir John Templeton.

He used enterprises to improve the lives of millions of people around the world.

• • •

The poor can't sleep
Because their stomachs are empty.

The rich have full stomachs,
But they can't sleep
Because the poor are awake.

—COPPER MINER,
LUSAKA, ZAMBIA

• • •

Contents

· · ·

Fighting Poverty with Purpose

DR. RICK WARREN

• • •

POVERTY is a spiritual issue. It demeans dignity, shrinks the soul, wastes potential, and inflicts suffering on over half of our world's population.

Three billion people on our planet live in poverty. Over one billion live in extreme poverty, existing on less than one dollar a day. Does that matter to you? It matters to God. There are over two thousand verses in the Bible about the poor. That is how much God cares about the poor and how much he expects us to care, too.

The Bible says, "Do not withhold good from those who deserve it when it's in your power to help them" (Proverbs 3:27 [NLV]). The authors in this book, *In the River They Swim*, are finding creative ways to empower the poor to break out of the generational cycle of poverty. They have worked, cumulatively, for hundreds of person-years against the backdrop of globalization where, as you shall read, "everything mixes with everything else." In a world marked by scarcities of raw materials, disruptions of technology, and mass migrations of peoples and where the rich have gotten richer and the poor, especially in Africa, have gotten poorer, these authors have chosen lives of hard travel, separation from their loved ones, and difficult, sometimes dangerous, conditions to empower others to escape poverty.

Poverty is also a leadership issue. We are told, "Without wise leadership, a nation falls" (Proverbs 11:14 [NLT]), and "Leadership gains authority and respect when the voiceless poor are treated fairly" (Proverbs 29:14 [Mes]). Actually, this book is as much about leadership as it is about poverty. You will read about genuine leaders doing outstanding work in some of the poorest countries of the world.

Some of these authors lead nations. Ashraf Ghani, an esteemed academic and high-ranking world banker became one of the founding fathers of a new Afghanistan and an architect of the world's first constitution that integrated the needs of a democracy with the principles of Islam. He writes about using the centuries-old institution of money exchangers to do in months what the International Monetary Fund (IMF) said would take years.

My close friend, His Excellency Paul Kagame, the president of the Republic of Rwanda, grew up in refugee camps in Uganda, rose through the ranks of the Ugandan army, mounted a campaign to end the genocide in Rwanda, built institutions such as rule of law and democracy, invested in education, and rebranded his country among the community of nations. He writes that entrepreneurship is the backbone of new Rwanda. He understands the biblical principle that "good planning and hard work lead to prosperity, but hasty shortcuts lead to poverty" (Proverbs 21:5 [NLT]).

Recently, during a thirty-day tour of P.E.A.C.E. projects in Latin America, I met with government, business, and church leaders in Colombia. There I saw firsthand the dramatic turnaround in that country. Luis Alberto Moreno was a cabinet member in charge of economic development in Bogotá during the violent reign of drug lord Pablo Escobar. He was perhaps the first person in the developing world to see the need for growth led by export competitiveness. He became a legendary ambassador to Washington, leading the way to Plan Colombia, and now heads the biggest development bank in the region. His essay is about how to change institutions that, in turn, change economies.

Donald Kaberuka was minister of finance of Rwanda for seven years after the genocide and is recognized as an instrumental figure in rebuilding the nation. He is now the president of the African Development Bank where his insight and experience are being leveraged across the entire continent. He writes about his powerful personal experiences with private sector development and, perhaps more than anyone, is integrating this vision into the future of Africa.

There are other leaders in this book, perhaps less well known than these men, but just as dedicated to empowering the poor in the world's most challenging environments. There is Sally Christie, a Canadian with a Wharton MBA, who has worked in Asia, the Caribbean, and all over Africa; and Diego Etcheto, a Venezuelan-American who served in the Marines in East Timor. Their laments on the frailties of oil-based economies will be widely appreciated. David Rabkin worked in the Palestinian Authority and became a well-known columnist in the Caribbean. David writes with an ironic style that amuses but always goes straight to the heart of the issue—the way he and others attach meaning to life.

The Bible points out that skill, not merely hard work, is a key to prosperity. We must work smarter, not merely harder. "If the ax is dull and its edge unsharpened, more strength is needed but skill will bring success" (Ecclesiastes 10:10 [NIV]. These leaders have brought new skills, new ideas, and new expertise to some of the most remote places on the globe, and the results have been dramatic. But skill development is often a two-way street. As Rob Henning explored the ancient trading relationship between India and Afghanistan, he recognized that he, the imported expert, had much to learn from his clients before he could equip them with the skills he understood.

Michael Fairbanks and David Rabkin write about the development industry and its potential as a force for positive change. Their unusual candor about how they have been negatively influenced in their own lives by some of the industry's enervating norms of behavior should serve as a warning to all of us: stay true to your mission and to yourselves. Michael is one of the most brilliant friends I have, and I always learn much when we are together.

One of the delights of this book is the way that many of the authors featured the work of their clients to whom they have dedicated themselves and who have obviously become their friends. These leaders model the first sentence of *The Purpose Driven Life*: "It's not about you!" Eric Kacou, an Ivorian who returned to work in Africa immediately after receiving his Wharton MBA, writes so warmly about his respect for his clients—a coffee farmer and a fruit-juice exporter—that one is left with the feeling of wanting to meet them and know them equally well.

Michael Brennan's essay about Macedonia pays homage to a brilliant

tourism entrepreneur, a man who might succeed anywhere in the world
in which he was placed. Michael Fairbanks' vignettes on presidents for
whom he has worked surprise and delight us with the brilliance, foi-
bles, and humanity of these world leaders. See how Mandela constructs a
speech, how Castro learns, how Kagame envisions the future of his postconflict nation.

Malik Fal tells us about Claver, a bright executive who each and every
day faces the irrational challenges of economic growth with social equity,
always learning and searching for perspective. The reader will end up pull-
ing for the Clavers of the developing world, never looking upon them the
same way again.

Jesus taught that the essence of leadership is service to others. He said,
"Whoever wants to become great among you must be your servant"
(Matthew 20:26 [NIV]). That statement kept coming to mind as I read
these essays. The authors all model "servant-heartedness" by giving their
time and effort, by providing their informed yet humble advice, and by
training others. They help the poorest of the poor enter new markets, cut
costs, change regulations, and find new distribution channels and new
markets. They develop new models of business where the workers' wages
increase and where the value of each human being is recognized by both
managers and shareholders. This is not just good business practice; it is the
way to positively impact people, our environment, and future generations.

Eric Kacou outlines this approach in his essay titled "Archimedes'
Formidable Dare," and Marcela Escobari-Rose, a Bolivian who runs
Harvard's Center for International Development, develops these ideas at
the national level on her sojourns through Mexico.

Mother Teresa once said, "It is not what you do, but how much love you
put into it that matters." It is all about love. Love is the secret of a great legacy. You will never be more convinced of the power of these words in rela-
tion to economic development than when you read about Kwang Kim's
love of his work in the digital sectors of Brazil; or about the passion of
Malik Fal as he reflects on racism in global commerce; or about the profound introspection of Andreas Widmer, who begins his story as one of
the pope's elite Swiss Guard and then brings you to his present role as a
high-tech entrepreneur.

Focusing on yourself will never bring you lasting happiness. Self-centeredness is a dead-end street. Jesus said, "If you try to keep your life for yourself, you will lose it. But if you give up your life for my sake and for the sake of the Good News, you will find true life" (Mark 8:35 [NLT]). In this book, you will meet some people who are serving God by serving others. And they are doing it in the most effective way: by giving people a hand up rather than merely a handout.

The tired and discredited government approaches of simply handing out money to the poor do not work. Charity robs people of their dignity, creates dependency, and stifles initiative. We must not do for others what they can do for themselves. Instead, we must provide what we have been blessed with—knowledge, training and opportunities. We are blessed to be a blessing to others. The poor are not inferior; they just have not had the opportunities we have been given.

These new models of enterprise solutions to poverty are not really new. Anyone who has studied the Old Testament knows that, thousands of years ago, God gave us simple business-enterprise models that are transcultural solutions to poverty. Instead of thinking in terms of poverty reduction, the Bible focuses on wealth creation.

Today, it is heartening to see so many practitioners of development, political leaders, academics, and other professionals discovering the value of partnerships between all three sectors of society—public, profit, and faith—in creating enterprise solutions to poverty. Governments have a role that only they can play. Businesses have a role that only they can play. And churches, along with other houses of worship, have a role in economic development that neither government nor businesses can provide. Like a three-legged stool, economic development requires all three legs in order to work.

Of course, good work all starts in the heart. It must be personal before it can be professional. Anne Morriss shares her warm and amusing reflection on how she moved from building latrines in Ecuador to working inside the Internet bubble. You will enjoy Aref Adamali's affectionate remembrances of growing up in a merchant family in Kenya, Elizabeth Hooper's plea for seasoned professionals to work across traditional boundaries, and Marcela Escobari-Rose's self-admonition not to forget that all the things she learned in other nations could be applied in her homeland, Bolivia.

The factors of poverty are many, and the causes are complex. That is the reason we need a holistic strategy. The global P.E.A.C.E. Coalition is a network of networks that enables strategic partnering among businesses, governments, and churches to attack five global problems including poverty, pandemic diseases, illiteracy, corruption, and spiritual emptiness. Each one affects all the others.

"P.E.A.C.E." is an acrostic for five global solutions: promoting reconciliation, equipping servant leaders, assisting the poor, caring for the sick, and educating the next generation. In the past four years, 7,766 members of my congregation have volunteered their services overseas in sixty-eight countries as a part of the global P.E.A.C.E. plan. You can be certain that we will be using *In the River They Swim* as a P.E.A.C.E. plan textbook and guide for assisting the poor and that I will be recommending it to the over four hundred thousand other churches in our worldwide network.

I admire you for picking up this book. It says much about you. Evidently, you care. My prayer is that these pages will provide you with new knowledge that motivates you to action. If I can serve you as you serve the poor, please e-mail me. "Happy are those who are concerned for the poor; the Lord will help them when they are in trouble" (Psalm 41:1 [TEV]).

Lake Forest, California
August 2008
rick@thepeaceplan.com
www.thepeaceplan.com

Acknowledgments

· · ·

I T IS IMPOSSIBLE to thank each person who has helped us bring this book together. We would have to mention all our families who supported our journeys with patience and encouragement; our colleagues who taught us the tradecraft of strategy and development work; our clients who believed in us and opened their hearts and minds to us; and all the guards, cooks, drivers, and translators who did their jobs so well just so that we could do ours.

However, we would be wrong not to mention a few individuals. This book would not have been written without the vision and friendship of Charles Harper, Arthur Schwartz, and Kimon Sargeant. We thank our team at Templeton Press, Susan Arellano, Laura Barrett and Natalie Lyons Silver, for their insight and forbearance, which enabled such a nontraditional project to be published.

We would like to acknowledge the contributions of His Excellency, the president of Rwanda, Paul Kagame; the former minister of finance of Afghanistan, Ashraf Ghani; President Donald Kaberuka of the African Development Bank; President Luis Alberto Moreno of the Inter-American Development Bank; and Pastor Rick Warren, the global thought leader. Each of these persons is a historic figure in the world of human development, and each graced our work with his experiences and ideas.

We the editors take the privilege of mentioning our spouses—Marylee, Beran, Lila, and Mark—for their loving support as well as their good taste and constructive remarks in reading drafts. All their contributions were critical to our project.

Finally, to our sons and daughters, who inspire us to try to make the world better: we hope that Sebastian, Ely, Sarah, Jasmine, and Nico grow up in a world of greater tolerance, prosperity, and justice and that, one day, they will read this book with pride.

IN THE RIVER THEY SWIM

Introduction

—————————— ••• ——————————

A SUFI MASTER once told his disciples about the different levels of knowledge. "There are different ways to know a river," he began. First, you can read books about it and learn its length, its source, its depth, its width, the power of its current, the types of fish it contains, and other tangible facts. Then you can undertake the long journey to see it. You invest time, money, and hardships to travel to that river so that you can one day sit on its shores and look at it. When that day comes, you have attained a greater level of knowledge because you know its smell, you feel the sand that borders it, and you watch the birds that play over it. Finally, at last, you take off your clothes, and dive in to swim in the river. You feel its current along your body, the gradients of temperature, its depth. You taste something of it. You wonder if you have the strength to swim its length.

HUMAN DEVELOPMENT

In the words of Thomas Sowell, the African-American sociologist, "We need to confront the most blatant fact that has persisted across centuries of social history—vast differences in productivity among peoples, and the economic and other consequences of such differences."[1]

1. Thomas Sowell, *Conquests and Cultures: An International History* (New York: Basic Books, 1999), 329.

Unfortunately, the development divide between Western nations and the developing world, with the exception of parts of China and India, is widening. One consequence of this fact is that millions of desperate people around the world are ready to brave the dangers of illegally immigrating to richer countries to escape the threat of poverty at home. Another is that millions of disgruntled youths, with no prospects for employment and the decent life it could sustain, become easy prey for the fringe elements of poor societies.

We must also acknowledge that, during the past fifty years, our collective record in international assistance to the least developed countries has been disappointing. This has been well documented by Jeffrey Sachs and William Easterly. One reason for this has to do with the mindsets with which development practitioners engage the very people they are trying to assist. Economics-based abstractions originated in the metropoles of Europe and North America have done little to help.

This book is the antithesis to the search for solutions in the next big theory of global poverty. It collects the voices of leaders and field practitioners who have witnessed the complexity of creating prosperity in poor countries. From the fresh perspective of advisors on the frontlines of development to the insight of leaders like President Kagame of Rwanda, it tells the story of *change* in the microcosms of emerging businesses, industries, and governments.

As these authors reveal, eradicating poverty will not lend itself to a generic list of good policy measures that make regions and peoples better off. The answers, we learn, are more likely to be found in a heretical mix of economic and management theory; business strategy and practice; psychology, anthropology, history, leadership; and that most precious of human activities, integrative thinking.

A common theme that emerges in this collection of essays is that prevailing local mentalities and ways of life have been underintegrated in the development discussion. Development programs that do not draw from local knowledge to refine their global perspective fail to contribute to sustainable solutions. This book is, in great part, about what it means to cull the wisdom of localities to find answers to the world's greatest challenge. It is about establishing new rules of engagement with local leaders who have the overwhelming task of creating wealth for the world's poorest peoples. It is about nontraditional solutions that are hard to measure, begin at "the bottom," and are slow to enact.

We ourselves are credible messengers for doing it the wrong way. Molly, a legendary union leader from an island country who had worked for twenty years as a hotel maid, was confronted by one of our economic advisors. He handed her a fifty-page document, which contained his rigorous analyses of the local tourism industry. He immediately made his case in his usual direct style: "According to my analysis," he said, "many hotels on the island have closed in recent years because their labor costs are too high—local hotel workers make too much money for the tourist markets you're currently targeting." Molly slowly flipped through the spreadsheet-filled pages, put the document down, looked straight at him, and declared, "To me, this is nothing but numbers on a page. It does not relate what we go through, nor does it show how these hotel owners exploit us!"

Molly was an essential player in the local tourism industry. The consultant was factually correct, but that was not enough to persuade Molly that she would be better off at the end of a radically new kind of economic journey. The detailed map my colleague had drawn was barely a starting place. He needed to demonstrate empathy, an understanding of the local context and Molly's own experience and, ultimately, a commitment to a fair solution. Change would require levels of mutual respect and understanding that the island had never experienced. Learning to foster that type of shared humanity was the consultant's own journey of a lifetime.

This collection of essays is written by people just like this advisor to Molly. They learned, the hard way, that in order to be effective as a development worker, one needs to understand not only how to apply economics and business strategy and the art of influencing donors, cabinet ministers, and presidents, but also how to listen to Molly.

They tell stories of developing country leaders who struggle to find solutions to the complex problems that assail them. They depict the frustration of well-wishing aid workers who use body and soul to fight hopeless causes. They describe the contradictions of the international aid community and the myriad of regrettable side effects that arise from today's dysfunctional donor-recipient relationships.

These authors bring diverse perspectives, cultures, and voices to their writing. They are all highly trained professionals with backgrounds that span a wide spectrum of social, ethnic, religious, and geographic affiliations. Most of all, they are field-tested leaders and advisors who confront, problem solve, and, in many instances, overcome *the most blatant fact* everyday of their lives.

WHY THE ESSAY?

The essay represents a long proud tradition of a humble form, that of Montaigne, Bacon, Johnson, Woolf, and Orwell, to cite a few of its masters. And though we cannot pretend to reach the height of their eloquence, we do attempt to take the rules of their form and to apply it to the domain of economic and human development—specifically to enterprise solutions to poverty.

We asked ourselves several questions: What if we changed everything about how we work? What if we used a "second-class genre," the essay, that reached the height of its popularity a century and a half ago and that some have called the "formless form"? What if we adapted the premise that we can hardly advocate the merits of change without changing ourselves first? What if we stopped preaching and eschewed the epic pretension of advisors to nations, and revealed our greater discontentment with our ability to change the world than with the world itself? What if we displayed all our warts: our vanity, exaggerations, misplaced hopes, rage, and ignominious failures? If failure speeds up learning, would it help to show others what worked and did not work for us? Could it help others who want to try to help the world to feel grounded and less lonesome and freakish? If success comes after learning to fail fast, frequently, and most importantly, originally, would writing essays be a start?

Essays allow us to become the crucible in which our own experience is tested. There is a personal nature to our work that rigorous analysis alone cannot explain. We have the freedom to explore, in these pieces, a learning process that is iterative, messy, and sometimes deeply introspective.

The essay is supposed to be digressive, reflecting the sloppy process of how one learns; more than any other genre, it shows the learning taking place, almost in real time. We want to show life itself as it is forming on the pages. Though some of the authors achieve it better than others, there is merit in the struggle that each has faced.

These contributors come from and know every part of the world; they speak over twenty languages including Swahili, Wolof, Pushtu, and Kinyarwanda, but that is not what was important to us. What was important was whether they could turn an eye inward to find and know better places in the mind; to know that, while education exists outside of oneself in the mundane world, each person is an education unto herself, interminably engaged in the apprenticeship of knowing himself better, through his or her relationship with others and, in some instances, with God.

We, the editors of this book, gave the contributors the following instructions: from your experience working in the world's poorest countries, tell about a personal journey you have had doing enterprise solutions to poverty. Teach us something about the work, a useful experience, or a framework you have developed or used. Tell us about something you contributed that turned out to be wrong. Give us your beliefs, goals, attitudes, and assumptions. Do not settle just for self-expression, though; give us a high level of craft and try for art. Your writing can be loose, exploratory, and digressive; it can be about failure with or without redemption. But locate yourself in the solitary endeavor of writing, at the crossing of the self and others, process and outcome, experience and meaning. Recognize that it is important what you write. It shows what you do, who you want to be. You can be confident that some development experts will read our essay book, but will some lovers of the essay read our development book?

We assured our authors that these pages would be a safe place for their idiosyncratic voices, the margins of their drafts, a happy hunting ground for their best ideas. In an era of total global competition for resources, of hollow advice, of poverty that degrades and destroys progressive human values like trust, civic-mindedness, and tolerance for others, we asked them to write as if these essays may be our last resort.

We also told them to reconcile with the fact that they may never rise above the nameless unproductive babble of practitioners and celebrities in development. Above all, they should bear in mind what the Marxist theorist and literary critic György Lukács referred to as the "wonderfully apt" label of *essays*, which means simply to try.

That Sufi master taught us about the different levels of knowledge, the "different ways to know a river." We could have written about its length, its source, its depth, its width, the power of its current, and the life it contains. Then we could have taken the long journey to see it, invested time, money, and hardships to travel to that river so that we could sit on its shores and look at it, know its smell, feel the sand that borders it, and watch the birds that play over it. Instead, we took off our clothes and dove right in to swim in the river. We felt its current along our bodies and the gradients of its temperature. We tasted something of it. We wondered, briefly, if we had the strength to swim its length, and now we know.

The Sufi told us that swimming gives the highest level of knowledge a man or woman can ever have of a river. It is the type of experiential knowledge no words can ever convey to those who do not wish to share it.

So it goes with every thing worth knowing. If the work of human and economic development is a river, the authors in this volume, and perhaps some readers, will no longer be satisfied to stand along its banks.

PART I: THE JOURNEY

• • •

"The factors of poverty are many, and the causes are complex."
Rick Warren on one of his frequent trips to Africa.

1. The Backbone of a New Rwanda

H. E. PRESIDENT PAUL KAGAME, REPUBLIC OF RWANDA

KIGALI, RWANDA

• • •

RECENTLY, I spoke to a young person on the streets of Kigali. I asked him, "What do you want to be when you grow up?" He said he wanted to start his own business and move into the private sector. This is wonderful news. I felt as if I knew this young man by the height of his ambitions. It is very exciting and interesting that people are beginning to think like that young man; indeed, it shows the shifting in mindset away from when people thought the only jobs they could do were with the government.

In the old Rwanda, everyone looked for a job in government because of the benefits and the security. But nowadays they are thinking that the private sector holds the promise of a better life for their families and themselves. More meaningfully, I think that it is better if they join the private sector because there are more opportunities, opportunities that have a higher payback than simply working for the public sector. I believe that this is a huge step forward for Rwandans, given our history, given the whole history of Africa.

Rwanda is a nation with high goals and a sense of purpose. Our vision is to create prosperity for the average Rwandan citizen. We are attempting to increase our gross domestic product (GDP) by seven times over a generation, which increases per capita incomes by almost four times. This, in turn, will create the basis for further innovation, creative thinking, and a host of progressive human values: interpersonal trust, tolerance, and civic-mindedness. All this together will strengthen our society.

We know that this is a tremendous challenge given our status as a land-locked nation, emerging from conflict, with few natural resources, little specialized infrastructure, and low historic investment in education. But, in fact, we have reasons to be optimistic: we have made a clear and explicit strategy to export based on sustainable competitive advantages. We sell coffee now to the most demanding purchasers in the world for very high price points; our tourism industry attracts the best customers in the world, and Dubai World invested $230 million to participate in our tourism vision; and market research reveals that perceptions of Rwanda tea are improving at a rapid rate. In all three cases, we have learned to integrate a complex customer experience with product development. This has resulted in wages in key sectors rising at more than 20 percent on a compounded annual basis. While these developments are encouraging, we believe the road to prosperity is a long one.

We understand that achieving prosperity requires a metamorphosis of our economy. We are fundamentally changing our economy to move away from a dependence on agriculture toward a knowledge economy. The Rwanda of tomorrow will be a regional hub for Eastern and Central Africa.

Rwanda must become a world-class competitor in information and communication technology (ICT), logistics, financial services, and education. This metamorphosis will significantly increase average wages and help us graduate into a middle-income nation.

How can Rwanda join the ranks of the more successful developing countries, those that have transformed themselves in a single generation?

It is increasingly clear to us that entrepreneurship is the surest way for a nation to meet those goals and to develop prosperity for the greatest number of people. In fact, government activities should focus on supporting entrepreneurship not just to meet these measurable targets, but to unlock people's minds, to allow innovation to take place, and to enable people to exercise their talents.

In all people, you find different kinds of talents, and entrepreneurship is about harnessing those talents and making sure that it takes people to another level in their personal development. So, for us in government, it is essential to develop the private sector and to create an environment that enables entrepreneurs to flourish. We have much more to do, and it will take time. We are focused on lowering the costs of electricity, providing access to finance, building roads, and training managers.

We decided after our liberation struggle that if we could develop economically, then there might not be the basis for conflict. To achieve this goal, we needed to create our own strategy. Many leaders are overly influenced by the multilateral institutions and by bilateral donors. We have had the strange benefit that, early on, not a lot of nations wanted to give us foreign aid, and we turned that into an advantage.

We insisted that Rwandans would create their own strategic vision. We began by seeking to change some of the thinking that is common with many of our people. And that is the belief that aid will come and solve everything or that people will come from somewhere else and do what we ought to be doing for ourselves.

It is very simple: nobody owes Rwandans anything. Why should anyone in Rwanda sit back and feel comfortable that taxpayers in other countries are contributing money for our own well-being or development? Why should we not be doing what we are able to do and raise ourselves up to higher standards and achieve more and better and get out of this poverty that we find ourselves in. Change has to start in the mind. And that is what we have been working on over time. Once the mind gets correct, the rest becomes simple.

This is the reason that we are focusing on creating an entrepreneurial mindset in every Rwandan. This mindset begins with a sense that one's life, choices, and actions matter to the whole country. It begins with a clear understanding that business as usual is not acceptable. Every day, every Rwandan from all walks of life has a unique opportunity to change our country for the better.

The Rwandese entrepreneurial mindset must be characterized by ambition, moral purpose, respect, openness to new ideas, and self-determination. This entrepreneurial mindset must inform our actions whether we are in the private sector, government, or civil society. This mindset must inspire our entrepreneurs to aim ever higher. It must compel our civil servants to reinvent government. It must encourage our civil society to work for the greater good.

Ultimately, this mindset holds the key to our prosperity, our development, and our future.

We do appreciate support from the outside, but it should be support for what we intend to achieve ourselves. And no one can assume that he or she knows better than we what is good for us. Our supporters should also start to value the fact that we really want to be the ones to decide where we go and what we do and that we are capable of defining what we want to achieve.

One thing we have decided is that competition in an economy is good for poor people. I think competition is good everywhere. Competition is compelling because it stimulates people and unleashes people's capacities and potential.

The most interesting part I see in competition is that it gives people a feeling that they are valued and have meaning, that they are as capable, as competent, as gifted, and as talented as anyone else. Asking our citizens to compete is the same as asking them to go out there into the world on behalf of Rwanda and play their part.

On the other hand, shielding them is something that travels deep in the mind. If you allow a process where some people are shielded from the forces of competition, then it is like saying they are disabled.

Our job in leadership is to provide opportunities. We must use all the means available institutionally to do the things that will help people develop their capacities, their potential, and their talents and then allow them to compete.

I consider entrepreneurship to be, simply, the backbone of a new Rwanda. It is, indeed, my hope that others will come to know Rwanda, as I came to know that young person on a Kigali street, by the height of our ambition for the private sector and our commitment to achieve it.

2. Flight VS 56: Riding the Cultural Divide

MALIK FAL

OVER THE NORTH ATLANTIC OCEAN

• • •

THE FIRST-CLASS CABIN on Virgin Atlantic's flight VS 56 was dark, quiet, and glossy. The bright red and purple upholstery, the Belgian chocolates, Scandinavian delicacies, and French pastries spread on an extravagant all-night buffet, the massage therapist on board, the reassuring humming of two 747 Rolls-Royce reactors were all clichés of Western comfort and sophistication.

A legion of overpaid, overcaffeinated New York executives and I were making our way to London. My duties as a young PepsiCo operations executive involved frequent trans-Atlantic travel, and I would sometimes be on flight VS 56 twice in as many months. This time I was with a team of managers who worked for a wealthy African franchise-bottler in the process of buying new production lines. Our consultation meetings at Pepsi Cola International's Somers, New York, headquarters had been intense. We were still above the Atlantic, a few hundred miles away from the British Isles, and my fellow travelers, as well as the rest of the people in the cabin, were now fast asleep. My watch indicated that the time for *Fajr* was at hand.

I was a yuppie caught in the lightheartedness of the boisterous 1990s. To some, kneeling and pressing one's forehead on the carpet of a first-class trans-Atlantic cabin did not exactly fit with that picture. For a Muslim, having the courage and detachment to pray on airplanes could, therefore, be a spiritual challenge. As I approached the only remaining stewardess "on watch" in the cabin, the words of our *ulema*, the morning Muslim ritual prayer, echoed in my mind: "Do not fear people, who are created beings, but fear your Lord who created you and created them."

My praying-in-airplanes routine had been tested and so far had never failed me. With an engaging grin on my face, slow and reassuring body gestures, and as friendly a tone of voice as I could muster, I made my move. "Excuse me, Miss. I am Muslim, and I need to pray the morning ritual prayer. The morning prayer is the only one of five daily prayers that cannot be postponed. Since people can become uneasy when they see a Muslim praying, especially on an airplane, is there a small place in the cabin where I could pray without causing a riot?" As expected, she responded without the slightest hesitation: "That's absolutely fine, sir. Why don't you set yourself up to pray in the galley over there, and I will make sure that you do not get disturbed."

I then proceeded to the small bathroom to make *wudhu*, the obligatory ablution. Having to do the three-times washing of head, hands, forearms, face, and, most importantly, feet in miniscule airplane bathroom spaces was always a challenge to my body's flexibility as well as my dexterity at keeping spurts of water within a microscopic sink. However, this meant that I would not miss a compulsory ritual prayer, and I was happy to comply. In a sense, I felt that I was defying the clash of civilizations, and I loved every minute of it. I was also conscious that such moments were more the exception than the norm. September 11 was going to make things more difficult.

Several years have passed since those flight VS 56 PepsiCo days. During that time, I went to graduate school and spent a few years working in America. I have returned to my continent of origin, Africa, and continue to ride the cultural divide. For me, this means being a Frenchman who does not drink wine, a Senegalese who speaks better English than Wolof, a Muslim in America, a busy consultant who prays five times a day, and a dad who wears business casual in the morning and *jellabiyahs* in the evening. In my new life as an economic development advisor to African leaders, I look at intercultural dynamics on a far larger scale than just through my own experience.

Two interesting observations are increasingly catching my attention. The first is that intercultural interaction issues are no longer a matter of geography. They are no longer an issue of North versus South, or West versus East. Waves of modern migrations in the 1960s, 1970s, and 1980s have transformed thousands of living and working communities around the world. Both developing and developed countries are experiencing such tensions and have to revise default understandings of their national identity. France has its North and West African communities. Senegal has its Lebanese, Beninese, and Guinean communities. England now has to deal with a freshly arrived wave of Polish immigration that is profoundly changing its labor landscape, as well as with a Muslim community whose allegiance is being increasingly questioned since the July 2005 London bombings. Countries like the United States, Australia, South Africa, or New Zealand have long been cultural melting pots and are still struggling with community integration issues.

From an economic development perspective, these demographic realities matter tremendously because they affect firms, and firms are the ultimate creators of wealth. In order to create wealth and lift millions of people out of poverty, firms in developing countries need to develop unbeatable competitive advantages. The ability of firms to develop competitive advantages depends on their ability to foster work environments where innovation and seamless communication occur. Creating work environments where people with different backgrounds, religions, and experiences interact well with each other, innovate, and communicate is hard. For leaders who are able to create such environments, the benefits can be outstanding because, when it works, employee diversity can be a very powerful problem-solving asset. Firms in developing countries face increasingly complex problems, and when the people tackling those problems bring a diversity of perspectives, solutions are easier to find than when everyone thinks from the same perspective. In fact, it is often the way that innovation and competitive advantage occur.

I saw this happen in Mauritius. The Pepsi franchise bottling operation was owned and run by an originally Indo-Pakistani Muslim family. It had a white Christian marketing director, a Hindu corporate affairs director, and a mixture of all of the above in the workforce. Our meetings were invariably held in English. My counterparts would all switch to French or Creole over lunch and switch back to English in the afternoon when returning to the meeting table. Planning marketing promotional campaigns with such a diverse but functioning group was always a pleasure.

We would do sales forecasts, discuss logistics and tactics, choose reward prizes, and organize prize-award ceremonies with an acute sense of the cultural sensitivities present on the island. One such task involved coming up with the earliest possible promotion launch dates. To do this, we would gather data on when foreign suppliers could deliver give-away prizes, when promotional labels and bottles would arrive, and when printing shops would print required point-of-sale materials. At that point, people around the table would invariably inoculate each other with doses of cultural awareness. Mr. Raja, the corporate affairs director, would stop us and say, "We cannot have the promotion at that time! September is when the Hindu community celebrates the *Diwali* festival, and during that period, our families become oblivious to anything else." A new date would be proposed, and Clifford, the sales manager, would say, "Well, those dates will not work either because they are three weeks away from Christmas. This means that families in the Creole community will be focused on storing rather than consuming food and drinks for the festive season right at the peak of the promotion." The business successes of Mauritian companies in India, South Africa, Europe, and beyond are a testimony to the fact that the cultural diversity of Mauritian management teams is a blessing to this well-performing developing economy.

The second observation that I make on modern intercultural dynamics is that traditional race, ethnic, or nationality divides are being supplanted by other and often far more subtle types of cultural divides: social, generational, and even "accent" divides. This trend pertains to both developed and developing countries. It has the potential to deeply impact wealth-creation capacity in developing countries.

In many parts of Africa, the social divide within countries exposes profound differences in people's cultural attitudes toward wealth creation. People who are part of the elite seem naturally to favor the status quo and are less receptive to calls for change. These people tend to be more educated and more exposed to the outside world than the general population. They often blame Africa's poverty on Europe's lack of generosity toward its poor southern neighbor. They believe that, for a country, wealth comes from the availability of natural resources or from foreign aid, while, for an individual, it comes from one's ability to get access to the dividends emanating from natural resources or foreign aid. They revere the past but still have an avid urge to indulge in the trappings of modern consumerism. People in the lowest fringes of society, on the other end, tend to be far more entrepreneurial and used to fending for their own well-being. They do not have government jobs and have no access to the privileges and benefits that come from being preferred citizens of the educated elite. Their ability to survive day to day in very difficult environments is a testimony to their resilience and creativity. Most have commercial activities in the informal sector. However, this segment of African society also tends to have far less formal education and, thus, less capacity to articulate alternative models of development for their country.

These two groups define specific subcultures in African societies. Both have a critical role to play in the development of Africa. Unfortunately, very few African leaders have been able to bridge the cultural divide between these two segments of society. With better technical support, investments in specialized infrastructure, deeper knowledge of foreign markets, and business-friendly rules and regulations, the spirit of entrepreneurship that exists throughout the lowest fringes of African society could blossom into myriads of wealth-creating businesses. With a deeper moral purpose, a more acute sense of responsibility, and a higher level of dignity enhanced by independent thinking, the African elite could provide the capital, knowledge, and language "accents" needed to succeed in global markets.

Bridging the generational divide is another critical challenge in the development of Africa. This divide is not new. However, thanks to CNN, MTV, and many of the other flagships of global satellite television, the generational divide has grown deeper and stronger in the recent past. In societies from Senegal to Afghanistan and from South Africa to Macedonia, younger generations are more open, more exposed to new ideas, and better traveled than their elders. This is also true in developed societies where younger members of immigrant communities have an easier time integrating in their host societies than their parents.

In a world where seamless communication, access to information,

and knowledge are the means by which wealth gets created, older generations who still control their community's capital and decision rights
and younger generations who have better communication and interpersonal skills need to trade the respective assets they possess more efficiently.
Hundreds of thousands of young, educated Africans who fear frustration
at home leave for Europe and America every year in search of better opportunities. This African "brain drain" is one of many indications that the
generational divide is getting deeper and wider. In fact, many of my own
personal choices were made, at least in part, because of the generational
divide.

My family comes from Senegal, one of France's oldest outposts in *"la
Françafrique."* My parents went to a university in France. My older sib-
lings were educated in France. We were among the few who had French
passports and apartments in Paris. Up until very recently, history books in
Senegal taught local children about *"nos ancetres les Gaulois"*—our Gallic
ancestors. In spite of being personally unaffected by such inconveniences,
hearing stories of Senegalese students standing in line at three o'clock in
the morning, night after night, in order to get return visas to study in
France was disturbing to me.

Despite such humiliations, most decision makers in Senegal feel an
almost visceral attachment to France. I grew up in a world where French-
owned businesses dominated the economy. French military bases occupied
the best seafront real estate. French expatriates went through life walking
on a continuous red carpet. And in return for such treatment, local French
expatriates invariably voted for the Far Right in French elections root-
ing for the expulsion of African immigrants in France. Older Senegalese
people felt that such a relationship with France was normal. Many of my
friends and I did not. We understood the importance for newly independent African countries to be open and receptive to foreign ideas and capital for the sake of progress, but to us, the prevailing situation felt more like
a total abdication of sovereignty and a lack of self-determination. Many of
us who had the opportunity chose to learn English and study in England
and the United States.

Today, our fluency in French and English; our understanding of African,
French, Anglo-Saxon, and other cultures; and our wider exposure to the

world are affording us greater opportunities than the previous generation had. A famous African proverb says that "a crocodile may stay in the water a hundred years, but it will never become a piece of wood." To me, this means that, at the end of the day, I have remained and will always be an African.

Being able to ride the cultural divide is important and continues to be a great part of my life. Looking back, I realize that many of the spiritual principles that guided me through my own intercultural journey came out of the religious tradition I grew up with—namely, West African Sufism. I vividly remember a personal episode in the early 1990s that perfectly illustrates this point.

It was a typical September Surrey-county night. I had arrived in London a few weeks earlier to enroll as an economics student at Richmond College. I had traveled many times during my childhood to the United States and Canada for short holidays, and I had consistently been one of the best English learners in my class throughout high school in Africa and Europe; but this was different. From now on, everything would have to be done in English. I was not worried about activities inside the campus, which was a welcoming microcosm designed to make foreign students feel at ease. What really worried me was the outside world. I was going to have to find an apartment, open a bank account, get a phone line, and set up my own utility accounts. Having to do all this in English, with people who had that challenging London cockney accent, seemed overwhelming.

As I sat in the hotel room pondering my fears, my gaze fell upon a book that I could not even remember packing but that was going to play a critical role in my life over the coming years. It was a paperback edition of Malian author Hampathé Ba's biography of his Sufi teacher in the late 1930s, titled *Vie et Enseignements de Tierno Bokar, le sage de Bandiagara*. I picked it up and instinctively turned to page 122. The beauty of what I was reading still sends chills down my spine:

> *Bigotry* and its twin sister called *ignorance* come from deficiencies in one's spiritual development. They are not confined to one particular race or community. They are a general human disease. All times and all places have known them. Even at this

moment, they lie buried in the darkest corners of our hearts, and they threaten to show their ugly heads as soon as we find, in *the other*, a difference that we cannot comprehend. That is why we all need spiritual guides whose role is to also be doctors of the heart.[1]

I have come to learn over the years that many other religious traditions teach similar principles. I sometimes think that intercultural communication would be so much better if people went back to their own cultures to find those principles and internalize them. That night in London, I was embarking on a part of my life where I would meet with many new *others*, and these words from the old 1930s African Sufi Sheikh became an inspiration to me. They mentally prepared me to be far more inquisitive and tolerant about the differences I was about to see in the people I was about to meet. They, at once, began to shape my own mental technology to ride the cultural divide.

These words, and others from our Sufi tradition, against the backdrop of the accoutrements of Western comfort—bright upholstery, Belgian chocolates, Scandinavian delicacies, and the white noise that emanated from Rolls-Royce engines—became a source of great comfort and enabled me to practice detachment while appreciating differences.

1. Amadou Hampâthé Bâ, *Vie et Enseignement de Tierno Bokar: Le Sage de Bandiagara* (Paris: Edition Poche-Sagesses, 2004). Italics added.

3. A Space Alien in Chaps

ANNE MORRISS

COTOPAXI, ECUADOR

• • •

A PRECONDITION of the development dream has always been patience. Change takes decades, if not generations. Complex problems must be solved before progress can inch forward. But having come of age in the United States in the 1990s, I found that narrative to fit awkwardly into my worldview. Change happened in an instant, it seemed, in the moments that individuals named Bill and Steve found the audacity to turn ideas into companies and change the way billions of people lived.

I started my career as a health worker in rural Ecuador. The global payoff on building toilets in the Andes was too emotionally remote for my twentysomething soul, and as I watched from the sidelines as the "dotcom bubble" inflated, I knew that my days in the health field were numbered. Even from my oxygen-hungry post, it was clear that a bubble was the wrong metaphor. The talent being unleashed was not blowing air into a delicate and unsustainable trend. It was kicking open a fire hydrant.

My public-health training had taught me how to help people manage poverty, not overcome it. The digital revolution invited me into a different conversation, one where individuals could control their economic destinies. The truths I internalized in those years had nothing to do with sock puppets or *irrational exuberance*. The central thing I learned, mouth hanging open, was the speed at which entrepreneurs could transform a society. What if that kind of shamelessness reached Quito? What if the next Guillermo Gates were somewhere in these mountains? Better yet, what if

Ecuador could learn to *invent* him, to pull him out of the thin air that kept its poverty in such sharp relief?

As my work in Cotopaxi came to an end, I did a final survey of project sites. I was leaving behind fifty new latrines but no new hope for a more secure existence, for a reality where sanitation was simply a given. For the last time, I climbed into the open bed of the truck that ferried community members down the mountain to the region's central market in Ambato. I wore layers of neutrally colored fleece, having abandoned most of my other ridiculous efforts to mute the contrast of our life experiences. (Imagine a space alien wearing chaps to help her connect with the good people of Houston, Texas—the strategy did not work for me, either.) Hiding sentimental tears, I assured my friends that I would be back. One woman told me to stay away. In broken Spanish, without the emotion that animated her native Quechua, she said, "I am poor, Ana. You are not. Do the things I cannot do."

The market was everything to them, but they felt powerless to influence its forces. The communities I worked in had few things to sell (mostly variations on a potato theme), and they came to find out every week what prices they would get for them. The idea that these transactions might offer an exit from a relentless cycle of poverty and disease was absurd, to all of us, but something was being created from nothing in garages in Silicon Valley. That was the type of magic this region needed.

I walked through the market again, past the identical stands of Chinese plastics and used American clothing, and committed myself to try to understand the dynamics of untamed economic growth, the type of growth that might reach as far as this place. The subsequent journey took me from producing treadle pumps for African farmers to helping "Fortune 50" clients sell things to insecure Americans. I chose Harvard Business School over public policy or foreign affairs degrees. I joined a technology start-up with an economic empowerment mission. I apprenticed myself to good capitalists.

At the OTF Group, a firm dedicated to transforming the economies of poor countries, I finally grappled directly with the Bill Gates-for-Ecuador question. Our work brought me back to the Andes and well beyond them and gave me the opportunity to talk with hundreds of entrepreneurs, policymakers, and development experts about how to cultivate entrepreneurship in developing nations. Not all of these individuals were succeeding, but most were effectively tackling some part of the challenge, and everyone had a strong point of view on the practice of entrepreneurial magic.

The Indians taught me that government can foster private sector creativity, even without the promise of capital. The Brazilians taught me that combining science and business education can create a biotech frontier in places most Americans cannot pronounce. The Vietnamese taught me that promoting the values that drive entrepreneurship, including comfort with risk and diversity, requires active engagement with young people. The Ghanaians taught me that local role models matter, sometimes more than anything else.

Most of the conversations focused on creating the optimal conditions for entrepreneurs to thrive, the right laws, the right mindsets, the right access to markets and skills. This collection of inputs was sometimes called the "enabling environment," but when that began to sound too paternalistic, the conversation would shift to the "business environment." The perspective was a reasonable one. The emergence of an entrepreneur's paradise could neatly explain Silicon Valley and Boston, increasingly Israel and Hong Kong. And it made sense that, in a sector informed primarily by economics, we were all looking for the solution in better systems.

It was certainly true that in the majority of places where the entrepreneurs we studied were thriving, their own talent was one of many inputs in their success. Bill Gates may have brought his own brilliance to the table, but that spark caught fire because Seattle was ready for him. The city embraced diversity of thinking and behavior. His elementary school offered a rigorous computer science program in the early 1960s, and he found the resources to start his first venture at age seventeen. His parents valued traditional achievement but also endorsed his decision to drop out of Harvard College and launch a software company before he could legally drink alcohol.

Had Gates been born on a mountain outside Cotopaxi, he probably would have lived a short life as a frustrated farmer. I was persuaded by our work that environment is the driving force in entrepreneurship, that influencing environments will produce different outputs, and that the change process will take a significant amount of time in some places, even genera-tions. I dutifully coauthored a two-hundred-page report that affirmed this view, and I stand by my team's conclusions. I believe that building an entre-preneurship movement relies on public, private, and academic leaders' coming together to turn cities and regions into large, virtual incubators of competitive ventures. That kind of transformation will not be quick.

And yet entrepreneurs were defying dramatic weaknesses in their environments everywhere I went. In one of countless examples I found, men who used to survive by scavenging trash heaps in Brazilian slums had launched a business that now counts Rio's leading-edge recycling firms among its clients. They wear white to work every day, the founders explained, to remind themselves of the distance they have traveled from the filth and hopelessness that used to define them. The environment they escaped could not have been more toxic to entrepreneurship.

The most salient moment in this work for me came in a conference room in Mexico filled with one thousand women entrepreneurs, many of them speaking in indigenous languages still used in only the most iso-lated regions of the country. The atmosphere was electric. I was pitched a new product or service every three minutes and finally gave in when a sixty-four-year-old grandmother outlined in halting SSL (Spanish as a sec-ond language) why her water filtration system was a better fit for me than anyone else's, including her mother-in-law's. When President Vicente Fox walked in to hand out the awards, the room exploded. It reminded me of the Luis Miguel concert I had recently attended, without (quite) as many adolescent screams, but with the same number of beach balls bouncing around the crowd—three. Seriously.

These entrepreneurs' "enabling environments" in Oaxaca and Chiapas and Guanajuato were grim by any standards, but they were prevailing any-way. I had been asked to speak to the group, and as I searched for the right words, I initially came up empty, humbled by the odds these women had overcome to be standing in that room. This crowd could teach me infi-nitely more than it could learn from me. I finally chose to put their experi-ence in a global context, to link it to the army of women starting companies around the world, an army that is strong and capable but still risk-averse. (Women entrepreneurs often have a greater resistance than their male counterparts to dreaming big and taking other people's money to fund those outsized dreams.) The last thing I wanted to talk about was the thing I had been studying—the constraining relevance of their environments. These women had rejected the destinies the economists scripted for them. It was that choice that gave me hope for a world without poverty.

I surveyed the audience and tried to reconcile these thoughts in my now thirtysomething soul. Their faces revealed a mix of defiance and optimism, and it put me in touch with what I really wanted to say to the people I met who cared so much about their countries' futures, with the fundamental truth that had pulled me off a mountain in Ecuador more than a decade ago. Systems such as families and markets and economies are powerful, and we should work to make them better, but they are not all-powerful. Individuals also have tremendous power, much more than we choose to realize. As entrepreneurs in poor countries teach us, we can transcend the systems that seek to contain us. Unleashing that capacity will be the real precondition for achieving the development dream.

4. A Mind for the Poor

ANDREAS WIDMER

BOSTON, MASSACHUSETTS

• • •

"PEOPLE GO into counseling because they want to help," Father John told us. "They want to help their fellow human beings, a noble objective! But many end up not helping their neighbor, but hurting themselves and the very people they're trying to help."

He opened the course with this stern warning, not at all what I expected.

Six years ago, I started a master's degree in theology, which I see as my avocation. I love to explore ideas that go beyond what the eye perceives, and, as a Catholic, I love and revere the teachings and tradition of my faith. These studies were my "guilty pleasure," which I pursued separately from my career. I always struggled to find a balance where I could pursue the two successfully side by side, without one's hindering the other.

This was my first course on counseling. During one semester, Father John, an experienced priest in his sixties, explained the various situations a counselor might encounter and how best to approach each.

He warned us about four counseling traps: employing crisis intervention instead of counseling, having sympathy rather than empathy, being a codependent, and playing the redeemer.

As I listened further, it struck me that counseling and development are susceptible to the same set of traps.

As I listened to Father John's lectures, I closed my eyes and imagined sitting in a room full of development experts. His lectures would have been right on the mark. This was a message I needed to hear and one I needed to take to my colleagues. The issue helped me raise tough questions that are not easily answered but are very useful to ask.

THE CRISIS INTERVENTION VERSUS COUNSELING TRAP

Father John pointed out that crisis intervention and counseling are fundamentally different. Crisis intervention is a short-term intervention, focused on dealing with and overcoming a traumatic experience, as opposed to regular counseling, which is concerned with accompanying someone over a longer period of time as that person figures out patterns in his or her life. He warned us that it is easy to slip from one into the other and that a person should never have the same counselor for both crisis intervention and counseling.

Crisis intervention and counseling are both learned. Contrary to what many people think, there are qualitative differences in the approaches used to assist others in their decision making. Our "feelings of caring" or doing what we find "comes naturally" are actually not very good guides to facilitate emotional and spiritual growth.

My friend Leo, a successful entrepreneur, was diagnosed with cancer shortly before the birth of his third child. He fought with grace and ferocity and gained the upper hand twice in the following year. I met with him regularly. During one meeting, he told me, "It's not so much dying I'm afraid of; it's not being able to take care of my family. I don't have life insurance. What will they do when I'm not around to take care of them?" *Crisis intervention.* I was moved to tears when I was with him and his most immediate needs gave me something to focus on. I still cried, but I could focus on problem solving. We went so far as to discuss a new business we could start once he got better. I knew then that I had definitely slipped away from crisis intervention. But it was more comfortable for me to talk about life with a dying man than to talk about dying. *And that was the trap*: this was not about me.

I had particular difficulties with this, and Father John reminded me often that my approach "appears to be more counseling than crisis intervention." I would focus on long-term issues and opportunities, work with a person like Leo on life goals rather than on helping him deal with feelings and needs. Crisis intervention is not focused on solving underlying and long-term issues; it is meant to help the person come to terms with his or her situation. Father John's advice was simple: crisis intervention is done in four or five sessions; if you go beyond this, you have moved into counseling.

The Crisis Intervention versus Counseling Trap in Development

Humanitarian aid and economic development are different both in their nature and in what drives them. Humanitarian aid is for the short term. It helps people overcome an immediate threat to their lives. The urgent need for humanitarian aid was clear when a cyclone hit Burma in 2008, killing fifty thousand people and leaving two million homeless.

It is not always as clear when a humanitarian mission should end. After a few months, when people are no longer in danger of dying, many other longer-term issues remain to be tackled. The difference between crisis intervention and counseling seems to be a very useful analogy to apply to these issues. Humanitarian aid seeks to relieve imminent but passing threats. It is much like crisis counseling. Economic development comes later and is more like long-term counseling. It assists the local community to take stock of its economy and identify the patterns in its economic system. It encourages people to find solutions that need to work independent of the aid agencies, nongovernmental organizations (NGO), and development experts. In other words, economic development, like counseling, should strive for independence.

Many humanitarian agencies and organizations continue their work after the crisis has been addressed and shift their focus to economic development. After all, is not the lack of economic growth, the absence of prosperity, a disaster of some sort? Perhaps economic issues are not "fixable" like humanitarian issues. We cannot just give everyone a job in the same manner that we hand out bottles of water to the thirsty. The emotions of compassion and sympathy, which are so critical in organizing humanitarian aid, become an obstacle when applied to economic development.

What is needed is a longer-term approach, and the participation of the local population is vital. Economic development should aim at helping people help themselves.

THE SYMPATHY VERSUS EMPATHY TRAP

Sympathy occurs when we make someone else's problem our problem. It is useful only in the case of crises, when the person needing help is momentarily incapable of acting for him- or herself. Sympathy leads one to manage the other person's situation. I do not let a man with the intent of committing suicide make the next decision himself. I intervene at once.

Empathy is the ability to look at a situation from another person's perspective, to tune in to his or her feelings, to be present with that person as he or she goes through the present experience. This approach works more slowly, as it does not "take over"; but precisely because of this, it forms the cornerstone of effective long-term counseling.

It has been challenging for me to make the switch from sympathy to empathy. I always thought that caring for the other meant "fixing" his or her problems.

The sympathetic counselor takes the decisions away from the other person and makes the choice for that person. He brings his own experience to bear. For example, the counselor may have a habit of waiting too long to make decisions. In sympathy, he does not want the same to happen to this woman he is counseling, so he makes the decision for her. This demeans the woman by paternalizing her and hampering her free will.

In empathy, however, I will relate to the other person, listen to and acknowledge her feelings, accompanying her throughout her experience with advice and encouragement. But I will not be prescriptive, and most of all, I will not make decisions for her. My primary goal is not to have the person make one choice or another; my focus is to help the person find out how to go about making a decision.

Empathy is a three-step process: First, we need a basic motivation for human relations. Second, we need to be able to surrender our judgments to perceive and "enter into" the other's perspective. And third, having entered into the other person's experience, we must have the capacity to withdraw again. I remember Father John's saying that, in this sense, "a counselor is a member of every family he works with, but belongs to none."

The Sympathy versus Empathy Trap in Development

It is noble to help the poor. But what does that help entail? A friend of mine once said, "Most people have a heart for the poor, but very few have a mind for the poor." What he means is that many good people who want to assist the poor identify with them and want to help them directly. That usually means "solving" the problems of the poor for them, through government or other outside intervention. These solutions are driven by sympathy; they take over and attempt to act in place of the poor themselves. In that sense, they paternalize the poor and deny their right to self-determination. We treat them as children, telling them what to do and then expecting them to do what they are told. If they do not, we resent them and judge them as having little sense, which reinforces our behavior. "Having a mind for them" means having empathy and recognizing that we would probably act similarly in their situation.

THE CODEPENDENCY TRAP

A codependent is someone who exhibits too much, often inappropriate, caring for persons who depend on him or her. The dependent party or parties may have emotional, physical, or financial difficulties or addictions he or she is unable to surmount. The codependent party exhibits behavior that controls, makes excuses for, pities, and perpetuates the needy party's condition.

If the counseling sessions seem interminable, this might be a good indication that the relationship has become codependent. If you feel that the person you counsel is not ready to cope with the situation without your help, then you are not effective or you suffer from codependency or both.

The Codependency Trap in Development

"If poverty is your business—more poverty is more business," the saying goes. That is a sad truism and a sure sign of a codependent system. If our aid is used to feed our own good feelings, then we lose sight of the aided person's progress. When "helping" others becomes a form of enabling them to perpetuate their need for our help, then that is a form of codependency. In the extreme case—and I think we arrived at that point some time ago—development aid becomes a business, an entire industry feeding upon itself.

It is understandable that someone who sacrifices for others expects some gratitude in return. But what should the one who is receiving help expect? Should sixty years of development aid show some tangible results? Whether aid comes from nations or NGOs, there should be a clear path to independence. Economic development aid cannot be accepted as a perpetual state.

THE REDEEMER TRAP

Father John made us repeat over and over, "I'm not the redeemer, I'm not the redeemer, I'm not the redeemer." He would say, "Before starting a counseling session, repeat that to yourself a few times, to make sure that you go in with the right attitude." We may interfere in matters of survival (suicide prevention, abuse, etc.), but when it comes to pursuing sustainable solutions, if we respect the dignity of the person, then we support him or her in the process of finding solutions to the problem, but we do not solve it for that person. We can't "want" for another person.

The Redeemer Trap in Development

Being a redeemer in a humanitarian disaster saves lives. Imagine if the locals at an earthquake site resisted the Red Cross dog handler's instructions on where to dig. That handler might walk away. The same thing happens in economic development. Western specialists go "over there" with a blueprint for the economy, ready to take charge. They want action. And then they meet with local resistance. Their initiatives start but then die off the minute they leave. So they end up feeling resentful. I have met development staff members so disillusioned with their work that the only thing they looked forward to was retirement. The "locals" did not do what they were told and were not "grateful" for what was given. The locals, of course, noticed this attitude and no longer cooperated, reinforcing the bad situation.

The redeemer trap is at the core of this situation. Westerners enter the stage of economic development thinking of the help we can offer and the good we can do. Under the current economic development playbook, we see ourselves entering to sounds of trumpets and fanfare to rescue the poor and bring justice and prosperity to all. We are the heroes in our own movie. But if that is so, what will these poor people do when we leave?

I continually ask myself, "How do I not fall into Father John's 'traps'? How do I ensure that I will not end up disillusioned with economic development?" The key is, just as Father John said, to act with the right attitude and expectations: I am not the redeemer with all the answers, and I am not the protagonist. I am just accompanying someone on his or her economic journey, willing to listen, share my experience, allow for opportunity, and offer encouragement.

The real protagonists in economic development are the local entrepreneurs. I should not tell them what to do or treat them as my pet charity project. I can help them by being a partner, ready with advice and encouragement and offering access to networks of productivity. Some questions that we have to answer are: Do our development solutions enable the target countries to participate in competitive global markets? Are our solutions focused on reducing poverty (the problem) or on creating wealth (the solution)? Would we be more effective by opening our own markets to trade with developing nations and doing business with them, rather than engaging in the aid cycle?

The answers, I believe, will have a transformative effect on our approach to economic development.

Reconciling my work and my theology studies was not that difficult in the end. The questions I learned to ask from Father John evolved into two key principles by which I guide myself: Can I enter into the other person's experience and retain my capacity to withdraw again? And do I have a mind for the poor as much as I have always had a heart for them? I finally realize how to make the two support one another. I wonder, now, if they were ever really apart.

5. Waiting for Mr. Anderson

KENNETH HYNES

FISH RIVER, JAMAICA

· · ·

"So who's all of this for?" I asked Murdoch and Gibson, surveying the two thousand acres of dasheen that grew as far as the eye could see. Dasheen is a hearty root vegetable that grows easily in the western parishes of Jamaica, an ideal crop for poor farmers who cannot afford irrigation or fertilizer. "It's for Mr. Anderson," replied Murdoch, "He'll be coming soon to buy it all."

Murdoch and Gibson had been farming this secluded area of Jamaica for years. Their plot of land was just thirty minutes east of the tourist resort of Negril, but I doubt many tourists ventured this far off the strip. A muddy, unmarked road was the only way into their fields. It had taken me a while to find their farm, but, no matter, I was on a mission. I was a newly minted consultant who had just arrived in Jamaica as part of an economic development project that focused on agriculture. I was confident that, if I were armed with enough research and analysis, I could provide Murdoch and Gibson with the solution to their problems.

Although neither Murdoch nor Gibson had much of a formal education, they knew their stuff when it came to dasheen. "We pick the crop as late as possible because the higher the water content, the heavier the plant. The heavier the plant, the more money we can get from Mr. Anderson," explained Gibson.

"What's the going price on dasheen these days?" I asked.

"Not sure," responded Gibson, "but Mr. Anderson will tell us."

"Well, who does Mr. Anderson work for?" I asked, stepping out of the mud that was steadily engulfing my shoes. "I'd like to speak with him. Do you have his number?"

"Don't have any need for his number. He told us last year that he'd be back again."

Mr. Anderson never did arrive. In fact, Murdoch and Gibson never heard from him again. What did not rot in the field was bought for pennies on the dollar by higglers, more formally known as middlemen. And that was it for Murdoch and Gibson. They had no idea why they had lost Mr. Anderson's business or why they had ever won it in the first place.

This episode troubled me. I did a bit of digging into the fundamentals of the dasheen market. It turned out that much of the dasheen grown in Jamaica was destined for the manufacture of root chips, an increasingly popular alternative in North America to the more mundane potato chip. Mr. Anderson's buyer in the U.S. was not pleased with the high water content of the dasheen he received the previous year because it prolonged the drying process necessary before the root vegetables could be fried. It made perfect sense for Mr. Anderson to bypass Murdoch and Gibson and, instead, buy his dasheen from a group of farmers that used dry-land farming techniques.

The mystery of Mr. Anderson's disappearance was solved, but I remained bothered on a deeper level. It still struck me as unjust that the livelihood of two men and their families was effectively dependent on the whims of high-end snack food consumers in North America. Grow dasheen with water content of 60 percent and you can earn a decent living. Grow dasheen with a higher water content, and you faced financial ruin. And how could farmers like Murdoch and Gibson ever know that?

Little things matter in today's sophisticated global marketplace. This is true even with products we commonly think of as being commoditized, like agricultural goods. For example, when it comes to salmon, color means money. Market research has shown that consumers believe darker salmon colors are indicators of higher quality and better taste. In response, a Swiss pharmaceutical giant developed a series of dietary supplements for farm-raised salmon that allows farmers to choose the exact shade of pink they desire from a fan deck, essentially a paint swath, called the SalmoFan™. Farmers need only select the shade they want from the SalmoFan™ and then add the corresponding chemicals to the feedstock of their fish to obtain the exact coloring that their buyers desire. Customer preferences in this regard are very specific: consumers in the United States prefer SalmoFan™ color 33; anything below color 25 never makes it to the U.S. market.

The fact that seemingly minor nuances driven by subtle consumer preferences can mean the difference between economic success or failure has significant consequences for the field of economic development. This has consequences not only for firms in developing countries trying to compete, but also for governments and donors trying to foster development.

There was a time when government could coordinate industrial policy by choosing national champions and allocating resources accordingly. Those days are gone. In an era where products, capital, and technology flow across borders with ease, global consumers have an abundance of choices. Consumer tastes are more sophisticated and evolve more quickly than they did years ago. It is these preferences that provide an opportunity to realize a competitive advantage. But often governments are too slow and too distant from the market; they cannot identify or even react to the fast-changing peculiarities of consumer demand. Furthermore, the importance of understanding and meeting consumer preferences highlights the limitations of a purely macroeconomic approach to development. Concepts like total factor productivity are important, but you first have to make a product that someone wants to buy.

Fueled by these insights, I realized that, in order to give answers to farmers like Murdoch and Gibson, I needed to focus my efforts as a development professional toward understanding the evolving needs of their target customers. My market survey was strong, and my interviews with key distributors had yielded some important facts on what it took to compete in the dasheen industry. Upon completing my report, I called Gibson's cell number.

"Gibson, I think you'll be impressed by what I found. I've spoken with at least three other dasheen buyers who are a much better fit for you and Murdoch."

"That sounds great!" Gibson replied. "Please come see us soon as you can. We'll be here waiting."

That is when it hit me. Instead of waiting for Mr. Anderson to buy their crop, Murdoch and Gibson were now waiting for me to arrive and provide the answer.

Development professionals must change how they contribute to the quest for economic growth in developing economies. I have come to the conclusion that it is not about a detailed set of recommendations drawn from elaborate research efforts performed by development professionals. It is certainly not about resumes and promises and not about elegant proposals and polished reports. It is definitely not about development professionals like me providing what we see as "the answer." Rather, in a world where the answer is constantly changing, my role is to help managers and farmers understand and anticipate those changes and to build their capacity to gather data, do analysis, and make inferences about the market.

Firms need to be engaged in a continuous learning exercise that provides them with the ability to determine their own way forward in today's constantly evolving marketplace. After all, business strategy is simply a set of hypotheses that must be continuously tested in the marketplace. This means equipping managers and farmers like Murdoch and Gibson with the ability to make informed choices and take timely action. This depends upon the ability of managers to identify the tastes and preferences of demanding consumers and to anticipate their evolving needs. A one-time market analysis by an outsider cannot accomplish this. Firms need assistance to understand market signals and to identify business opportunities on their own. My role needs to shift, from merely supplying information to helping firms learn from the market. This is very much a collaborative process that focuses on helping firms to formulate their own business strategies and develop the skills necessary to revise those strategies.

I replaced my color-copy, bound report with a set of less glamorous but more impactful training materials for Gibson and Murdoch and set off for Fish River. As I carefully drove along the unmarked roads leading up to their farm, a young man approached the car and began to walk beside it. He asked, "Are you looking for Mr. Murdoch and Mr. Gibson?"

"Yes, I am. Can you point the way?" I asked.

"No problem, they're just a mile up the road." "Mister," said the young man, "are you Mr. Anderson? My grandfather has been waiting."

"No, I am not," I replied.

As I made my way farther down the path, I thought to myself, *No, I certainly am not Mr. Anderson. But I almost was.*

6. My Faith in Capitalism

ANDREAS WIDMER
VATICAN CITY

• • •

As I hunch over my BlackBerry to check for new e-mails, the domain *vatican.va* jumps out at me. It is the first message from my twenty-one-year-old nephew, a newly appointed Swiss Guard enlisted in the protection of Pope Benedict XVI.

He writes to me that he got lost on his way to his first assignment in the apostolic palace. He describes his increasingly panicked attempt to find his way among the labyrinth of corridors, stairs, and rooms in the ancient edifice. "I reported late to my first assignment—I was so embarrassed," he admits, "but I knew you would understand."

Of course I would—the same thing happened to me twenty years ago.

I was to report at 2 p.m. I had left the barracks one hour early in order to make my way to work. I had passed the main gate, noting the startling bronze of the Portone di Bronzo. I headed to the papal palace, and I climbed up the first set of winding stairs, which led to a large, open courtyard. I recall being flooded with a warm, red light from the stained glass window in front of me. Greeting every priest, nun, and layperson passing me, I walked slowly. I lingered as I crossed the courtyard, looking up at the loggias, the open galleries that sit atop one another and connect the palace offices. As I kept my face upturned, I noticed that the afternoon light was reflected in the hundreds of windows.

When I was a member of the corps sworn to protect the late Pope John Paul II, I shared one telephone with 113 other men. In many ways, the

A Swiss Guard: Andreas Widmer in the Vatican.

Vatican had changed so little that I could easily imagine myself as living hundreds of years earlier in my Medici-colored uniform. It is hard to imagine that as I walked among some of the most celebrated artworks of the Renaissance, students at MIT in Boston were developing the Internet. It is even harder to imagine that one day I would help to bring that technology to the market.

In a serendipitous way, after my tour of duty with Pope John Paul II, I immigrated to the United States and joined the Internet boom. It led me on a wild roller-coaster ride, with capitalism charting my course. The money flowed. At age twenty-eight, I managed over one hundred employees and was part of one of the first large high-tech initial public offerings. The speech recognition company I worked for was sold for six hundred million dollars. At thirty-four, I was in my element, giving TV interviews, being quoted in leading business journals, and meeting with mainstream magazines.

Although I did not fully realize it at the time, I was in the middle of the greatest capitalist boom in human recollection. My hardworking, blue-collar father-in-law would look at me skeptically when he got a hint of my salary and bonuses or heard about my business-class flights around the globe. But I saw my lifestyle as a given. I could not relate it to anything else; it was the only work experience that I knew. The day-to-day operations of a rapid-growth business became second nature to me, an instinct, almost a drug. Without fully understanding why, I learned to equate success with earning a hefty salary and with shooting for unsustainably high growth rates for the company, whatever the costs.

Beginning in 2000, when the Internet bust hit us like a slow, suffocating mudslide, I began to have an inkling that capitalism might be a bit more complicated than penny stock options.

These experiences defined my love/hate relationship with capitalism. Although capitalism was responsible for so many of the professional opportunities that I had been given, I felt it was also responsible for destroying the companies for which I cared so deeply. I had big questions. Are these self-destructive tendencies in capitalism inevitable? Is there a form of capitalism that does not self-destruct? And, most importantly, is my drive for status and money intrinsically bad? I had no answers.

Up another set of stairs. Every few steps there were indentations in the wall, where white marble statues silently looked on with empty gazes, frozen in motion for eternity. The stairs led to a long corridor with windows all along one side. Every square inch of the walls and ceilings were painted in minute detail. All kinds of small creatures, insects, birds, and flowers were painted in photographic likeness. I started to wander off, as I would so many times during the next two years. Having all these keys to the doors of an ancient palace at age twenty was an invitation to explore.

Perhaps the companies for which I had worked deployed the wrong business strategies. The quest for an answer weighed heavily on my mind as I thought about my next career move. I wanted to go back to basics and learn more about business strategy and the theory of capitalism.

The search led me to join a business strategy–consulting firm that is making strides to solve the oldest problem of all—poverty. Over one-half of the world's population lives in poverty (on less than two dollars a day), and that number increases each year. The people at the OTF Group believe that the free-market economy can help solve this problem. In order to implement this vision, the company directors advise heads of state and business leaders in developing economies on how to build thriving private sectors that use sound business strategy to compete better in the global economy.

My first visit to a project was to Skopje, in the former Yugoslavian Republic of Macedonia. A decade later, the country was still paying for mistakes under the communist regime. As the taxi left the airport, we drove past a faded sign announcing the free-trade area of Macedonia. Its original wooden supports were rotted and buckling, and the sign leaned on a tangle of untamed brush that grew around it. My driver, Dragan, commented disdainfully that "Macedonia is, supposedly, open for business." Now the government was telling the people that they should wait patiently for the business to come.

I told him a little about why I was there, and he looked at me suspiciously as he declared his fears about foreigners coming in to take all the money. Dragan knew that he would remain poor. He said that Macedonia was a great nation. "The nation of Alexander the Great and Mother Teresa doesn't need capitalism!"

As I sat in the conference room during our presentation to Macedonia's government and business leaders, Dragan's words echoed after me. Is capitalism really just another way the "West" can rule this nation? On the drive back to the airport, I attempted once more to convince Dragan that we had a good plan, one of which I thought Mother Teresa would approve. We were trying to help people find prosperity and happiness, among other things, by bringing businesses that would invest in the workers' knowledge and raise salaries for people like Dragan. Our philosophy, I explained, was to find a solution where it was not just the foreign consumer or the owner of the firm who would win through cheaply produced goods from his country. In our proposed interaction between the foreign consumers, the owners, the workers, and the country as a whole, the local worker would gain adequate wages and would be treated with dignity. "There is a solution where all the participants in an economic transaction can win," I exclaimed. His suspicion did not abate, though I saw that my ideas intrigued him.

Finally, he grunted, "Even with capitalism, the old ways will not change.

People will still steal, cheat, and bribe. Your system does not take this into consideration." Dragan had sensed my discomfort with my own proposal. I realized that my way of thinking depended heavily upon my own beliefs about capitalism, the type of capitalism that had shaped my life so strongly. But I began to realize that business strategy alone is not going to pull anyone out of poverty. There was a missing piece in the equation of prosperity, but I did not know what it was.

I could hear my own steps echo throughout the hall and into the adjacent rooms. It was siesta time, and there was not a soul around the palace. (The Vatican follows the Italian custom of closing all offices and stores for a four-hour lunch break.) I entered an open door, which led me into a frescoed room. I recognized the depictions of Bible stories: the Creation story and several scenes from the life of Christ. The marble floor was so worn down and polished that the entire room was reflected in it, making me feel as if I were walking on water. There was a large mirror on one of the walls. As I walked by, I caught a glimpse of myself; however, I didn't realize that it was me. My colorful uniform made me look as if I were another man, one who belonged in that room.

I turned to the only other paradigm I had in my life, my faith. Before this moment, I purposely tried not to mix faith and business. I had kept them in two separate silos, afraid of the paradoxes I might find. The big unanswered question was whether my Roman Catholic faith would support my advocacy for capitalism.

Appealing to Mother Teresa for business advice, as Dragan had insinuated, at first seemed like an odd idea. But she did build a religious order with over five thousand members and five hundred shelters that feed over half a million poor families per year.

During my time at the Vatican, the petite nun (she must have measured no more than five feet, which is a stark contrast to my six-foot-nine frame), single-handedly convinced John Paul II to open a soup kitchen inside the Vatican. I helped serve meals there during my off-duty days. Thinking back, I realized that Mother Teresa's objective had always been to restore dignity to individuals by fulfilling their basic physical needs, along with a dose of love and appreciation for who they were. I witnessed firsthand how many of her guests escaped poverty through this treatment. Contemplating this in the back of my mind, I realized that Mother Teresa's aspiration and our goal had much in common—except that she acted out of her deeply held religious beliefs and we acted out of our beliefs in competitiveness. Mother Teresa also deployed sound business strategy, but, more importantly, she firmly put the human person, the self-realization of the individual, at the center of all she did.

One restless night, with all these ideas swirling in my head, I had the faint memory that, while serving as a Swiss Guard at the Vatican, I had heard Pope John Paul II speak on such topics. The next day I went on to rediscover his teachings. I realized that I had been standing guard at his side (in service) the day he released his encyclical *Sollicitudo Rei Socialis (On Social Concern)* in 1987. I had listened to John Paul II state that Catholic social doctrine defined the freedom of economic initiative as a basic human right. He explained that "poverty in today's circumstances is primarily a matter of exclusion from networks of productivity and exchange; it is not to be understood simply or simplistically as a matter of having an unequal and inadequate portion of what is imagined to be a fixed number of economic goods." This had not meant anything to me at the time. A few years later in *Centesimus Annus*, he went on to describe democracy and a free economy as basic human rights, as he said that we must think of the poor "not as a problem to be solved, but as people with potential to be unleashed." The pope added that, due to the tremendous forces of good and evil, which could potentially be set free by democracy and a free economy, there is also a need to develop a "robust public moral culture" as a foundation for these basic human rights to be exercised effectively.

The pope argued that systems of free economy and democracy needed to conform to a moral compass. Society has to agree on what is acceptable business behavior in the pursuit of profit and what is not. He used the example of child labor as something that no moral society should condone but is sometimes used in the pursuit of corporate profits. John Paul II described capitalism and democracy as being built on moral norms. He stressed that the best way to ensure that these freedoms are indeed built on moral grounds is to place the human person firmly at the center of all economic activity. To John Paul II, work was not just the means by which one earns a living. He suggested, as George Weigel has eloquently summarized, that if a company encourages and enables an individual's self-realization through his or her work, ". . . we do not simply make more; we become more."[1]

I had found that missing piece. What had inevitably occurred at my high-tech start-ups was that the human person no longer stood at the center of the activity. The aim had become only money. People no longer identified with the company in a personal way; instead, they felt used. Could that phenomenon have led to the eventual and, sometimes inevitable, self-destruction I had so often witnessed?

Some of the people in the paintings wore similar costumes to my own. I remembered how my recruit master told us that a colonel of the guards had designed our uniforms (some one hundred years ago) after studying the old paintings: he used the Medici colors of red, blue, and orange to commemorate the sacking of Rome in 1529 (where some 150 guards died defending Pope Clement VII, a member of the Medici family). It made me feel good to be part of such a proud history. I was a small link in a long chain.

Another stairway led me to yet another room. I realized that I needed to pick up my pace. Ten minutes to 2 p.m. But where was I? I tried to retrace my steps. I thought I had passed just a couple of rooms, but as I retraced what I thought had been my recent steps, I became increasingly confused by the many doors and stairways I could take. I began to pick up my speed. The paintings melded together as I ran through the rooms—they all started to look alike. I began to sweat and became increasingly desperate until panic set in, to no avail. I was completely lost, and there was no one around to help me find the way.

Reviewing the thoughts of Pope John Paul II on capitalism and morality helped to fill some of the gaps that existed in thinking and provided me with a moral compass. For economic development, it is not enough simply to help people create great business strategies that enable them to become more competitive in the world market. The other half of the equation depends on whether a people's moral culture can implement capitalism in a way that puts human capital at its core. Do Macedonians agree

1. George Weigel, "The Free and Virtuous Society: Catholic Social Doctrine in the Twenty-First Century" (The Fourth Annual Tyburn Lecture, Tyburn Convent, London, May 19, 2004). To read the complete texts of Pope John Paul II's encyclicals, go to www.vatican.va/holy_father/john_paul_ii/encyclicals/.

with each other on what moral business behavior is and what it is not or about how capitalism should be implemented? Had this debate ever been held? The economic switch to a free market is, in my view, easy. The tough part is to stimulate the local culture to define moral tenets that guide the forces that are unleashed by the free market—toward the greater good of the society.

I had the other half of my argument for Dragan. Helping developing nations create great business strategies that enable them to become more competitive in the world market is only part of a sustainable solution. The other, equally important, part is to stimulate the local culture to define and implement moral tenets that can guide the new forces that are being unleashed by the advent of the free market. Financial gain itself does not furnish the answers to the questions it raises: Which means are acceptable to generate financial profits? How does human dignity fit into the pursuit of economic prosperity? What is the role of government in regulating business? Does each individual businessperson have a responsibility to the society at large? Without that guidance, without these answers, economic development is like giving someone a car without teaching him or her to drive. How could I have seen these two parts as separate from each other?

I jammed away at the keys on my BlackBerry, pounding out an answer to my nephew's e-mail. I did in fact, twenty years ago, get lost in the apostolic palace, on the way to my first assignment as a pontifical guard.

I stopped, resigned to the fact that I would have to wait until someone came along to show me the way. I was going to report for duty seriously late, if at all. My thoughts raced. I would be the first Swiss Guard to get lost in the Vatican, the first one to miss his initial assignment, and I would have to face the commandant and be punished. I would be marked from the start as a loser. When I managed to calm down, I heard the sound of a Gregorian chant in the distance—the beautiful ancient music of the Church—I followed it. The corridors in the papal palace carry sound very well and the music quickly became louder as I came down a small stairway. I crossed an ornate room with sculpted and painted drapery across the middle of the ceiling. And there was the source of the sound: the Capella Paolina—the Vatican's private chapel—my assigned post was right next to it. Just in time for the 2 p.m. changing of the guards.

7. Nature Is Destiny, and the More Nature, the Worse the Destiny

SALLY CHRISTIE

LIBREVILLE, GABON

• • •

THE PLANE landed in Gabon. I was optimistic and energized as I walked into the colorful bustle of Libreville Airport. I had heard a lot about this obscure African nation. Everything I had heard or read had been positive: it was the country with the highest gross domestic product (GDP) in sub-Saharan Africa. It had a stable government, little ethnic tension, and plenty of oil and timber, as well as unexplored mineral wealth.

In my experience working in developing countries, I had learned that "development" could not be boiled down to just one or two or even three factors. Development was a complex recipe, and getting it right was a mix of many factors, differing in their importance depending on the country. I had worked previously in Asia and had lived through the impressive emergence of Asian miracles in South Korea and China. Had Gabon, I wondered, created its own miracle? Had Gabon gotten the "African recipe" right?

My first impressions were good: the tree-lined boulevards of Libreville, the gleaming ministry buildings, the well-stocked shops—with imported cheeses and designer labels, and the polished Land Rovers were clear signs of affluence. I met with many people in the government and was impressed by them: they all seemed to be saying the right things.

My optimism was quickly shattered, however. In the weeks and months that followed, I came to reassess my initial opinion of the country. Instead of a tropical paradise and a case study for development, I discovered that

Gabon was essentially a "waste-ocracy." Massive amounts of oil had been pumped out of the ground and out of the sea over the past twenty years. It was a disappointment to learn that Gabon's black river of oil wealth had flowed straight out of the country, mostly into the Swiss bank accounts of the Gabonese elite.

I found that Gabon appeared rich, but it was only a facade. Beneath the surface, the reality was very different. Between the enormous ministry buildings were empty plots choked with weeds and shantytowns. The paved roads stopped almost immediately outside the capital. Foreign companies largely dominated private business, and there seemed to be few business opportunities for the Gabonese. More than 60 percent of the inhabitants of Libreville lived below the poverty line. There were rumors of starvation in the remote southern provinces. I was overcome by sadness witnessing the missed opportunity in this country.

I also came to realize that the political and economic systems were rife with corruption and cronyism. The wealth of Gabon was concentrated only in the hands of the elite who tightly controlled the future of the country. Government officials were saying all the right things, but action and a real desire for change were missing. I saw firsthand the pernicious effects these elements had on the overall culture of the country. I came to feel something I had not been prepared to feel—rage.

I fantasized about something stronger than the New Partnership for Africa's Development's (NEPAD) African Peer Review that would point a finger at a government that had destroyed the future of its country. What about an International Hall of Shame for the leader who has done the *least* for his country? Gabon was at the top of sub-Saharan Africa in terms of GDP; but when compared with the Human Development Index (HDI, which measures nonfinancial development indices like literacy and life expectancy), Gabon falls thirty-two places, one of the worst discrepancies of any country. I began to ask myself an important question: why was this country, with so many natural resources, so poor? We like to say that nature is destiny. *But if nature is destiny, does more nature bring a worse destiny?*

It is an interesting fact that, in Africa, natural resource wealth often has an inverse correlation with the health of the economic situation:

countries with higher natural resource endowments are also the ones most likely to experience conflicts and economic crises. The recent history in Angola and the Democratic Republic of Congo are just two striking examples.

Gabon, despite its natural resource wealth, has not experienced any civil war or ethnic strife since the end of colonialism in 1960. The last thirty-nine years have been spent under the seemingly benign dictatorship of just one president. Nonetheless, despite peace, Gabon has not been able to transform its natural resource endowments into sustainable wealth.

There are many types of wealth that contribute to the development of a country. Michael Fairbanks' "Seven Forms of Capital" framework highlights the various forms that wealth can take. While the Seven Forms of Capital acknowledges the importance of natural endowments, it also states that wealth is about much more than that. Capital, or wealth, takes many forms: it is about the intangibles of human, cultural, and knowledge capital that create long-term sustainable wealth and a rising standard of living for the average citizens of a country.

According to the Seven Forms of Capital, countries should not rely solely on natural advantages (physical capital), or *comparative advantages*, but rather should focus on the higher forms of capital (social capital) to create *competitive advantages.*

Natural resources can be a good start for development, and many (but not all) of today's economic powerhouses started off with a strong physical capital base. They then transformed that base into long-term sustainable growth by reinvesting the rents from their natural resources into the "higher forms of capital"—investing in strong institutions, moral values, knowledge, and human capital. And, along the way, they developed a culture of competitiveness and economies built off of sophisticated industries and products.

Some countries in Africa do understand that long-term prosperity does not come from diamonds or oil or timber. Botswana is an example of a country that has used the rents from its impressive natural resources to create higher forms of capital. Botswana invested its diamond money not in guns, but in schools; not in showy government buildings, but in health clinics and hospitals. In another part of the continent, Rwanda is a good

	REPRESENTATIVE ELEMENTS	REPRESENTATIVE EXAMPLES
CULTURAL	• tangible articulations • norms • mental models	• architecture, music, language • range of acceptable behaviors • trust, wealth-creation attitudes, long-term thinking
HUMAN	• health and population • education and training • attitudes and motivation	• nutrition, medical and mental health • primary and secondary, technical • self-responsibility, action-orientation
KNOWLEDGE	• qualitative, quantitative data • frameworks and concepts • knowledge generation	• statistics, opinions, records • theories, processes, procedures • universities, R&D, market learning
INSTITUTIONAL	• "good, clean governance" • justice system • connective organizations	• transparency, no hidden costs • property protection, predictable regulations • chambers of commerce, unions
FINANCIAL	• financial systems • private wealth • public wealth	• banks, stock markets • bank deposits • bank reserves, taxes, duties, macroeconomic stability
MAN-MADE	• transportation, communication • power • water and sewerage	• roads, ports, telephone systems • electric grids, generation capacity • pipelines, pumping stations
NATURAL ENDOWMENTS	• environmental issues • raw materials • climate and location	• conservation, restoration • agricultural, mineral, petroleum • proximity to markets

Figure 1: The Seven Forms of Capital

Source: Michael Fairbanks, "Changing the Mind of a Nation" in Culture Matters: How Values Shape Human Progress, ed. Lawrence E. Harrison (New York: Basic Books, 2001), 276.

example of a resource-poor country whose government is nonetheless dedicated to developing industries based on competitive advantages.

Gabon, by contrast, is "stuck" in the lowest form of capital. The natural oil wealth of Gabon has made the government complacent and unwilling to reinvest in any other forms of capital. As long as the rents from its oil and timber wealth are enough to satisfy the needs of the elite, then there is little incentive to invest in developing the strong institutions, technology,

knowledge, and human capital that are so crucial for the sustainable development of a country.

I met many wonderful Gabonese during my year in Gabon. These were
lively, interesting people who were always ready to sit in a restaurant over
beer (always served warm) and talk about their country and their society.
They were generally open and honest about their country. What struck
me most was their passive acceptance, even their complicity, in the current state of affairs. Their lack of desire to rock the boat or attempt change
always puzzled me.

I knew that they were not inherently bad or lazy people. Rather, they
were simply living, working, and trying to survive in a system and a culture that rewarded only absolute obedience to the status quo. They lived
in a system where innovation had no value. In Gabon, decision making,
wealth, and power are concentrated in a small circle. The only path to
riches or advancement is to get into that circle. There is no benefit in rocking the boat or in advocating change.

I worked in the Ministry of Finance. It was a ministry so bloated by
bureaucracy that two soccer-field-size buildings were needed to house its
staff. I made friends with many of the young Gabonese who worked with
me. One of them was a young civil servant of my age, named Jeanne-Yves.[1]
One day, I asked Jeanne-Yves about her future and dreams: did she really
want to be like the bureaucrats with their mournful eyes with whom we
worked, many following in the footsteps of people full of flowery promises, but ultimately trapped in a cycle of soul-sapping indolence? I also
knew her pay was terrible, insufficient for subsistence in the fantastically
expensive import culture of Gabon.

Jeanne-Yves sighed. She was bored by her job, but there were not many
other options for young, educated Gabonese. "Well," she said slowly. "If I
wait long enough, one day I might be in a better position. One day I might
be in charge of a budget, and then the work would become more bearable."
The straightforward manner in which she said this sent chills down my
spine. There was no ducking of the head, no licking of the lips, no apolo-
getic laugh. This was it. The future of the country, the best and the bright-

1. Name is a pseudonym.

est graduates, had no other aspirations but to seek out moribund jobs in stifling ministries for a "chance to be in charge of a budget."

It is easy to be cynical about people like Jeanne-Yves, but I came to realize that Jeanne-Yves is a product of a flawed system. She is part of a social arrangement built around cronyism, nepotism, and strict adherence to a predetermined order. The government tightly controlled *all* the opportunities in the country, even private sector opportunities. The only way to benefit, to survive even, was to buy into that system.

When I think about Jeanne-Yves and the other young Gabonese with no future except the one predetermined by their government, I do feel rage. I compared Jeanne-Yves to the people I had worked with in the fast-growing economies of Asia. In Asia, I saw people with a sense of personal implication in the development of their countries. The sense of *personal contribution* to the country's development is ingrained in the minds of the workers in the fast-growing, upwardly mobile tigers of East Asia. The Korean salary-man working the late shift in a grim office tower in Seoul believes that by working until midnight, he is directly involved in the development of his country, a mission that is dear to him.

In Gabon, that personal implication, a crucial ingredient for development, was missing. In Asia, development was something you made happen. In Gabon, development was something that might someday fall from the sky.

There is a body of development literature that blames poor governance for Africa's ills. Then there is another point of view that says, no, the problems of Africa have nothing to do with poor governance but more to do with health, social, macroeconomic, or even weather-related issues.

Before coming to Gabon, I would have laughed at the thought that poor governance was a key determinant of development. I had worked in China and had experienced corruption and poor governance firsthand, especially in local government circles. Yet in China, in addition to the corruption and cronyism, there was also a lot more: growth, many people benefiting from the wealth spreading throughout the country, optimism, and upward mobility. In Gabon, I found only corruption and not a lot of anything else.

I used to believe strongly that the strength of the private sector and

the will of the people could overcome bad governance. I underestimated
the impact that poor governance could have on the culture of a country.
Working on the ground in Gabon, alongside Gabonese colleagues, was a
frustrating, exhilarating, and challenging journey that changed my mind
about many aspects of development. It did not change my mind about the
complexity of the development recipe, but it added one or two ingredients
that I now realize are very important.

Poor governance is now definitely in the recipe, as well as the impact it
has on shaping the culture of a country. I have reassessed my opinion about
the role of the government and how crucial and deterministic it can be in
shaping a country's future. And I have seen firsthand how natural resources
can be both a blessing and a curse: in Gabon, I saw a country "stuck" in
poverty, largely because of a predatory government that has relied too long
(and too effectively) on natural resources.

I was at the airport in Libreville, saying good-bye to the friends I had
made. I got on the plane, and we took off over Libreville. Further down
the coast, we flew over the port where the oil ships were moored, waiting
to sail away with wealth from the country. Out the other window, I saw the
rich equatorial rain forest, full of exotic timber that covered an unexplored
depth of mineral wealth.

There was so much potential here. Leaving the country, I felt robbed of a
certain naïveté, that optimism that I had had when I arrived. Development
was, indeed, a complex recipe, and getting it right was a mix of many factors, differing in their importance depending on the country. I left Gabon
wiser but sadder, though my cookbook of ingredients for development
was bigger than when I arrived.

8. Locomotives, Needles, and Aid

MALIK FAL

DAKAR, SENEGAL (IN MY FATHER'S HOME)

• • •

THE PREVIOUS DAY'S incident in Nairobi kept playing back in my head. The brief argument I had with Richard Woodburn,[1] Pepsi's operations director for East Africa, had been my first-ever corporate skirmish. It left me puzzled and surprised. I had joined the company's New York world headquarters three years earlier upon graduation and had gotten married a year after that. I was about to travel when Richard and I had that difficult session.

It all started well. We were going through routine business checklists before my trip. Our chat began to derail when I brought up a sticky compensation issue. "Richard," I said, "you know that I am going to Paris in order to visit my dad who was just released from the hospital last week. The human resource folks in New York told me about an expatriate compensation policy before my transfer here. They said that being hired as a French citizen posted in Kenya, I qualified for home travel leave from Nairobi to Paris twice a year. I also checked with Michel, the only other French expatriate in the office, who confirmed the policy. So, I intend to expense this ticket back through you and wanted to flag that." I had mentioned these words casually on my way out of Richard's office but did get a glimpse at an immediate sense of discomfort in his facial expression.

"Actually, you can't," Richard said with a voice in which I detected a

1. The names in this essay are pseudonyms.

little bit of embarrassment. "Michel is entitled to it, but you're not. It is a bit complicated to explain, but you are not, technically, an expatriate."

"Well, what am I then?" I asked.

"You are a regional hire," was his answer. "Home travel leave policy applies to people who are culturally estranged. Since you are an African, this does not apply to you."

At that point, I was confused and could not figure out whether to howl or scream. I opted for a third option, humor.

"Well," I said with a smile, "you must remember the time when you and I had lunch at a Kenyan restaurant, a few days after we both arrived in Nairobi. You asked me to order for you and got baffled when I started speaking to the waiter in English. I remember the look on your face when you said, 'Hey, I could have done that; don't you speak Swahili?' It was quite funny actually but you know, Richard, I still do not speak Swahili, and Senegal is still further away from Kenya than Britain is. So how does this *technicality* work in my case?"

By then, Richard's awkwardness showed on his face, and he retreated by saying, "Listen, I do not make the rules here, but I will look into it and get back to you." I was surprised to see that an educated person like Richard could not fully register the fundamental cultural differences between a Senegalese and a Kenyan. In any case, as I walked out the door, my mind had already moved on, and the next morning I arrived in Paris.

To the seasoned traveler, Parisian cab drivers seem to be some of the most obnoxious people on earth. Their degrees of rudeness work according to an elaborate social order. Blacks and North Africans who speak French but have strong accents and ordinary clothes get the worst treatment: no help with the bags, offensive remarks, and scores of never-heard-of charges added on the fare. Other foreigners who do not speak French but look like easy prey for unwanted tours of Paris come next. Upper-class Europeans with crisp Parisian accents or aristocratic demeanors sometimes get a little bit of respect, on a good day. A Chinese general once observed, "The French fear the strong and bully the weak." Parisian cab drivers, even *black* ones, are the embodiment of that statement. As I stood in the taxi stand outside Charles de Gaulle Airport after the grueling nine-hour flight from Kenya, I thought of my Senegalese origin and where it placed me in the social order of the over-unionized but highly class-conscious Parisian cab driver. I decided that during this two-day visit to Paris, I would have no time for abusive French nonsense. My altercation with Richard the day before had put me on the defensive. I was ready for a fight. My turn finally came, and I got into the cab, where a surprisingly pleasant fellow greeted me with a cheerful "Bonjour, Monsieur, where to, *s'il vous plaît!*" "*Avenue de Suffren*," I said with a grin on my face. There would be no fight on that day.

As we made our way through early morning Parisian traffic, I thought that, apart from checking on my dad's health, there was now a second thing I needed to inquire about. I was going to ask my dad about the expectations he had as an African living under French rule. He grew up in the city of St. Louis, Senegal, under colonial rule. Later, he became one of the first African graduates of a French elite engineering *grande école*. He was part of Africa's independence generation of the 1960s. Unlike many of the younger African leaders who embezzled their way to great riches, he never felt guilty about his status. Rather, he felt secure in his knowledge that he had earned everything he had the hard way. For him, it would have been poor manners to speak about one's private life struggles. The little I knew about his experiences I got through eavesdropping on adult conversations that he would have after dinner with close friends. However, I was on a mission. I decided that I was now a young African professional trying to make his way in the world and that the time had come to ask my father a few things that I may never again have the chance to hear him speak about.

A few hours later, as he and I were sitting in the living room of his Paris apartment having gone through the mundane chitchat and the outcome of his recent operation, I went on the offensive. "Dad," I began, "you remember that my best friend in Abidjan when I was growing up was this white kid, Olivier Cadeac. He and I were always together, learned to swim together, played soccer together, and built little tree houses in the bush together. All those years and throughout school in Africa and Europe, I never really felt different or prevented from accomplishing anything I would wish to accomplish. Now something has happened to me at work, and I want to know what it was like for you growing up under foreign rule and how you dealt with this."

As I said those words, my dad leaned back in his chair and went into a sort of dreamlike state. "Ah, expectations," he said. "Things were not the same in our time, and you kids have it better nowadays." He was getting animated, and a faint smile appeared on his face. "Did I ever tell you about Professor Rousseau, who used to teach us at Lycée Faidherbe in St. Louis? It must have been in 1935 or '36. We were one of the first integrated classes in the colony. Every morning, Rousseau would start his history lesson with the following statement: '*Whites make locomotives; Negroes cannot make simple needles. Whites are civilized; Negroes are savages.*'"

His smile grew wider as a sheer expression of incredulity invaded my whole body. I managed to hesitantly ask him, "And how did you black kids react to this?"

He began to laugh and said, "What could we have done then? Many of my African classmates got really affected by this and became under-achievers. Others began to think about becoming a locomotive driver or a worker in a needle factory, although none of these things existed in Senegal at the time. For me, people like Rousseau were a source of moti-vation. They made me want to excel and prove them wrong. The trials and tribulations of this life are the food of the soul!" He concluded before standing up, while I remained glued to my chair, "Let's go get some lunch," he said. "You'll figure this out on your own."

He was right. Many years after that fateful Paris visit, I became an eco-nomic policy advisor. Because my work involved client engagements with high-level officials, very soon I was finding myself roaming presidential offices, ministries, and local donor country missions in Africa. There were plenty of opportunities to observe how peoples' subconscious attributions about Africa continue to affect economic development and the donor-recipient discussion. As time went by, sets of stereotypes began to emerge in my mind. Within minutes of meeting a Western official, I was able to tell whether I was dealing with the dismissive or the benevolent type. With African leaders, it took longer, but eventually I was also able to tell whether I was dealing with the aid-addicted or rebellious type. Of course, many people I was meeting were on the fence of my arbitrary mental clas-sifications. Overall, however, my respective experiences with each member of these subsegments were pretty consistent.

The encounters in which dismissive Western aid bureaucrats were most readily exposed were the ones where I would be accompanied by a junior white colleague. A meeting my colleague Clay and I once had with an aid organization official in Nigeria named David Baldwyn stands out in this category of encounters. Clay was walking behind me as we entered Mr. Baldwyn's office, I suppose out of deference for my more senior status. Our host was standing behind his desk. "Good morning, Mr. Baldwyn," Clay and I both beamed with extended hands while moving around the two visitors' chairs Baldwyn was pointing to, "and thank you for making time to meet with us," I added. By then, already, Baldwyn's body had somehow fully shifted to face Clay. He shook Clay's hand, gave me a brief nod, and motioned us to sit down. "You are welcome. What can I do for you?" he asked while sitting down at an angle that gave him direct eye contact with Clay. I was feeling a growing sense of discomfort but pressed on. "We are here on behalf of a client called People's Energy, a Boston-based non-profit organization that wants to work on improving the competitiveness of Nigeria's agriculture-based industries. We would love to hear your views about the Nigerian economy, the types of agribusiness programs your organization funds in Nigeria, and perhaps get names of economic actors you think we should meet," I said. Clay and I deposited business cards on the desk, which Baldwyn took and proceeded to examine.

"I see," Baldwyn said while looking up toward me in an inquisitive way. "Well, apart from oil, which only benefits a corrupt oligarchy of Nigerian officials, and a little Lebanese-run manufacturing activity that serves the basic needs of the 120 million other impoverished Nigerians, there is not much of a Nigerian economy to speak of," he said directly to me with a mischievous smile. "We are trying to support a few agribusiness initiatives here and there, but the dreadful infrastructure and sheer chaos we see in this country make it impossible to achieve anything meaningful," he added, now turning again to face Clay. As the meeting continued, Baldwyn almost stopped acknowledging my presence and went on lecturing Clay on how hopeless a development case he felt Nigeria was. The virulence with which he was making his negative statements about Nigeria made Clay feel uneasy. Throughout this sermon, he kept insisting on the notion that the rest of the donor community felt exactly the same way he did.

I had long learned to detach myself from the grief generated by such instances. Being ignored, I would naturally withdraw and become an observer in a conversation I had initiated. Doing so involved letting my mind wander in spaces where disturbing thoughts and questions would assail me. Baldwyn's argument had valid points, but what kind of "development partner" could a person like him possibly be to the Nigerian leadership, however corrupt that leadership may be? Why were African governments not more concerned about the need to reduce their dependence on donor funding? Having been in Nigeria for the best part of twenty-four hours, I had already experienced the folly of the Lagos airport and the suffocating pressure of the crowds. I had also met brilliant entrepreneurs and had been exposed to an amazingly vibrant culture. Could someone so deeply negative about the country he was supposed to help ever rise up to the challenge?

It has been said that everything in this world was created in pairs: night and day, action and reaction, elation and sadness, courage and cowardice, honesty and deceit, heat and cold. As my professional network grew, I discovered that dismissive westerners personified by Baldwyn had counterparts on the other side of the donor-recipient table: the aid-addicted African bureaucrat. Aid-addicted African officials could display the same body language to my junior white colleagues and me and make the same gloomy statements about their own country as people like Baldwyn. I began to notice that many such "African Baldwyns" were quite senior in the hierarchy of their organization, for example Emile Diakite, a former minister of education I came across while on missions in West Africa.

At first glance, Diakite's ministry looked like a center of excellence. Outside of the Ministry of Finance, the Ministry of Education was the best-funded ministry within government. Donors would run over themselves to award the ministry projects. The minister himself was a poster boy at donor party conversations. He was a savvy "charmer" who knew what to say and when to say it in order to get projects funded. He would dance and sing to whatever donor tune was in vogue: governance, gender, AIDS, you name it. Even if the current theme of the day had nothing to do with his department, Diakite would become the spokesperson for that theme and would thus endear himself to potential funding providers. All this he saw as a critical component of his success, and he was relishing the reputation of a "doer" within the expatriate community.

The problem I saw with Diakite's approach is that there was never any coherence in what he was doing. His ministry would get funding from literally scores of different donors who all had different agendas, different requirements, and different objectives. Resources would flow into Diakite's coffers, and he would just do what he was bid to do, regardless of whether his portfolio of programs had consistency or impact. On one end, local television news shows would invariably have a segment on a new Ministry of Education initiative being launched somewhere in the country, which created the impression of success. On the other end, the quality of primary and secondary school graduates was getting so bad that the number of first-year university students who could barely read and write was alarmingly growing.

There was no comprehensive and well-thought-out education strategy. The country's education policy had been outsourced to ten different foreign countries that were all competing to outdo each other with favors to the minister, rather than cooperate to support sensible solutions to the education challenges of this developing nation. Donors had found measures of success that satisfied their constituencies but did very little for the country. Unfortunately, Minister Diakite acted like a person who had given up his prerogative as a leader but did not even know he had. My calls for fundamental reforms aimed at training future generations of leaders with the capacity to manage the country's key commercial industries were falling on deaf ears.

Not everyone in Diakite's government behaved like him. In fact, I would often meet some of his cabinet colleagues who could hardly conceal their resentment of his aid-addicted ways. Chief among these rebellious ones was Minister Joshua Barenge, the minister of agriculture. Minister Barenge had been a youth union leader. He had been trained as an agroeconomist and had spent time in Cuba. In his midlife years, he had become a nationalist who only wanted to deal with African advisors, African institutions, and African solutions to Africa's problems. "We need to stop this culture of begging that prevails in our leadership," he would say. "Our brothers who think development will just be handed out to us are fools. Look at the

Asians. They have understood long ago that sustainable prosperity is not something one receives. It is the result of hard work, wise judgment, and independent thinking."

As a result of his beliefs, Barenge tended to be overly abrasive with all westerners, but especially with westerners who worked for donor organizations. Using the stature of his high office, he would play embarrassing power games with western visitors that made everyone uncomfortable. To him, this type of behavior was a way to turn the tables a little bit. To me, this type of behavior was unproductive and potentially damaging to the interest of his country. Western ambassadors, heads of multilateral missions, and even cabinet colleagues were beginning to raise concerns about his style of engagement. Some started gunning for him. The president was close to him, but, nonetheless, he was eventually removed from his high-profile post and placed in a less preeminent office. Barenge was a rebellious African leader who felt that Africans should not let others set expectations for them. The problem is that he did not understand that, regardless of his intellectual values, he was at a level of leadership where interpersonal skills are paramount and can make or break a career—not to mention the fact that engagement with the West would remain an essential component of the development equation for his country for years to come, albeit in the terms he was advocating.

Encounters with benevolent aid officials carried their own baggage but would, nonetheless, be far more pleasant than most other encounters. Bernard Rakas was one of my closest benevolent Western acquaintances. He worked for an American nongovernmental organization (NGO) in Kenya and would travel for weeks at a time in remote villages up-country. We would meet socially, and I truly appreciated his dedication and concern, but I had a fundamental problem with the way he thought poverty should be dealt with.

Bernard would say things like "I feel very sorry for those poor-but-smiling Kenyan kids who run after my four-by-four yelling *muzungu! muzungu!* (white man) every time I go to the villages. They're the ones who are getting the short end of the stick. The Kenyan government does not care about them. And the bureaucrats in Washington are too busy playing politics and looking for ways to cut my funding. I wish our Western leaders would be more sensitive and send more money to solve Africa's poverty problem."

I always knew that Bernard's intentions were noble and well meaning when he made comments like this. However, it was still important for me gently to highlight some of the flaws in his line of reasoning. "Well, Bernard," I would say, "we both feel bad about those kids, but, frankly, the line of thinking that says Western leaders should be more generous and more willing to come and save us poor Africans perpetuates the problem. Aid and handouts will not create prosperity in Africa—not just because large chunks of that aid have been embezzled by corrupt African governments, but mainly because what Africa needs most are dynamic businesses and industries that can create employment and income for the average citizen." At that point, Bernard would frown, and I would add, "Yes, my friend, this means that a bunch of African businessmen must be supported to access capital, generate capital, and become very rich. Isn't it how every single G8-country did it? If while creating great products and services, a few Africans get rich and help the vast majority of other Africans live more fulfilling lives, why should we have a problem with that?"

I knew that Bernard was uncomfortable with such statements. He believed that all good and smart Africans should be doing what he was doing: wearing Birkenstock sandals and providing health or education services to the poor in the most remote parts of Africa. I kept pointing out to him that, while his line of work was inspiring and noble, it could never be a long-term solution to Africa's problem. "Bernard," I would say, "in most of Africa's fifty-three countries, donor funding accounts for more than 50 percent of national budgets. The schools, clinics, books, medicines, pickup trucks, uniforms, and equipment with which you assist the poor in rural areas cannot indefinitely continue to be funded by Western handouts. Some people within the local leadership need to start thinking about how local fiscal revenues will eventually be sufficient for African governments to provide all those things to their own people. This means that African private businesses and industries need to be enough of a fiscal base for our governments to generate adequate amounts of domestic fiscal revenue." Bernard and I agreed to disagree but remained good friends.

My dad went back to Senegal shortly after his Paris operation. He stopped traveling and went on to spend his twilight years reading, watch-ing the news, and meeting friends in his Dakar house. The trophies, awards, works of art, heads-of-state pictures, and framed letters lined up in his liv-ing room bear testimony to his long and fulfilling life of service. During my sporadic and short visits, he would ask me about my family, about my brother and sisters who all live in different countries, and occasionally about my work. We would sit in deep, leather couches, glancing through the large windows that overlooked the Atlantic, sipping tea, chatting, and enjoying the mild ocean breeze. We were in that exact situation one after-noon in July 2005 when Tony Blair appeared on the flat-screen television hanging on the wall behind us. We clumsily attempted not to pay atten-tion while soft blurbs of the British prime minister's speech distracted our conversation.

With a couple of presidents, an opulent Scottish mansion, and a legion of journalists standing in front of him, Tony Blair was making an announce-ment: "Today, as I close this historic summit of Gleneagles, it is my great pleasure to tell you that Britain and all of its G8 partners have decided that in the course of the next few years, we will erase the debt and double our aid to Africa. . . ." My dad faintly moved in his chair and said, "That looks encouraging. The West is finally deciding to help the world's poorest con-tinent. What do you think of that?"

"Well," I replied, "it is indeed encouraging, but I wonder how many African countries are ready to use this money wisely. Very few African leaders understand that it is only through the improved competitiveness of their key industries that poverty will be eradicated. If this money goes exclusively into unsustainable poverty-relief programs, in fifty years Africa will end up at exactly the same place where it is today."

"Hmm," he added with his trademark smile, "I see. By the way, have you kids figured out how to make locomotives and needles yet?" he asked.

I was taken aback by his question but tried to hold my ground. "Actually, Dad," I replied, "we should not think about Africa's success in those terms anymore. It is no longer about being able to *make* locomotives or being able to *make* needles, although many foolish African leaders still insist that we should do so. Hundreds of Africans now own shares in privatized railway networks, and importing needles from China makes more sense than manufacturing them on the continent. What matters now is that we should be pragmatic about ways to generate wealth for the average African, whether that means manufacturing goods ourselves, importing, or outsourcing."

As I was talking, I could see an increasingly active twinkle in his eyes. "Well," he concluded, "that sounds like a civilized approach to me! Even at my age, life continues to be a series of rude awakenings. When I was growing up, whites were to make locomotives, and we were expected to start making needles. Today, due to aid, Europe's declining esteem for our abilities, and the thoughtlessness of many of our leaders, no one expects even that anymore."

9. On Globalization

MICHAEL FAIRBANKS

BOXFORD, MASSACHUSETTS

• • •

W HAT IS GLOBALIZATION? What is the effect of it on me and of me on it? Am I not just an aspect of globalization, but also a determinant, a fractal of it? Or, put brusquely, can I push back? Do I have choices of how to interact with globalization? Is there a journey to be made through globalization, and if so, what are the points of reference, the way-points along a planned course, in a successful personal expedition?

A famous economist at Harvard once lectured to a group of us: "Globalization is where everything mixes with everything else." I asked him, "What is everything?" He gazed over the group of us, his acolytes for the evening, held his hands on his hips defiantly, and repeated in an even more assertive tone, "Everything."

So I set out to taxonomize *everything*, for the purposes of understanding globalization. I considered the common features and outcomes of it: popular culture, politics, consumer items, and costs of transportation, energy, and communications. I thought of a few specific illustrations: the Beatles, communism, American TV, Coca Cola, papal pronouncements, *Newsweek*, Chinese soccer stadiums in Africa, Google, flows of investment, the diffusion of innovations, asynchronous communications, and the impact of medical breakthroughs.

I decided, after some efforts at finding models that explained globalization to me, that I must return to the uses of language, to metaphors, and to the anecdote. After all, the challenge to each of us is not merely to observe globalization or to move smoothly, if unconsciously, through its ether, but to participate fully and to become, over the time of our lives, forces for positive change within it.

I began with several principles: globalization is socially constructed, and each of us is a fractal of it, a self-similar, small (though not diminished) aspect of it; personal narrative can convey the meaning of globalization better than any abstraction; and good stories happen to those who can tell them. So I set foot, back nearly three decades for the first of two anecdotes, to my second full year in East Africa.

Somewhere South of Juba, Sudan, December 1980

It felt to me as if it were 150 degrees Fahrenheit. I was hungry and tired and did not know where I was. I regretted that I had left my comfortable Peace Corps post in the western highlands of Kenya, a small village school I was helping to build. The lorry hit every hole in the dried-out tributary of the Nile that we used for a road.

The lorry hit a rut, and my head banged off the side of the railing. It was hot, and I was so uncomfortable that I used the next rut as an opportunity to take my head and bang it deliberately off the side. I wished that it would knock me unconscious and that I would awaken some hours or days later, nearer to a cold glass of soda, a shower, and the cool side of a pillow. It did not work.

I was lucky to have a ride, but I was miserable. I had not eaten for two days, and though I drank a lot of water, I was not sure how long the water would last.

The driver looked back at me. I sat on bags of cement and used a sack of the local plant drug *miraa* as a pillow. He motioned to me to get off the sack. My weight would ruin its value. Then he motioned for me to look ahead. A vehicle was coming.

Africa was always a chessboard on which strong nations played. These nations wooed countries in Africa with foreign aid that local leaders stole. Capitalist nations sent teachers and doctors; they provided credits for fighter jets and surface-to-air missiles. Communist nations built soccer stadiums, roads, and hospitals.

The productivity of capitalistic states was greater than the putative productivity of the Soviet Union, and in the end, the power of Russia and their client state Cuba weakened. When the communists left Africa, the capitalists lost interest. Soon communism in the region died. You no longer saw billboards that proclaimed "All Glory to the Revolution." Instead, democratize, liberalize, privatize, and stabilize were the pithy aphorisms of the time.

This was apparent everywhere. I traveled five thousand miles from Lake Victoria along the Nile River to the Mediterranean Sea. I saw famines and skirmishes that fell just short of wars, the kind of wars that are ubiquitous in Africa, so much so that foreign correspondents are exhausted from covering them and not getting column inches in the newspapers and magazines for which they worked.

I saw Coca Cola in almost every village: warm, sugary, less carbonated, but nonetheless satisfying. I saw boys and girls with t-shirts that read "Who Shot J.R.?" from the American TV show *Dallas*. There were countless t-shirts of American football and basketball teams. While poverty was extant, the West reigned. Capitalism was winning.

The other lorry came nearer. It was the first one we had seen in three days. I wanted to stop and ask the passengers for food. We moved rapidly over the baked mud track and so did the other vehicle. I saw a white man standing up in the back of that lorry; he looked Scandinavian. His hair was blond and tussled. He had a red beard. He was elfish, fair skinned, and as pink as anyone I had ever seen. He saw me standing likewise on my lorry and motioned that he wanted to say something.

We would each have time to say one thing as the trucks passed. I shouted first. "How far to Juba?" He ignored me. He cupped his hands and shouted back, "Lenin is dead." He passed me. He waited for my reaction, a hand gesture, a shrug of my shoulders, something. I offered him nothing, perplexed.

I imagined he was a young northern European communist. He had decided to give me a dose of his ideology. Perhaps it was a reaction to the poverty and what we were experiencing there in the southern Sudan, during the famine and the civil war. All of this horror conjured up for him the image of Vladimir Ilyich Lenin.

We both had one thing to shout. I shouted out of my concern for self-preservation. I wanted to know where food and water was. Where was shade? How far to all that?

Western capitalism delivered only t-shirts and sugar water. It did not deliver food and medicine, but neither did communism. That was this Scandinavian's thesis; he cared so much about it that it was the one thing he wanted to say to someone.

I admired him, though. He shouted out of a sense of justice. I did not agree with this young Marxist, but I envied his ability to hold a belief so deeply that, even in the dire circumstance in which we found ourselves, he demonstrated the depth of his values. I wondered how I could be the same. I wondered why I was not the same.

In some hours, we stopped at a village where I found tea and biscuits. A day later, I obtained a large bag of potatoes that lasted me some time. Two weeks later, I walked into the Khartoum Hilton, where the Blue Nile from Ethiopia and the White Nile from Lake Victoria comingle for the first time. I was exhausted, thin, and emotionless; I patted down my clothes to get off some of the dust. I put down nine Sudanese pounds onto the counter in front of a puzzled waiter for an all-you-can-eat buffet. My hardship was over.

I left the hotel and walked into the street. I was satisfied for the first time in a month. I began to look for a small, cheap guesthouse where I could wash my clothes and put my head on that cool pillow. I wanted the sound of water. If I could get a toilet in my room, I would rig it so the water just ran and ran and ran.

I passed a kiosk where an old man sold recent international magazines. I picked through them to catch up on news; and that is when I saw it: the cover of *Newsweek* dated several weeks before, the second week of December 1980.

"John Lennon is dead."

KIGALI, RWANDA, THE OFFICE OF PRESIDENT
PAUL KAGAME, APRIL 2008

Clet Niyikiza and I sat next to each other at lunch. He was an important member of the Rwandan diaspora, a senior executive at one of the largest pharmaceutical companies in the world, and an expert in cures for cancer. We are both members of President Kagame's Advisory Council and meet regularly to discuss the broad issues of postconflict nation building. The committee consists of twelve men and women, such as Fortune Five-Hundred CEOs; Pastor Rick Warren, the best selling author; the president of the African Development Bank; and a Harvard Business School professor.

We had spent the morning discussing infrastructure investments, policy adjustments, and export competitiveness. The country was growing and secure, wages were up in key export sectors, outsiders recognized Rwanda as a corruption-free nation. There were rumblings that there were small internal factions anxious to raise the specter of genocide once again, and some international human-rights activists insisted that quelling the ethnic discussion in political circles was tantamount to violating free speech. A member of the committee, the most prominent clergyman in Rwanda, Bishop John Rucyahana, responded, "If a government raises a miserably poor population toward prosperity, isn't that the greatest service it can provide to the cause of human rights?"

The president capped off the discussion by urging us always to think differently. "We have to do things that other nations don't do if we want to maintain our right to expect a better outcome."

Clet and I began to brainstorm about what we could do. I asked him if he knew about Lackawanna Biotech, a ten-year-old, privately owned company that was one of the pioneers in the field of network biology, looking for cures to cancer.[1] He did.

Clet had PhDs in physics and math and, due to a U.S. national security act, was invited to become a U.S. citizen as a young man because he had the

---

1. This is a fictitious name. The actual company and its executives are disguised. This is due to the strict guidance of the company's lawyers who, for regulatory reasons, felt it prudent not to mention the company's name.

kind of experience and training that the country valued. A then seventeen-year veteran of the pharmaceutical industry, he knew that 80 percent of the costs in traditional pharmaceuticals were from drug testing that never accomplished its goals and that network biology was the efficient way to do the testing with mathematical models on computers, looking for digital results before doing experiments on animals. The old paradigm was trial and error with chemistry; the new one was computer modeling with math and biology to find winning drugs before launching expensive animal and human experiments. This could drive down costs, focus efforts, and find more complex treatments with a hope eventually to discover cures.

I was an original small investor and knew that Lackawanna hoped to enter the public markets sometime in the future. If the company embarked on this path, it would approach the "quiet period" prior to a public offering and would no longer be able to speak directly with potential investors or to discuss its prospects with anyone, especially the press. I decided to approach the president and ask if he could take pension plan money to invest in Lackawanna. A number of things had to happen: the president had to agree, the government had to have funds available, and the CEO of Lackawanna had to agree. There were the complications of two types of legal jurisdictions, one based on the French system of codes, another on the English system of precedents. Most importantly, time was running out.

I asked the president for a private meeting. "Mr. President, you urged us to think differently on behalf of the country. Clet and I would like to pursue a strategy of getting Rwanda's pension money into a nontraditional, speculative investment." He listened to me. "Pope John Paul said that eradicating poverty is integrating the poor into networks of productivity. I think there is a way . . ."

We spoke for some time, and he authorized us to move forward to evaluate the opportunity. As a shareholder of the company, I would have to recuse myself. Clet would have to do the same as an official executive of a potential competitor. However, as a private citizen acting on behalf of the president, Clet was able to help guide the process.

The next discussion was with Ray Miller, the CEO. "I have a crazy idea for a new kind of investor. Please call me back," I said into his voice-mail.

Ray, to his credit, called and listened. Ray was used to speaking to the biggest venture capitalists and biotech investors in the industry. Lackawanna had no need for new money, though he did say he wished he had some long-term investors. He indicated he would think more about our proposal but that the answer would probably be "no" because he did not really know Rwanda and its leadership. And he was afraid that if the country lost the money, it would hurt its people.

I told Ray that the president was prepared to take risks to achieve superior outcomes. I explained how the pope said we need to link the poor to superproductive networks. I argued that Google set aside 1 percent of its market capitalization in its initial public offering to do development projects and that if we felt good about our prospects, we should behave similarly. I added that the president was coming to Boston on state business the following week, and I could ask His Excellency to meet with him. Ray listened carefully and said he would think about it.

The next day, Ray called and asked, "May I meet the president?" I asked, "What changed?" Both Ray and his wife had done development work around the world, and after a brief discussion between them, hearkening back to their roots as professionals, Ray decided to go one step forward.

The president and Ray spoke in a hotel suite, surrounded by a phalanx of U.S. Secret Service, personal bodyguards, and advisors. I sat back and let the two of them speak. It occurred to me at that time that they are much the same: though they are different by virtue of their life experiences and demographics, both are quiet and unassuming leaders, politely persistent in their objectives, which are to subvert political, economic, and commercial conventions and make discontinuous leaps in productivity to help people. I wonder to this day if they recognized in one another the aspect of an innovator.

After a time, their discussion morphed from polite salutations, through patient elucidation of perspectives, to a workable plan. These two men, I thought, could be a link between the needs of one of the world's poorest nations to a network of (potentially) unsurpassed productivity. But there was much work to do in a short period of time.

A high-level Rwanda team descended upon Lackawanna to evaluate the opportunity: the ambassador to the United States, the central bank governor, the permanent secretary of finance, their legal council, and a legendary cancer researcher from Harvard. They had been authorized to invest on behalf of the medical and social security funds of Rwanda.

Ray and five other executives, including the chief scientist from Lackawanna, welcomed them. Clet and I sat between the two parties, which, though they were separated by their experiences, languages, needs, beliefs, knowledge, expertise, and goals, were united by the possibility of creating something new, a link between Kigali and Kendall Square, between a post-conflict nation and the People's Republic of Cambridge, between the poor people of Africa and the most innovative cancer researchers and biotech investors. They came to an agreement after a tour of the facility, a shared meal, and seven hours of discussion.[2]

As I write this, in the summer of 2008 for publication in the spring of 2009, we hope and believe that Rwanda will benefit from its ownership in Lackawanna and that the stock will continue to rise after subsequent developments in Lackawanna's product pipeline.

Though we must regard this investment as speculative, it holds the possibility of such high returns that we might one day make a sovereign investment fund out of it to build schools, roads, and hospitals; to train workers; and to invest even greater amounts on behalf of the Rwandan people. If, as Pope John Paul II said, eradicating poverty is integrating the poor into global networks of productivity, then, perhaps that day, in the windowless conference room, high up in a biotech tower in the United States, Rwanda took another step forward.

I was informed yesterday, as I am nearly finished writing this essay, that President Kagame has invited me to become a citizen of Rwanda. I am touched by the honor, and it motivates me to find even more ways to help. I smile when I think that Clet was invited to become American and I, a Rwandan, both so we could help these nations even more. And it was the two of us working together who brought the people of Rwanda to invest in the efforts of the biotech community in the United States.

2. The lawyers called again. Due to the sensitive nature of the agreement, they have asked me to pull the level of investment, the stock price, and any discussion regarding the anticipated rate of return.

All this brings me back to my original question: what is the effect of globalization on me and of me on it? Am I that multitude of features and contradictions, of competitive international and intercultural outcomes, of collective wisdom and stupidity, at the confluence of the past and future, the only possible outcome of a terrifically complex system that is perfectly designed to achieve it? Or can I push back? Can I decide who I want to be within globalization?

The answer, it seems to me, is that there are waypoints on a journey through globalization: the first one, like mine in Sudan, is to be an observer: occasionally disgruntled, sometimes a little disoriented and fatalistic. The second waypoint, which is harder to reach but more fulfilling, is to be an integrator: to be generative with the concepts of globalization, to attempt to be deeply introspective, to cope with the ambiguity as one searches for one's own vision within it, to integrate between such domains as politics, commerce, science, the arts, and the law. The trick, after all, is not just to see that everything mixes with everything else but to accelerate those specific determinants that are in the service of humankind.

Time will tell, and due to the nature of writing and publishing, with its strange aspect of asynchronous communication, the writer of the words affixed on these pages will never know; while someday in the near future, the readers of this essay can know with ease (Google: Rwanda biotech) if I ever made it to my second waypoint.[3]

---

3. The lawyers just called. They said that due to the "unintended consequences of globalization," they felt it would be prudent if I stopped mixing everything with everything else.

10. The Merits of Change

LUIS ALBERTO MORENO

WASHINGTON, D.C.

• • •

DURING THIS TIME of global competition for resources, a time characterized by technology disruption, a widening gap between the rich and poor, and increased private flows of investments, we in the leadership of nations and in the multilateral system can no longer dictate changes to the world. We can no longer preach the merits of change without being willing to change ourselves.

I entered public life in the early 1990s. After a stint as a Niemen Fellow at Harvard, I became minister of development as my country, Colombia, began its difficult transition from a strategy of import substitution to an open-trade environment; I became Colombian ambassador to the United States as our nation fought to maintain its territorial integrity and reposition itself in the community of nations; and I became president of the Inter-American Development Bank in Washington during a time of increased pressure on the multilateral donors to remain relevant.

I have learned many things: that each of the above-mentioned national and international experiences are interrelated and, therefore, require an integrated solution; that the challenge to leaders is to produce people, organizations, and nations that learn fast by tolerating some failure and by creating the space in organizations for deep introspection of our underlying values.

I can illustrate by saying that the real challenge to opening the Colombian economy, a process begun by President Virgilio Barco and consummated with President César Gaviria, was not the policy debate. The appropriate policies, even then, were well understood. We had the recent experience of Chile's monetarist experiment between 1973 and 1983. We knew that South Korea and Taiwan had been saving money and investing in primary education and that the government and private sectors were making collaborative decisions since the 1950s. We could go back in history to the Meiji restoration in Japan in the late nineteenth century to see the impact of that country's open orientation to the world and even back to the Industrial Revolution to study how breakthroughs in technology and organizational structures were influenced by outside forces.

Colombia's priorities were well understood. We knew that nations had to stabilize their economy to create a predictable investment climate; to liberalize trade to introduce competition, which would spur innovation and foster human initiative; to privatize firms to create more demanding shareholders and distribute earnings; and to democratize and decentralize decision making. We also knew we had to invest in people and specialized infrastructure.

What we did not understand then was how to create a private sector vision to compel change: how companies improve their language system, practice new behaviors, and internalize change to the point where they become innovative.

As Colombia entered *the apertura*, the opening of its economy, President Gaviria and I agreed that I would lead the effort to learn and understand the strategic issues facing our companies. I introduced the concept of *competitiveness* to Colombian firms, created a broad consultative process between the public and private sectors, and made an agenda for legislative reform, which included privatization, to support this new direction.

Colombian firms were not succeeding beyond its borders, and only an in-depth understanding of their challenges would allow the government to play a meaningful role in building competitiveness. As we improved our understanding of the strategy issues, I communicated our insights broadly to the public and the government:

> Our leather producers were getting squeezed between two other nations' exporters, *estábamos atrapados en el medio*. We did not have the design capability of Italy or the cost advantages of China.

Our flower exporters were losing the advantages of labor costs to Ecuador, and the middlemen-wholesalers in Miami kept all the good customer information.

We had no advantages of scale in petrochemicals, and rival nations were subsidizing the cost of feedstock.

Tourism, despite Colombia's amazing natural advantages, was beset by problems of security.

Our textile producers produced a broad scope of products for a protected environment and did not invest enough in world-class machinery that allowed for small batches and fast turnarounds to more demanding customers.

The list was long, but we took on these issues one by one, so that, to this day, most of these sectors remain among the most important parts of the Colombian economy.

It was through this experience that I realized that strategy for economic development, for creating prosperity for all citizens of any nation, had to be made at the level of the firm. "Enterprise solutions to poverty" was a paradigm shift. Up until then, most other decision makers in Latin America and around the world believed that economic and competitive strategy should be set by government officials. They believed they were entrusted by the people through democratic institutions to take care of them. The thing was, this strategy was not working. Poverty rates were increasing. Traditional positive values were under assault. Social cohesion itself was threatened.

That experience led me to develop the following principles about the important, yet distinct, roles of the government and the private sector:

The world has irrevocably changed. Communication costs are going to zero; legislative and logistical impediments to trade are declining; human migrations mean that more and more people, especially in middle-income countries, believe they have choices. Competition has become a global phenomenon.

In this global environment of extreme competition, the *government* can no longer be the master economic strategist for all the firm-level actors in a nation. Government has a lot to do to create the rules of the game: laws that are fair, transparent, cheaply administered and that provide equal opportunity to all citizens. (A corollary to this is that the actors in the multilateral system cannot play the role of master economic strategist either.) In addition, investments in higher forms of capital (i.e., specialized infrastructure, human capital, knowledge) are becoming more critical, and government needs to focus on those investments.

Firms must spend more time investing in workers, upgrading their products, finding new distribution channels, and segmenting and understanding their customers' needs. They cannot do this if they spend all their time trying to decipher and influence the government's next moves.

Finally, every investment, every strategic action, from both the government and the private sector, have to be made with *the future* in mind, informed by a shared vision, and in particular, a firm-level vision.

However, many questions remained unanswered: How do those in government create higher forms of capital (knowledge, skills, and abilities) that increase the possibilities of each person? How do those in the private sector factor in workers not as fungible inputs, as costs, but as part of unique, sustainable, and competitive value proposition? Which value propositions not only do not degrade the environment but improve upon it?

When I accepted the job as ambassador to the United States, I had to do, essentially, the same thing again: learn a new system, the U.S. political system; learn how to understand how influence was gained and used as a force for positive change; and learn to align Colombian objectives with U.S. objectives. In addition, I had to work in a bipartisan way.

I traveled to many districts and met with congresspersons in their home districts. My goal was to learn about each political leader's goals for his or her district and to inform him or her about Colombia's needs and why they mattered to the congressperson's constituents. I built a small but very competent team and insisted that we be focused, be optimistic, and, above all else, be ready to take action. I reasoned that even if we failed initially, we would learn faster that way and then have time to self-correct and improve our performance.

Colombia is now the third-largest recipient of the American investment in peace and has a system of trade agreements that offer unique incentives for our private sector to grow. Our country has strong leadership and an emerging peace dividend and has managed to avoid most of the economic pitfalls of other nations in the region.

I began to see patterns in my ability to create change: optimism, seeing failure as something not to fear but from which to learn. Simon Bolivar said it well: "Good judgment comes from experience, and experience comes from poor judgment." I also believed in an action orientation, a willingness to learn new systems, building strong teams on which I could rely, and building new coalitions of sometimes unlikely partners.

I carried these principles with me when I became the president of the Inter-American Development Bank. The multilateral system, I assessed, was at a critical juncture. With increased flows of private investment and remittances, measured in the hundreds of billions of dollars, we in the multilateral system and the aid community are in danger of becoming less relevant. Still, there is much to be done if we can unleash the forces of human initiative. I reasoned, based on my experiences with the private sector and watching the beginning of the open trade movement, that the private sector was still not recognized in the development community for its possibilities to eradicate poverty, indeed, as a source of wealth creation.

I launched the Opportunities for the Majority (OM) initiative within the bank to find ways to instill a private sector perspective into everything we do. We reckoned that if development meant meeting the needs of the poor and if the needs of the poor, in the aggregate, were a large market, then we could play a role in stimulating companies to meet these needs by making strategic investments, creating role model projects, and improving information surrounding these markets. Furthermore, this could be done in housing, energy, health care, education, and even areas like climate change.

While the data are not yet in, we do have projects in our pipeline, a group of talented and dedicated bankers focused on the task, and a vision of what this could be that excites and inspires all who experience it.

We have also reconfigured our organization to support these new strategies. We instituted competitive processes and hired people with more private sector experience. We reorganized every facet of our institution, developed a complex consultative process with our board, and began to examine our values and relationships within the bank with a view toward greater effectiveness. None of this was easy, and we have a long way to go.

We in the multilateral system will need to develop some private sector skills while maintaining what has made us effective so far: our intellectual integrity, action orientation, and altruism. These new skills include an ability to cope with ambiguity, an appetite for some increased risk, the willingness to invent as we go, the self-knowledge that we cannot control everything, and the willingness to form new relationships with nontraditional partners, both in the private sector and with pro-innovation groups of the nongovernmental sector.

At this time of dramatic and rapid change, we in the multilateral system face the issue of our own relevance and can no longer dictate, or simply wish, changes to the world. We can no longer preach the merits of change without being willing to change ourselves.

We can upgrade our strategy, make it more informed, explicit, and more widely shared. We can hire people with a broader scope of experience, upgrade our intellectual assets, and change our processes, especially how we learn. We have a long way to go, and the path is fraught with difficulties. We will make our missteps and accept responsibility for them. We intend to control what we can control, learn from what we cannot, and do what Gandhi famously said, be the change we wish to see in the world.

PART II: STRATEGIES FOR PROSPERITY

· · ·

"Our job in leadership is to provide new opportunities."
President Kagame and Nicholas Negroponte distribute
personal computers for students.

11. Claver's Wall

MALIK FAL

KIGALI, RWANDA

◆ ◆ ◆

THE STORY of Rwanda is the story of Africa. Precolonial Rwanda is a story of kings who ruled over expanses of land the size of western Europe. It is a story of court intrigues, effective administration, and sophisticated culture. It is a story of war and peace, beauty and beastliness, a Shakespearean human epic.

Colonial Rwanda is a story of forced labor, anthropological deception, and the compulsory cultivation of newly introduced cash crops. Post-Belgian Rwanda is a story of ethnic strife, economic decay, corruption, and civil war. Independent Rwanda is a story of Western power plays, local heroes, and client-based relationships.

To most people, the story of Rwanda is the story of Africa because of the genocide. They see Africa as a land where genocide happens every day through poverty, hunger, AK-47s, and machetes. They forget that the Rwandan genocide happened more than a decade ago. In the West, once the CNN effect fades, no one ever bothers to look back. I am an African and was an economic advisor to the Rwandan leadership. I do not forget. I love Rwanda because modern Rwanda is a story of resilience, integrity, and hope. If the story of modern Rwanda continues to be the story of Africa, it will be a good thing for my children and for the whole world.

The Rwandan leaders I meet and hug at local functions, the little boys and girls I see carrying water at night in remote villages as I drive back from the countryside, the breathtaking beauty of the thousand hills and soft-featured Rwandan faces, all trigger the same feelings in me—epiphany, resilience, and pride. The development challenges of Rwanda are great. So is my determination to help Rwandan leaders overcome them.

Claver Gatete is the ultimate Rwandan national leader. He sits two doors down from the president's office. He is at the center of important economic decisions in the country. His office window opens on a magnificent tropical garden with exotic plants, fresh-cut grass, and birds with colors so beautiful they look like flowers. Business executives, industry association leaders, ambassadors, representatives of donor agencies, cabinet ministers, NGO directors—all come to him for advice.

An International Monetary Fund (IMF) delegation has just left. The delegates saw a lot of people and made demands but were not proactively helpful. Claver Gatete is a frustrated man. He leans back and throws his hands in the air. "When we were schoolboys in Uganda, we used to have a cruel game. We used to go to the weaker among us, bring them to a place with their backs against a wall, and tell them to step back three feet or get slapped. I just realized it today. This is what the IMF is doing to us!"

The frustration Claver Gatete feels is felt by thousands of national leaders around the world. Claver wants to invest in development; he cannot. His treasurer tells him he only has recurrent budget funds at his disposal. He wants to borrow from private and foreign partners to drive development; he cannot. The IMF tells him that his country's exports are too low and that he cannot exceed his debt sustainability ratio. He wants to boost exports by providing better support to local exporters; he cannot. The government has no money for that, and the donor community is not interested in supporting local businesspeople whom they feel have it too good already. He has a PhD in econometrics. He is looking for a way out. He cannot find one. His problems seem insurmountable. They are not.

Two mutually reinforcing goals matter to build the competitiveness of an economy and to solve Claver's problems. The first is about enhancing the competitiveness of key local industries or clusters.[1] The second is

---

1. Editors' note: Clusters have a deep history. Alfred Marshall developed agglomeration. Paul Krugman deepened the idea of competitiveness and trade as a regional phenomenon. Michael Porter coined the term "clusters" to describe this.

about creating a culture of innovation and competitiveness in the country. I have the privilege to work with Claver toward achieving these goals in Rwanda.

Enhancing the competitiveness of local industries is about business strategy and cooperation. It involves making critical business choices, securing tangible investment commitments, and coordinating the actions of several players that support an industry. The first strategic choice is deciding which local industries, by becoming competitive, have the potential to transform the economy. This choice is important because it encapsulates the notion that developing countries have limited human, financial, and institutional resources to allocate. Such countries must, therefore, carefully evaluate where their few resources will have the most economic impact in terms of sustainable jobs, revenues, and equity generation. Oil dominates the Nigerian economy, but in that country of 120 million people, only about 4,000 work in the oil industry.

The second set of strategic choices has to do with the type of customer segments, distribution partners, product, and marketing scope local industry leaders should focus on. These types of business choices involve a myriad of industry stakeholders who need to work closely together to articulate clear national visions for local industries. Once critical strategic choices have been made, financial commitments from all local industry players and close coordination provide the final critical ingredients for success.

Achieving all this does not happen by chance. Systematic approaches are required, and the five-step industry development process is such an approach. It is a collaborative approach where local stakeholders work together in industry workgroups to upgrade the competitiveness of their industry. Applying the five-step process to an industry takes months. It requires the participation of people who have full-time jobs and no prior history of collaboration.

National leaders like Claver are ideally suited to oversee such processes because of the status of their office. My role is to secure their participation and commitment. Playing that role is an easier task in Rwanda than anywhere else in Africa because Rwandan leaders are genuinely committed to change. Here is how the process works.

1. ANALYZE THE CURRENT SITUATION

The purpose of step one, analyze the current situation, is to understand local and international dynamics that are inherent to a particular industry. Research is conducted and presented to a carefully selected industry workgroup to help workgroup members reach a common view on the state of their industry. Step one is also about facilitating a productive dialogue among parties who may appear antagonistic. Efficient industry-level operations and the ability to create and deliver great products and services depend on a number of interdependent local relationships. Local suppliers, universities, businesses, government departments, donors, and industry associations are often critical players in manufacturing- or service-provision processes. Building such relationships requires sustained interaction and cooperation among public- and private-sector managers whose motivations, reward system, and aspirations are very seldom aligned.

My team assembled working groups in Rwanda's major industries: coffee, tea, tourism, information and communication technologies (ICT), hides and skins, fruits and vegetables. Mobilizing workgroup members and ensuring participation are always ordeals for our new consultants. It is a pleasure to see local professionals build trust and learn to work with each other. Through the dynamics of industry workgroups and the external facilitation provided to them, social, ethnic, gender, and age differences subside. Claver often joins these groups' working sessions and enjoys witnessing their dedication, energy, and openness to new ideas. Being a politician, he also likes the lively debates that occur at industry workgroup meetings. He gets to engage with Rwanda's top business community, and the business leaders seem to think that, at last, the government is trying to understand them.

2. SET DETAILED SECTOR OBJECTIVES

Step two, set detailed sector objectives, is about getting local industry players to quantify industry transformation goals in ways that are as specific as possible. Target export volumes and receipts for the industry reflect the strategic objectives of local industry leaders. Such targets must, therefore, be expressed in a detailed manner that shows not just aggregate numbers but numbers broken down by product and, if possible, geographic segment. For example, the targets that are set for Rwanda's coffee industry specify not just export tonnage and dollar receipts but also exports by different grades of coffee. Local coffee industry leaders are now able to declare, "In five years, our goal is to grow from an export level of twenty-five thousand tons/twenty million dollars per year to a level forty-five thousand tons/ one hundred seventeen million dollars per year, with 60 percent of these exports being of high-grade quality."

Getting Rwandan coffee industry leaders to agree on national targets was a delicate matter. Factual data about historical and other countries' performances had to be provided and discussed so that workgroup members could have constructive debates and make well-informed choices. Both step one and step two contributed to build the premise of a shared industry vision among previously unacquainted industry participants.

3. UNDERSTAND TARGET CUSTOMER NEEDS

Step three is the most research-intensive step. Primary customer research is compiled to inform critical strategic choices. Industry workgroup members get to learn about what customers want, how to reach them, and how to serve them profitably. As local industry players get exposed to insightful customer information and get engaged in debates about what customer segment to serve, a greater convergence of views occurs, and people from the same industry who may have previously ignored each other begin to develop a productive working relationship. In no time, they begin to make comments like "Specialty coffee buyers in the United States are increasingly demanding reliability of supply. It is not enough for us to be able to produce good quality beans once in a while. We need to maintain extremely high standards of quality *all* the time and for substantially larger quantities of coffee."

4. ARTICULATE A UNIQUE POSITIONING

This shift in perspective created in step three helps create the conditions for step four, where workgroup members are asked to articulate a unique positioning for their particular industry. This step becomes particularly important in industries where regional competition is stiff and the need to clearly identify and articulate one's unique features is essential. This is the case for ecotourism, because Rwanda lies just in the middle of a neighborhood in which some of the world's major ecotourism countries compete. Rwanda borders Tanzania on the east and Uganda on the north, while Kenya is an hour away toward the east and South Africa three hours away toward the south. Every single one of these countries has amazingly beautiful game reserves endowed with exotic vegetation and the renowned "big-five" savannah-based animals: lion, leopard, buffalo, rhinoceros, and elephant. With its nasty image and less-than-impressive savannah game reserve in the east, the Akagera National Park in Rwanda cannot compete with its neighbors in the overcrowded and price-based "big-five" safari segment. This reality can be difficult to convey to Rwanda tourism old-timers whose understanding of ecotourism is limited to what they have seen in neighboring countries. However, with the world-famous Virunga National Park in the north, home of some of the last few mountain gorillas, and the less-known Nyumgwe rain forest in the south, home of thirteen different species of monkeys, Rwanda has unique natural assets to dominate a growing subsegment in ecotourism: the primate safari subsegment. Step four is about making these kinds of strategic opportunities explicit.

5. DEVELOP ACTION AND INVESTMENT PLANS

By the time step five is reached and industry workgroup members begin to develop action and investment plans, buy-in for what will be presented as a national industry strategy has already been secured. This means that industry workgroup members have a clear understanding of how they can beat the competition and why they need to work together. Operational and financial requirements needed to upgrade the competitiveness of an industry have been identified. All participating parties can make financial, technical, or action commitments. The impact of all commitments can be monitored against tangible volume and receipt industry targets over a set period of time. In the case of the Rwanda tourism strategy, for example, the action-and-investment plan revolves around creating a seven-day visitor circuit around the Virunga National Park in the north and the

Nyumgwe forest in the south. Road and waterway infrastructure linking the two parks has to be deployed. Primate physiology and social study programs to train visitor guides have to be developed. Locally present international conservation agencies that are working on primate research have to be mobilized to support Rwanda's "Primate Discovery Tour" visitor circuit. Private investors who are interested in building high-end game reserve lodges have to be attracted. All this activity needs to be coordinated and planned carefully among parties who until recently had never even spoken to each other.

The five-step industry transformation process is the type of collaborative effort that forms the basis of long-lasting and productive public, private, and donor sector partnerships. Public and private organizations need mutually agreed industry objectives, plans, budgets, and commitments in order to work effectively together. High-level forums where top government officials and business leaders meet twice a year can be helpful, but such events can never replace the hundreds of interactions that occur between lower-level public and private decision makers who work together for the competitiveness of specific industries.

Claver is a national leader who has become immersed in the five-step industry strategy process. He is excited to have industry objectives validated by the most respected businessmen in his country. He likes knowing where government needs to focus its resources in order to drive growth and employment. He is happy to hear that the donor community takes part in the process and sometimes decides to support his country's key income-generating industries directly. He has tangible numbers on where his country's exports could grow in the next few years. The private sector feels energized to be working with the government on substantive issues. His boss, the president, is being praised by influential business leaders about his advisor's bottom-up approach to economic policy.

For the first time in a long time, Claver feels he is not alone. He feels a bond with other economic leaders in his country. He and those who are taking part in these industrial transformation processes understand what it will take to make the economy competitive. Claver has realized the power of business strategy, the power of innovation, the power of cooperation. He wants everyone else in the nation to realize that, too: cabinet ministers, schoolteachers, college students, business owners, hospital nurses, taxi drivers, restaurant managers—everyone. He wants to instill a culture of innovation and competitiveness in Rwanda.

Creating a culture of innovation and competitiveness is about changing the minds, attitudes, and beliefs of a nation on what it takes to create wealth. It begins with figuring out underlying beliefs and attitudes toward wealth creation, which can be done through a Mental Models assessment survey. This survey elucidates the Mental Models that are conducive to the growth of private enterprise and those that are detrimental to this goal. The Mental Models assessment findings can then provide content to national communication campaigns on competitiveness. These campaigns rely on the participation of opinion-leading change makers, on the discerning use of media and discourse outlets, and on the relentless infusion of inspiring content. They have the power to change the mind of a nation.

There is often a great discrepancy between what local leaders profess are the virtues of capitalism and how they act on those principles. Since the fall of the Berlin Wall and the widespread acceptance of capitalism, political rhetoric on the virtues of probusiness and procompetitiveness policy has become the norm in developing countries. In reality, government, civil society, donor, and even business leaders' underlying beliefs on how capitalism should work can sometimes be surprising. The result of such inconsistencies is depicted in the "ping-pong" story of Bob Choo, a Malaysian investor I came across in Central Africa.

The senior minister had gone on prime-time television to announce the establishment of a "one-stop-shop" government department to facilitate investment. Bob Choo got the go-ahead from his headquarters to set up a twenty million dollar wood processing plant. Five months later, Bob was still fighting to get the ten signatures he needed to set up his factory. He felt overwhelmed and worried. He decided to ask for an audience with the senior minister. Four months later, Bob got the appointment, went to see the minister, and started complaining about the poor way he had been treated by local government officials. He was hoping to arouse the minister's sympathy and personal concern. "That one-stop shop is not working," he said. "I am being played from pillar to post like a ping-pong ball . . . ping-pong, ping-pong, ping-pong for nine months."

The minister's reaction was unlike anything Bob had been expecting. "This is our country, and we can do whatever we want. We can even play ping-pong with you if we want to."

The way leaders of a nation think about business and, more importantly, the way they act on it matters for several reasons. First, developing nations cannot and should not be ostracized from the global economy. Since globalization is unavoidable, they must embrace it, find ways to do well in it, and develop attitudes that match those beliefs. Second, in order to succeed economically, public, private, and civil sector leaders must have a clear understanding of their respective roles and how those roles contribute to the prosperity of their country. Third, public, private, and civil sector leaders need business strategy skills as well as an underlying culture that fosters innovation, openness to new ideas, and trust. In other words, they need to develop the right Mental Models. The minister in Bob Choo's ping-pong story needs to develop the right Mental Model.

I was part of a team that conducted a Mental Models-assessment survey in Nigeria on behalf of the World Bank. The survey was administered throughout the country to more than eleven hundred respondents from all walks of life: local leaders, academics, nongovernmental organization workers, and business, health, and religious leaders. This effort and its subsequent analysis revealed a great deal about Nigerian leaders' underlying Mental Models. More than fifty questions on critical economic development issues such as "the role of government," the "impact of corruption," or "the competence of the private sector" were asked. On each of these issues, the nature of the answers provided great insights. The answers themselves exposed the positions Nigerian leaders held on wealth creation. And the demographic spread of the answers uncovered the level of consensus, or lack thereof, which existed in Nigeria with regard to wealth creation.

For example, the survey showed that 81 percent of Nigerian leaders expect the "government to take the lead in ensuring the development of the country." This was not good news from a competitiveness standpoint because it implied that Nigerian leaders are not in favor of a greater private sector role in the development of their country. The study showed that 56 percent of respondents felt that "economic growth comes at the price of social equity." This was also a disturbing finding because such a belief is both inaccurate and limiting. A dynamic communication campaign would be needed to address these findings. Media personalities who drive the content of newspaper articles and editorials, radio programs, and television talk shows would need to be mobilized to support a national debate on the "role of the private sector in economic development."

In Nigeria, Rwanda, and elsewhere, the problem of reconciling poverty relief with wealth creation has become one of the most serious Mental Models issues in the developing world. Poverty relief is a legitimate concern for leaders in the developing world. Over the past few years, it has become the principal issue guiding economic policy in developing countries. This trend is understandable but can lead to misguided policies when the concern for poverty relief takes precedence over the concern for wealth creation. Wealth creation is the only sustainable way out of poverty, and nations whose leaders do not believe this are nations in danger of remaining poor. Countries that tend to overfocus on poverty relief over long periods of time become foreign aid dependent and get trapped in the expectation that the rest of the world is responsible for their economic condition. In the end, these countries never "graduate" from humanitarian inflows and the culture of begging that goes with it.

Focusing on poverty relief and humanitarian aid is understandable in countries that are emerging from conflict or natural disaster, like Rwanda. However, after a few years of immediate humanitarian assistance, economic policy should shift its focus toward wealth creation. Unfortunately, we still see many countries throughout the developing world that remain dependent on foreign aid for their most basic needs many years, even decades, after independence. In such countries, government officials, the agencies they work in, and the modes of operation they design are all geared toward maximizing donor assistance. This whole approach becomes a self-induced dependency mindset. It is also one of today's most detrimental Mental Models to achieve sustainable development.

It need not be that way. Economic growth can happen together with greater social equity when it is based on the sale of high-value products and services. In turn, high-value products and services can be made only by highly qualified workers who are entitled to high and rising salaries. Nigerians, Rwandans, and all other Africans need to be aware of this. Donor assistance can be of great benefit to recipient countries that can use development aid inflows well while building the future self-earning capacity of the nation. Countries like Ireland, Mozambique, or Vietnam, for example, have been quite successful at achieving this balance. Ireland, one of the fastest growing economies in western Europe, invested much of its European Union aid money in education, while Mozambique, after a long and nasty civil war, invested much of its aid funds in rebuilding its tourism and aluminum industries. People who live in aid-dependent nations also need to be aware of this. The determining element that enables countries to make such mental shifts is the realization that sustainable economic transformation is based on commercial success. It is a mindset-related issue that ought to be treated as such in the framework of systematic communication efforts. Claver and I discuss these mindset change issues at length every time we have the opportunity. We agree on both the means to establish mindset change and the praiseworthiness of the end.

The Rwandan "culture of innovation and competitiveness" campaign has been active for a few years now. It has two main components: indirect communication via opinion leaders and direct communication to an internal target audience.

Indirect Communication via Opinion Leaders: These activities entail a number of outreach activities to ensure that key opinion leaders and influencers are exposed to the principles of competitiveness. It is based on the main messages captured from the Mental Models assessment survey that are then integrated with competitiveness principles in order to engage local opinion leaders. Messaging opportunities to engage opinion leaders and influencers such as speeches, university courses, presentations, public lectures, and panel discussions on local radio and television provide the platforms through which the national debate on competitiveness happens.

The president himself mentions the importance of competitiveness relentlessly at every speaking occasion. Rwanda's Mental Models survey revealed that many Rwandan decision makers fear making decisions and, when unsure, prefer to "do nothing." The president was taken aback by this finding. Sure enough, a few days after being briefed on it, he made the following public comment:

A recent survey confirmed a cultural trait we all intuitively know about ourselves: the propensity many Rwandans have for inaction rather than action in the face of uncertainty. We tend to fear the consequences that might arise from making bad decisions, and as a result, we tend to prefer not making any decision at all in the face of uncertainty. This is wrong. Rwanda has fallen far behind many other nations since the genocide, and there is no time for complacency at any level of leadership. Lack of decision making is a tax on our development, and we must discourage it as much as possible. One must look at the facts available and make decisions according to those facts. Making no decision is worse than making a decision that turns out to have been bad, after the fact.

Direct Communication: Ideally, a local public relations or advertising firm should be hired as part of a culture of competitiveness campaign. That firm should be directed to handle all direct communication activities and to disseminate all indirect communication events to broader internal audiences. For example, the above-quoted comment that the president of Rwanda made was captured on television. Some of the key points in that comment were inserted in a promotional poster that was plastered all over the country. The themes raised became topics for local radio programs where sociologists and traditional leaders were invited to talk about Rwandans' overrespect for authority. It was amazing to see how much media momentum could be created from a few presidential remarks. In no time, lethargy, inaction, and complacency became open targets in hundreds of Rwandan institutions. Cabinet ministers, school principals, businessmen, and civil servants were becoming agents of change in their own right, while Claver was becoming the poster face of the culture of competitiveness campaign.

Two years went by since the cabinet passed Rwanda's national strategies for coffee and tourism, and the culture of competitiveness communication campaign created tremendous momentum. Different ministers came together to support visions that had been formulated by the private sector, and out of that alone came a sense of accomplishment. The minister of health was excited about upgrading the quality of rural clinics around Rwanda's national parks. The minister of infrastructure became interested in providing water and electricity to all museums and historical sites around the country. The minister of gender decided to introduce hospitality industry training programs in the curriculum of activities her department provides to women's groups around the country.

The plans to raise coffee exports from ordinary-grade coffees to high-grade Arabica coffees were aggressive. The investment required in new coffee trees, washing stations, cupping laboratories, grower training, marketing initiatives, and specialized infrastructure came to eighty million dollars over eight years. In return, nearly five hundred forty million dollars in exports were expected over the same period, with a growth in annual coffee exports from twenty-two million dollars to one hundred seventeen million dollars. The country still has a long way to go, but already Starbucks customers in the United States have had a taste of high-quality coffee from Rwanda and have paid a premium for it.

In tourism, the chosen strategic course was to migrate toward high-end eco- and cultural tourism offerings. The investment in national park facilities, new lodges and hotels, guide training, transportation infrastructure, and cultural site upgrades amounted to one hundred million dollars over eight years. In return, nearly four hundred million dollars in tourism receipts were expected over the same period, with a growth in annual tourism receipts from fourteen million dollars to one hundred million dollars. Here as well, initial results have been phenomenal. Countless Hollywood celebrities, European aristocrats, and Asian tycoons have already made the trip to Rwanda. Some have "adopted" Rwandan baby gorillas, while others have become public advocates for the country.

Claver started to brief the president every month on all execution issues related to the national coffee and tourism strategies. The results were making them both look like heroes. In both industries, the country was beating the plan with regard to yearly volume and income targets. Both domestic and foreign investments in those two industries have soared. International press references to the country's tourism and coffee success stories have become too numerous to mention.

Claver was sitting at his desk during one of my recent visits, reflecting on the economic transformation under way in his country. His gaze stopped at the pile of letters he had received from coffee growers in the past few months. Many of those letters have endearing spelling mistakes and flowery language thanking him for his efforts. The authors talk about how they are now able to buy medicines for their families, open bank accounts, get cell phones, or do home repairs that were long overdue.

Another IMF delegation was scheduled to arrive soon. The lawn outside Claver's office window had been freshly cut. The smell of cow dung used to fertilize the soil made one's nostrils palpitate like butterfly wings. The bright sunshine pouring into the room brought with it a mysterious, almost mystical energy. Claver was thinking about the IMF delegation. He was thinking about how the delegates were going to make him stand back against the wall. He was thinking about how they were going to ask him to step back or get slapped. For the first time, he considered the possibilities for crashing through that wall.

12. Leadership, in Context

ASHRAF GHANI

KABUL, AFGHANISTAN

• • •

I RETURNED to Afghanistan in December 2001 after an interval of twenty-four years. I had spent the 1980s looking at the last four hundred years of Afghan history; thus, when I returned, the country was both familiar and new. The communist coup, the Soviet invasion, the internal conflicts, and the hijacking of the country by Al-Qaeda had taken a huge toll on the Afghan people. Five years of drought had also changed the physical face of the country. Areas I remembered as green and verdant were now brown and dry, and there were no trees in the capital city of Kabul, given the need for firewood. The western half of the city was completely destroyed, and there was hardly a government building, including the president's palace, where infrastructure functioned at all. I was seconded from the World Bank to the United Nations to help prepare the Bonn Agreement. Mr. Hamid Karzai, initially chairman of the interim administration, then head of state from June 2004 to December 2004, and subsequently elected president, asked me to join the government. He made it clear that the job entailed high risks with no pay or benefits, but I understood it as a duty to serve my country. I accepted the offer and resigned from the UN and the World Bank. I first became chief advisor to the president, dealing with both national economy and national security issues, and then served as minister of finance from June 2002 to December 2004. I had advised many governments during the course of my work at the World Bank, and my academic work for over a decade at The Johns

Hopkins University had focused on a comparative approach to state building across the world. The challenge in Afghanistan, however, required a
shift from leadership facilitation to assumption of direct responsibility for
positive change.

Reform of the currency was the first technical challenge that I had to
deal with as both a political and institutional process. In early 2002, the
currency of Afghanistan, the afghani, had declined nearly one-thousand-
fold in value, to the point where a basket of afghanis was needed to buy a
basket of goods. Counterfeit notes were common, and multiple curren-
cies were circulating within the country. The Central Bank had no deposits of currency, and the transitional government had to buy afghanis for
U.S. dollars on the open market and use the currency for the payment of
salaries. At the same time, the transitional government, composed of an
untried and untested group of people, had been given a mandate for gov-
erning and had to rapidly win the trust of the Afghan population and
establish credibility both with Afghans and the international community.
It was, therefore, imperative to devise a win-win approach for currency
reform and demonstrate the ability to develop coherent and effective
strategy.

As finance minister during the tenure of the transitional government,
I first received technocratic advice on this issue from the International
Monetary Fund (IMF), given that the fund is the embodiment of knowledge and capability on currency reform. However, the process of governance is political and not merely technical. Therefore, a second step
was to subject the advice provided by the IMF—partial dollarization and
issuance of a new currency over a two-year period—to a political reading.
The political test was how other key elements within the transitional government, and particularly the president, would react to the IMF's ideas.
It became clear through a series of consultations led by President Karzai
that the technical recommendations proposed would not pass through a
political filter given that it would be incredibly difficult to explain partial dollarization to the Afghan population. The Afghan people appreciated the symbolic importance of the afghani as a representation of
Afghanistan, and it was, therefore, a central component, at least emblem-
atically, of the state-building process. The meaning of currency reform

for the legitimacy of the state was central, and thus forced a reexamination of the assumptions upon which the IMF recommendations had been based.

A third step, therefore, was to develop leadership through problem solving and strategy making through sense and response. This required convening a task force to analyze the issues and recommend a pathway for change. I facilitated a discussion on the rules, a timeline for reform, and implementation mechanisms as part of an effort to allow all voices, both Afghan and international, to feed into the process. I sought to simplify the objectives and ensure focus specifically on the issue of currency exchange given that time was of the essence. We, therefore, rejected the proposal by the IMF to limit the amount of the currency that a single person could exchange to ten thousand dollars. Such a limit would have been necessary had our chief objective been prevention of money laundering, but we had to accept that confronting the challenge of money laundering required a set of capabilities that we did not have. The task force met every day for a month until it reached consensus on the way forward. This consensus was based upon a deep historical and social knowledge that allowed for mobilization of existing capabilities in Afghanistan to support the task—specifically the existing networks of *hawala* dealers, specialists in currency exchange and transfer.

Consultations indicated that the *hawala* network had a sophisticated infrastructure that could support the task and that their interests were aligned with those of the government—a new currency would simplify their transactions immensely. In addition, pride in putting their networks at the service of a national cause and a small commission were important enabling factors. This led to a process of social verification with these stakeholders and agreement on the rules for the currency exchange. The *hawala* dealers were assured of a space to operate with certainty, away from what they perceived as the predatory behavior of government officials and police officers, and were given access to the new currency a month before the general public to allow for the transition to take place. An uncontrolled printing process was also brought under control through mobilizing printing companies in Europe that could guarantee security for the new afghani notes to prevent leakage and preissuance problems. The cabinet endorsed the consensus, and the process of implementation oversight passed to the Central Bank.

This contextualized, entrepreneurial approach was risky and went against international advice. The process was inherently uncertain, and the period for exchange of the currency was set at only three months. Efforts to destroy old bank notes and old printing facilities proved challenging, but, ultimately, it was not the domestic capacities that had been mobilized by the government that proved the largest risk factor: the international community, which had promised to provide logistical support for the process, was the real problem. This support from the donors did not arrive in time, and the Afghan security forces were mobilized rapidly to stand in and support the process instead. This led to an implementation extension of one month, but the entire process was carried out in four months despite the inherent risks in an incredibly difficult context.

The building blocks of this approach are clear:

- ▸ defining a clear objective
- ▸ creating rules for reaching that objective, based on deep knowledge
- ▸ accounting for but moving beyond received wisdom in the implementation process
- ▸ reading and defining capabilities not only through a technocratic lens but through a social and institutional lens
- ▸ stitching together assets as the core of a strategy
- ▸ understanding interests, stakeholders, and methods for mobilization
- ▸ harnessing time to a task
- ▸ understanding risks through backward mapping and the careful building of consensus
- ▸ leading through definition and mobilization
- ▸ being willing to take risks based on careful analysis of the options

A reform process of this type can be built upon some or many of these building blocks, depending on the parameters and conditions within which it must take place.

The lessons to be drawn from the experience of currency reform in Afghanistan are threefold and derived from the fallacy of "misplaced concreteness" as first expounded by the mathematician Alfred North

Whitehead. This refers to the mistake of confusing a model with the physical reality that it is meant to describe. First, the international understanding of currency reform processes was transferred and proffered as a solution uncritically, without an in-depth knowledge of context. Implementation has to be tailored to conditions on the ground, and this does not necessarily involve enormously complex planning procedures as in other countries. Second, and a related point, the political implications of the technical recommendations were not considered—reform is political in that it requires consent and compromise beyond technical feasibility. Creation of a depoliticized space of governance is about imagination and problem solving, not just about the rigid application of rules. Finally, capacity must be considered holistically, as the capacity of society as a whole—from networks to hierarchies and social communities—that can be harnessed for the common good and not defined narrowly as just the abilities and skills that exist within government or the international community.

Success of the currency exchange in Afghanistan served as a symbolic means of unifying the country. It also went some way toward cementing the legitimacy of the transitional government with the Afghan population and the international community in a way that a protracted partial-dollarization process simply could not have done. The process demonstrated that a problem-solving and entrepreneurial approach to strategy and management can focus all of the relevant energies on resolution of a concrete problem. The key in today's interdependent world is to create these types of linkages rather than accepting conventional wisdom and received practice that become quickly outdated in a rapidly changing global political and economic environment.

The experience of devising a solution to currency reform in Afghanistan has changed my views on both the skills and capabilities required of international organizations and national leaders. I have reached the conclusion, as argued in my recent book *Fixing Failed States*, coauthored with Clare Lockhart, that international organizations need to be fundamentally transformed to acquire the capabilities to coproduce change with national actors, rather than to remain purveyors of abstract technical knowledge that is applied to different countries regardless of societal capabilities and conditions on the ground. I also believe that the capacity to understand design and coordination is a core function of national leadership. Above all, the lesson I learned from my experience in Afghanistan is that if one focuses on the problem of implementation from a contextual perspective, the right solutions emerge much more easily than if one relies on standard approaches. With this understanding, I believe that leaders can bring about the systemic change that can transform the least developed countries and allow them to take advantage of, rather than to miss out on, the process of globalization.

13. Selling Culture without Selling Out

MARCELA ESCOBARI-ROSE

KINGSTON, JAMAICA

• • •

THE RED-EYED youngster slumped in his chair, moved the dreads off his face, and gesticulated slowly: "It's part of our culture. We can't let 'em water us down." He was referring to toning down the lyrics in Jamaican dance-hall songs. There were slightly embarrassed nods around the room. As half of the audience was (likely) stoned, it might have been wise to drop the discussion there.

The purpose of the meeting was to explore how young Jamaican artists can succeed internationally, and it was hard to ignore the recent news. Beenie Man, a Jamaican dance-hall artist, had to cancel his European concert tour and had been dropped from MTV's Video Music Awards due to the inclusion of homophobic lyrics in his songs. Gay-rights organizations had demonstrated outside his concert, and Virgin, the label that had recently signed him, was being sued. This talented group's ability to capture value in international markets was at stake.

Tackling a sensitive, culturally ingrained topic so very early in a project aimed to improve the competitiveness of the Jamaican entertainment industry was not ideal. Yet, no matter how authentic a rhythm and its lyrics might be, if a record label has to worry about being sued, it will walk away from the deal. In the group meeting, a dreadlocked producer disputed this view: "How about Eminem?"

My years of schooling in economic development had not prepared me for a project like this.

That was only the beginning of many surprises. The question was straightforward: how could the people in the room (and many more in the industry) make money from utilizing their talents?

Cultural goods and unique experiences are an important niche market for developing countries. Unfortunately, members of these industries usually lack sophisticated intermediaries to connect with the buyers of their products. Today, clients are often mass buyers of services (for example, of tourism packages or musical talent) that suppress prices and, in the end, compromise quality. A systemic lack of trust within these fragmented industries exacerbates the inability to collaborate. As a result, Jamaican artists cannot position themselves to compete.

Can members of these industries move away from the base of the value chain and connect directly with final customers? Can the industry be mobilized to upgrade its offerings and to collaborate to reposition itself in global markets? This dilemma has to be tackled so that developing countries can reap international success for some of their most distinctive and innovative assets: cultural and knowledge products.

The music industry in Jamaica has had the classic problem of not being able to capture the value end consumers get of its collective talents. Usually, as is the case with many products in the developing world, the most challenging hurdle is to upgrade the innate quality of the product to fit international demand. In the Jamaican case, the music was so ingrained in the society that it seemed to hold great promise.

Jamaica is an extremely musical country. Most people have experimented with music at some point in their lives—the recent prime minister P. J. Patterson was a member of the band Skatellites, and the opposition leader Seaga owned a music studio. People sing not just in the shower but everywhere. It is not rare to have your neighbors on a plane or bus break into song, with authentic emotion. Independence Park in downtown Kingston has reggae blasting from fake rocks to accompany early morning joggers. Music in Jamaica is like soccer in Brazil. Every youngster from the ghetto experiments with music as a way out of poverty and as a way to earn the respect of his peers. It is not surprising that there are more studios per capita in Kingston than in any city in the United States except Nashville.

Jamaica has historically been a creative source of new rhythms that have been successfully adopted internationally. From genres such as ska, dub, reggae (through legends like Bob Marley and Peter Tosh), to modern dance hall with stars like Shaggy, Elephant Man, and Sean Paul, Jamaica keeps coming back to the radar screen of major music trends worldwide. Jamaican influences have pervaded the international recording scene for the past three decades and have left an imprint upon the sounds of many, from The Rolling Stones to Ben Harper.

I, on the other hand, had not heard any reggae other than the songs of Bob Marley, and dance hall seemed like unintelligible garble to me. I was not about to mention this or the fact that I was kicked out of my high-school choir or that "Happy Birthday" stretched my singing abilities to their maximum. After all, my colleagues were leading the lamb-and-cheese cluster in Macedonia or marble in Afghanistan. While others were study-ing rocks and dairy products, I was going to be leading world-renowned musicians to the Top 40. Besides, my role was not to teach them to sing but to help them create better businesses.

As I landed in the number one murder capital of the world, the situ-ation was not so glamorous. It became clear that the success of the few Jamaican legends was not easily replicable and that the economic value of that success had not helped most of the island's population. Jamaica's income per capita had decreased in the last thirty years. The music indus-try for the most part was not a profitable business, the industry was frag-mented and divisive, and the informality in the business served as a front for much of the drug money laundering in the island.

Reggae, Jamaica's landmark genre, represents a flat 0.8 percent of world music sales, and total revenue numbers have continued to slide since the mid-1990s. Moreover, Jamaica represents an ever-decreasing fraction of that percentage as Japanese, German, French, and American reggae bands have taken share in their own local markets. While Jamaica is still a hotbed of creativity, other countries have been taking the rhythms to more suc-cessfully tap international markets.

Jamaicans have not found the structure of the industry to be advan-tageous. The producers, writers, and musicians are at the bottom of the music industry's value chain. The artist, usually represented by a cousin passing for a manager, is the commodity in this business. In the best-case scenario, he receives 10 percent of CD sales. The latter part of the sup-ply chain, where most of the value is created and retained, is dominated by four major world companies that are vertically integrated to reach the final consumer.

Members of the Jamaican music industry viewed all of this as blatant exploitation. A history of vague contracts and never-paid royalties rein-forced this belief. Without trained managers, musicians and producers were out of their league when it came to the complicated legalities of intel-lectual property. The local competition to get access to the few industry labels that dominated the access to retail and international channels was fierce. The result was a deeply distrustful and fragmented industry. During our initial Mental Models survey, which is designed to expose and map the hidden beliefs and associations that drive an individual's actions and choices, 65 percent of cluster members responded, "You could not be too careful," when it came to doing business within the industry.

This distrust also led to fragmentation: although there were many cre-ative business initiatives, they lacked the critical mass and the coordination to be widely effective. For example, there were over forty different reggae festivals in Jamaica, with only a handful having sufficient size to attract an international audience. One producer noted, "This is a land of lead singers. No one wants to be backup." These circumstances contributed to several market inefficiencies over the years, such as the necessity to transact on a cash-only up-front basis and low levels of international industry awareness and investment. Jamaica had become the clichéd bucket of crabs that does not require a lid—all the crabs will pull down any crab trying to get out.

My job was to help this group work together to create more value and earn high and rising incomes for its members. The first and biggest barrier was not a strategic one; it was building trust. In the beginning of the pro-cess, I inadvertently benefited from the fact that no development project had focused on music before; the government did not want to invest in an informal industry that did not contribute to tax revenue and thought it was a lost cause to try to get the fractious artists to work together. While faced with initial skepticism, the group of fifty to sixty producers, studio owners, and musicians became increasingly intrigued by the cluster pro-cess and its potential benefits.

The lack of trust within the industry, in some ways, actually helped me be able to lead this cluster. Although the white man represented the exploitative colonist, the participants were not sure where to place me. I was a female in a mostly male-dominated industry; I came from Bolivia, a country poorer than Jamaica, yet had the U.S. pedigree. Most importantly, I came with no attachment to the ingrained interests in the island and was unapologetic about my intentions to change things. The group members were willing to be guided by a complete outsider—better me rather than anyone they already knew. In the end, what made me effective was at the core of what was wrong with the industry.

As a banker in a previous life, I had a ferocious attachment to data, which allowed the group to get past the initial pontification and to be blunt about the situation of the industry. Many of the long-held beliefs about what the industry might have to do to succeed (for example, build a new multimillion-dollar performance complex funded by the government or a reggae-only TV channel) were quickly discredited with benchmarks and valuations that showed that such projects would have negligible impact on the economics of their business. With an open agenda, I presented a decision process that was based on real data gathered by members of the industry. The members debated the significance of the data and decided what were and what were not worthwhile investments.

The group was starting to work well together. Cluster members found the process of creating business models energizing. The group had grown from fifteen original members to close to one hundred. The contributions of insights, data, and time were considerable. However, once we had eliminated all the conspiracy theories and quick fixes, there was a vacuum: what should we do now? We had arrived at the difficult place of looking inward. The answer was disturbing. Despite a deep culture of individualism, self-determination, and pride in its own music, the industry had left its most important source of livelihood, its strategy, to others. It had left its fate up to everyone else: the global labels, the distribution channels, the tour organizers, etc. Jamaican music was being imitated around the world, its brand eroding, the quality diluted. The few successes were being decided in an office in New York, not Kingston. The lack of decision on how they were going to compete in the changing industry was in itself a choice: a choice to continue a slow path into poverty because when you do not make a choice, others make it for you.

We had gotten to a standstill. It was much easier to blame the government, racism, colonialism, the world order, and the lawlessness in society than to admit that the members of the music industry were the only ones who could change their situation. And to some degree, each individual's success required cooperating with the others in the room—the same people with whom they had once ferociously competed to be the one chosen by the U.S. label.

The dynamic was not foreign to the Jamaican landscape. Blue Mountain Coffee had missed the same type of opportunity. With a distinctive brand and superior quality, Blue Mountain Coffee commands a price of sixty dollars per pound. However, the average Jamaican is not capturing the value of selling it. Jamaica sells 90 percent of its coffee in bulk to wholesalers in Japan for eleven dollars. Foreign companies blend it, package it, and are able to sell it for an attractive profit. In the end, this is where competitiveness happens, in the ability of firms to create products and services that can provide unique value to demanding customers willing to pay a premium for it.

When Jamaicans sell commodities, from bauxite to coffee, they are competing solely on prices or on the ability to lower salaries more than their global counterparts. Countries can continue to compete this way until their societies disintegrate. This was happening throughout the Jamaican business community, which was a factor driving the diminishing standard of living and the escalating violence. The move toward creating value for demanding consumers involves a conscious choice to invest in higher forms of capital. The choice is to invest in human capital, specialized skills, technology, knowledge centers, and dependable institutions.

As the group grappled with the question of how to proceed, I also struggled internally. I remembered why I entered this business in the first place. At the core was a similar feeling that I had sensed in this group at the beginning, a feeling of anger about injustice. Growing up in the second poorest country in Latin America, I found the destitution hard to ignore. Both my parents were physicians who devoted much of their time to public hospitals: juggling death, more from poverty than from disease. Conspiracy theories are also rampant in Latin America, from the brutal Spanish colonization to the CIA operations of the 1970s. Dependency theories are appealing and a good outlet for anger. For me to contemplate that future prosperity could be in the hands of Bolivians, and not prevented by the oppressive and immutable world order, was paralyzing.

I struggled with this larger question as we sought a way forward for the cluster. Will Jamaicans stay poor because they have not yet decided they want to be rich? Could we figure out a tangible way forward that they could implement immediately, by themselves?

The solution could not just be theoretical. We needed to determine a path that the cluster could implement immediately, one that would show results in the short term to fuel momentum. The locus of responsibility had to be switched back to the cluster members if any change was to happen. The answer could not be dependent solely on new donor money, government subsidies, or philanthropic sources. While all of these would be helpful, the development industry had taught me about the fragility and undependability of these sources.

One of the patterns of uncompetitive behavior in developing countries is the lack of vertical integration in most business models. In music and industries based on intellectual property (IP), it is not as easy as setting up a retail outlet in New York. The oligopolistic structure of media conglomerates and their controlled outlets makes entering that industry extremely difficult and often unprofitable. High capital costs, lack of local market knowledge and economies of scale, and the network effects necessary to make music popular made such a move prohibitive for the Jamaican players.

There were three moves open for these businesses, which we explored and started to act upon:

(1) *If it is hard to touch the final consumer, at least move up the value chain.* Part of the problem for Jamaican singers trying to break into the international scene was their lack of managerial knowledge. In a survey sent to reggae and rhythm-and-blues labels, we found that while the music was attractive, no one wanted to deal with Jamaican managers, given their lack of professionalism and business knowledge. We looked at the few success cases: Bob Marley had Chris Blackwell to represent him and ultimately

created his own record company, Island Records. Shaggy and Sean Paul, current idols in the hip hop/dance-hall movement, had also been able to navigate the large company rules. Improving the quality of management and intermediation, which were the weakest parts of the industry, was a key part in upgrading the business model.

(2) *Find alternative distribution channels.* While large multinationals like BMG and Virgin dominate the music business, alternative channels of distribution are growing. For the first time in two decades, the trend has reversed so that now niche, independent distributors were increasing their market share to over 20 percent of final sales. Peer-to-peer Internet programs were a free way to disseminate music, and the advent of iTunes made e-commerce a much more affordable model of distribution. The independent film industry had a comparable model, where many producers skipped the billboards and went directly to DVD or independent chains. Local markets can be a good way to start if the end consumer is sophisticated.

Jamaica is not Bollywood and does not have a huge internal market to fuel its growth, but the tourist market was a distribution channel that had not been exploited at all. Most of the live entertainers in the hundreds of hotels on the island still performed Frank Sinatra songs, instead of Jamaican rhythms. Exploiting the tourist market and the independent channels would allow Jamaican music to reach the final consumer with limited intermediation. The cluster analyzed web-based selling platforms and created a series of "music tours" for the tourist market. Studios made four times more per hour entertaining tourists than they previously had and at the same time recruited new fans of their music—who sent the message abroad.

(3) *Change your business model.* The last move on the table was the most radical—change the business model. If it is hard to reach the final consumers in their own lands, bring them to you. We worked to turn Jamaica into a music mecca, by creating an offering of the best studios, producers, and musicians to bring labels and bands to record on the island. This strategy would bring the market of sophisticated consumers to Jamaica and lead to joint productions and partnerships. Instead of trying to sell CDs to the masses, the cluster would sell production expertise to bands and foreign

musicians who wanted to incorporate new and old Jamaican rhythms into their music. There was a precedent, with bands like No Doubt and Heavy D spending over one hundred thousand dollars on a "working vacation" in sunny Jamaica.

The ideas took hold, and the cluster mobilized into action. We created a new entity called Jamaica Signature Beats (JSB) to implement the new business plan. Collaboration was a must. If it was to attract new bands to record on the island, Jamaica had to offer myriad expert services in a one-stop-shop model. A representative committee developed strict rules for quality control for musicians, studios, and producers to show Jamaica's best side. Studios needed updated technology, and producers had to have compelling track records. Service standards (of punctuality and professionalism) would be monitored for members to continue to be part of JSB. Leveraging the tourist board, we publicized broadly in music publications. Cluster members put their own money into building a collective website and into launching the marketing plan. Such a group investment would have been an inconceivable notion at the beginning of the project.

Within a few months, JSB had started to make inroads into the music industry as the first bands were trickling in. A percentage of the proceeds of the new business were to be reinvested in JSB in order to continue to represent the industry well and to prepare younger producers to join.

A year later, the meetings had changed in nature. For one thing, we started on time, and I was not leading the conversations. The discussions were no longer about how the industry was being ripped off, and I no longer had to halt passionate debates about issues such as what was an authentic rhythm.

The cluster members' anger has turned to resolution and to a collective sense of possibility. They now discuss the market share of reggae and how to represent the cluster in MIDEM, the largest music exposition in France. The white man is no longer the enemy; instead, he is a customer.

I had more questions than answers after going into the trenches in this economic development experiment. This intervention had allowed the industry to start moving forward instead of backward. Many in the industry realized they had power over their own destinies. Still, despite the industry-wide collaboration that astounded even the prime minister, the projects were fragile in their nascent state, and donors continued to be dubious about continuing spending in such a nontraditional industry.

When I got back to Boston, I searched through my desk for the business card of a presidential candidate in my homeland of Bolivia. He had asked me to call him if I were ever ready to come home. I pinned his card up on the board above my desk.

So far I have not called—there are so many challenges there, the problems as large and entrenched as the mountains that have defined the country's landscape and politics. And yet this unusual group of Jamaicans, with all their differences and individual aspirations, had banded together to move mountains in their own country. Their example has inspired and challenged me.

14. The Afghan Method

DIEGO GARCIA ETCHETO
KHOGIANI, AFGHANISTAN

• • •

T HE PEOPLE in the village of Khogiani, Afghanistan, are accustomed to the sounds of explosions echoing out from the surrounding hills. A remote village of a few hundred people, located four hours from Jalalabad over rough dirt roads, Khogiani is in an area near the Pakistani border that has played host to bases of Russians, Mujahideen, and Al-Qaeda—often at the same time. This place was made famous as the last stronghold of the Taliban and Al-Qaeda; it is known to the world as Tora Bora.

The echoes of explosions still rattle through Khogiani, years after the battles that made the region famous, no longer for the purpose of war but for private enterprise.

During the fighting that uprooted vast sections of the Afghan population, the villagers of Khogiani were faced with a stark choice. Staying meant risking their lives, but leaving would guarantee lives of destitution in crowded refugee camps across the Pakistani border. The villagers chose to stay.

For twenty-five years, they employed effective strategies that allowed them to live through the ravages of war. The villagers grew a sufficient amount of basic crops to feed themselves; they supplemented their income by planting hardy, drought-resistant poppies. At one point, the region provided one-third of Afghanistan's poppy crop. To diversify away from agriculture, the villagers chose to quarry a large marble deposit on a nearby hill. It is this quarrying that today can be heard for miles around.

In the course of just one year, the government crackdown on opium production has turned Khogiani's hills of poppies to less lucrative but more donor-friendly hills of wheat. But as the villagers come to rely more and more on quarrying, they find their techniques to extract the marble deposits are woefully inadequate in an increasingly competitive environment.

General Amrullah Nazari has the mining rights to a portion of the Khogiani marble deposit. "No one else can provide security," he bluntly explained. He is a soldier recently turned businessman, with little experience in quarrying. The way the general has so far chosen to compete, which is typical of the entire industry in Afghanistan, allows him to capture only a fraction of his marble's value.

While Khogiani is a testament to the adaptability of people under extreme circumstances, today the village must adapt again and face a challenge every bit as difficult as the threat of war: the promise of prosperity.

My colleague Michael Fairbanks has identified the patterns of behavior that hinder development. Most firms and industries can be seen to engage in one or more of these Seven Patterns of Uncompetitive Behavior:

1. *Overreliance on basic factors of advantage*—a focus on export of raw materials prevails, with little regard for value addition.

2. *Poor understanding of customers*—lack of customer knowledge prevents the industry from effectively marketing its products.

3. *Ignorance of relative competitive position*—little understanding exists of how to position oneself to compete (and how other industries are competing) in global markets.

4. *Failure to forward integrate*—the industry controls only the portion of the value chain closest to the raw material.

5. *Poor interfirm cooperation*—members cannot work together to overcome common obstacles.

6. *Defensiveness*—there is a lack of recognition that the industry is responsible for, and can solve, its own problems.

7. *Paternalism*—companies attempt to use government intervention to secure profits, rather than focusing on improving competitiveness.

From what I have seen of General Nazari and other Afghan business-men, Afghanistan is seven for seven. But there is a good reason for that. These patterns of behavior allowed industry in places like Khogiani to sur-vive in an environment where "cutthroat competition" has often been taken literally. It is only now, as the conflict recedes, that men like Amrullah Nazari are able to redirect efforts that may have worked in the past but that are no longer considered reasonable.

And so we return to the sounds of war. Afghanistan has two things in abundance: marble deposits and stockpiles of munitions. In the breathtak-ing peaks and valleys of the Afghan countryside, the two have combined to form the backbone of the marble industry.

Marble processing starts at the quarry. An efficient system of produc-tion utilizes diamond-wire saws to cut large marble blocks from the rock face. The blocks are then loaded onto trucks for shipping to the process-ing plant, where they are run through multiblade saws that can quickly cut large blocks into numerous slabs. The slabs can then be polished and fur-ther processed into tiles, cladding, countertops, etc.

Although any one of those products is export ready, successful indus-tries tend to focus on slabs and further processed goods since they cap-ture more value. For example, a block of marble may sell for two hundred dollars a ton; when cut into slabs that same marble can sell for upwards of $480; and when cut into large, thin tiles (a difficult process), the identical ton could fetch up to $530.

Afghanistan currently exports none of these products.

Afghanistan quarry workers extract marble with a method that, I believe, is unique in the world and that leaves little worth exporting. In Khogiani, this method involves going down to the ammunition dump that is located in the valley just below the quarry, breaking apart shell casings or mines to extract the powder and explosives (I could not make this up if I tried), drilling a hole in the quarry face, stuffing the explosives inside, and detonating the whole thing—one hopes after everyone has managed to find some cover. That is the Afghan method.[1]

When the dust clears and the results are revealed, even a layman can

1. There is a blasting method called "dynamic splitting" or the "Finnish method," which in-volves the use of slow-expanding explosives to minimize damage to the stone; although

see this method of blasting is the root of the industry's problems. Over half of the marble pieces are too small to be of use and are left strewn in the quarry. The larger pieces are cracked and irregularly shaped, leading to a great deal of wastage in further processing. Much is lost in "dressing" the stone (cutting off the uneven edges); much more breaks when cutting slabs and tiles, due to the fractures created by the explosion. One hundred percent of Afghanistan's marble exports consists of these stones, shipped to Pakistan for a meager thirty dollars per ton. Furthermore, blasting can "kill" the quarry by causing microfractures throughout the entire site, drastically reducing the value of any future marble extracted.

For my first few months in country, I could not help but wonder why anyone would process marble this way.

1. Overreliance on Basic Factors of Advantage

The best model for processing marble involves investing in the latest technology and techniques—diamond-wire saws, hydraulic jacks, good derrick cranes, earth-moving equipment at the quarry, and large gang saws and polishing lines at the processing plant.

Why is the Afghan model designed to blast the quarry with anything handy and then to ship the stone to Pakistan for further processing? Anyone looking to quarry in Afghanistan needs to be sure that he can defend his investment against competitors—in a country where defense is traditionally carried out at gunpoint. With such an investment climate, most production hovers near the resource, and there is little incentive to invest in expensive (and easily seized) machinery. Hence, marble is extracted as cheaply as possible (by blasting) and processed at the nearest safe distance from conflict (in Pakistan).

Men like Nazari are acutely aware of the shortcomings of the marble industry. They are selling their marble at a fraction of the final value and have nothing nice to say about the Pakistanis who realize that value. But in the middle of a war zone with no insurance and only the vaguest rules

---

normally used for granite and not ideal for softer marble, it is far preferable to the Afghan method described above in this essay.

of ownership, who in their right mind would invest a million dollars in a quarry? Nazari and his partners control Khogiani because, as he bluntly put it, "When [anyone else comes] to the quarry, we shoot into the air, and they run away." But even Nazari and his cohorts are not confident enough to put down a large investment.

Diamond-wire saws, large derrick cranes, and top-of-the-line cutting and polishing equipment do not exist in Afghanistan for the same reason skyscrapers do not exist: anyone foolish enough to set one up would have seen it come tumbling back down in a barrage of rocket fire. The Ruham marble factory is a great example. It was established by the Afghan government in the early 1970s with state-of-the-art Italian equipment. It managed to survive the Russian invasion and the civil war, albeit with drastically reduced operations; suspected of being a munitions factory, it was finally bombed into extinction by the United States in the aftermath of the 9/11 terrorist attacks. All that is left is a heap of twisted metal.

In fact, the only factory in Afghanistan that has survived the fighting is the onyx processing plant in the province of Helmand. Helmand was famous in the 1960s and 1970s for its onyx deposits. Legend has it that Afghan onyx is among the best in the world and was once much sought after by Italian processors, the leaders in the industry. Today, Helmand is famous for being one of the most lawless provinces of Afghanistan. It is considered a no-go area for most nongovernmental organizations (NGOs), and the few in the region are at the U.S. military base or another secure compound—under lockdown. The main road through Helmand, despite being heavily traveled by police and military, is bordered by vast fields of poppies. When I drove through at the peak of the harvest, workers were collecting poppy resin in the fields with little regard for passing traffic. Some fields had a few feet of wheat acting as a screen from the road—a subterfuge spoiled by the fact that the poppies grow taller than the wheat and on an upward slope—but most farmers do not even bother with pretense.

The Helmand factory's vintage equipment was installed in 1947; only one of the two gang saws works, and it can run with only half of the blades at one time. The blades are warped and bent to the point where they have a troubling tendency to shatter the onyx—a process aided by the fact that the onyx is quarried with the Afghan method. No one has invested in the plant because, in their struggles to control the quarry, the various warlords have not ensured consistent and dependable shipments of onyx to the plant. Since no one from the plant has thought it wise to travel to the quarry to raise the issue with the warlords, the matter remains unresolved.

2. Poor Understanding of Customers

Haji Kaseem is the owner of a small marble processing plant in Kandahar. He currently sells all his marble locally. Kaseem wants to expand his factory and begin to export. However, he admits, "I am Afghan; what do I know about the world? The only country I am allowed to go to is Pakistan."

International trade drives the marble market. Fifty-four percent of all marble produced in the world is installed in a different country from which it was quarried. International trade is even more important for developing countries since local demand is not large enough to absorb the industry's production capacity. By some estimates, Afghanistan is already exporting 80 percent of the marble quarried in the country, but it is not realizing the full value of its exports.

Afghan producers do not have the customer knowledge required to market their products overseas successfully; in addition, they are not sufficiently "forward integrated" to have the customer contact that can help them acquire that knowledge. Pakistani trucks drive right up to the quarries and take the stone to plants across the border. Without access to the outside world, how can Afghans learn about world markets?

Before setting up the Ruham factory, the engineer in charge traveled extensively throughout Italy on a fact-finding mission. Over a cup of tea at our office, he insisted that Afghanistan should quarry red marble because that is what the Italians liked—in the 1970s. I contradicted him by stating that the buyers I had contacted suggested focusing on white, beige, and black: more "classic" colors. We then had a lively debate on the subject, the crux of my argument being that many things that were widely popular in the 1970s are not necessarily popular now.

Afghanistan today is in a time warp and desperately needs to update its market knowledge. Most Afghans know this, but few know how to go about changing it. Short-term market research projects can boost knowledge; but over the long term, the best way customer knowledge is gained, maintained, and made useful is through forward integration.

The closer the industry moves to the end customer, the more knowledge it can gain about what customers want, and it is necessary to integrate that knowledge into an ongoing competitive strategy. For example, there are close to three thousand different types (colors) of marble and six different finishes a marble tile can have. What are the odds that the truck driver picking up the stone at the quarry knows which are the most popular? Pretty slim.

The bad news is that customer knowledge is never complete; the good news is that, with the right systems in place, every sale becomes a customer survey.

3. IGNORANCE OF RELATIVE COMPETITIVE POSITION

A great deal of the finished marble sold in Afghanistan comes from Pakistan and Iran. Herat, a northwestern province in Afghanistan, is flooded by Iranian imports. Iranian marble sells for six dollars per square meter, while Herat producers can barely break even selling at fifteen dollars per square meter.

On a trip to India, I was able to observe just how cheaply one of Afghanistan's regional competitors is able to bring marble to market. Despite the fact that it is quarried almost a thousand kilometers away, Rajasthan marble sells in Bombay for five to six dollars per square meter, in 8' x 4' sizes that cannot even be produced in Afghanistan.

Production costs for marble in Rajasthan are $3.50–4.50 per square meter, compared to around thirteen dollars per square meter in Herat. Indian processors pay three times more for their raw material than do Herat processors, yet their final cost is one-third that of their Afghan counterparts. The processors' cost structure is lower because they waste less than 40 percent of the marble during processing; wastage in Afghanistan is over 60 percent. Furthermore, with their large volumes, Indian factories achieve economies of scale that Afghan producers are not even aware exist.

It is difficult to get information on companies in Iran, but I imagine their cost structure is similar to India's and thus the main reason they can sell their marble in Herat for less than half the price of Afghan marble. Afghan processors do not have a good understanding of the industry dynamics that allow Iranian exports to underprice their own products. Until they invest in the proper knowledge and equipment needed to improve the efficiency of the industry, they will not be able to compete with imports, much less develop an export market.

4. FAILURE TO FORWARD INTEGRATE

As I have mentioned, 80 percent of Afghan marble is currently exported, but Afghanistan is not realizing its full value. Exports are exclusively of unprocessed marble and go to Pakistani buyers who own the customer knowledge required to process and sell the marble at a premium. Afghanistan's failure to forward integrate has left the processing and marketing of its resources in the hands of others.

Figure 1 is a value chain analysis of marble exported from Khogiani. The figures for processing in Pakistan are not exact since the information is difficult to source; however, even if we include a healthy margin of error, it is obvious that Afghanistan is missing out on the bulk of the value.

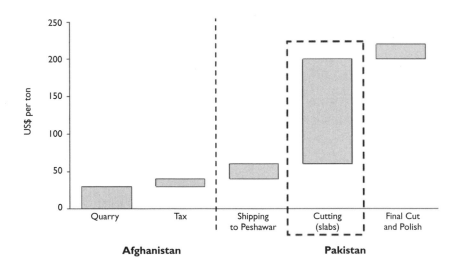

Figure 1. Exports of Khogiani marble to Pakistan
Source: OTF Group

Quarries like the one run by Nazari are trying to survive on thirty dollars per ton, while in Pakistan, processors get approximately $220 for processing that same ton of marble into polished tiles. Even without upgrading his quarrying capacity, Nazari could capture more value by forward integrating into processing. This shift would require not only equipment but the customer knowledge necessary to serve markets willing to pay for spotless white marble of the quality found in Khogiani.

5. POOR INTERFIRM COOPERATION

As part of our work in Afghanistan, helping improve the competitiveness of the marble industry, we conducted a survey of two hundred business, government, and civic leaders to get some insight into the belief systems at work in the country. One of the most interesting results of the survey was that 80 percent of those polled do not trust people outside of their clan. It should come as no surprise to anyone who has worked in Afghanistan that trust among Afghans is a scarce commodity.

Lack of trust is like an invisible tax. It makes every business transaction more expensive. I have seen many examples of this in action; here are just a couple:

> ▸ Almost all of the marble processors in Afghanistan use their own trucks to bring the stone from the quarries, despite the fact that it would be cheaper to centralize shipping. They simply do not trust anyone else with their raw material.
>
> There is a great picture in the office of a Herat marble factory of a truck stuck in the middle of a raging river. As the owner of both truck and plant informed me, the river between Herat and the quarry is not passable for three to four months of the year. In this case, the unfortunate owner tried one trip too many. But despite the fact that there are five factories operating in Herat that obtain over 90 percent of their marble from that quarry, the factory owners cannot organize to get a bridge built. The truck in the picture sat in the river for almost a year before it could be pulled out.
>
> ▸ The Coca-Cola plant in Kabul, a twenty million dollar investment, is using imported marble tiles in its building because the one marble

company it contacted in Afghanistan does not have the equipment to make tiles in the appropriate size. Just down the street is another plant that has the correct equipment, but information is not something Afghan businessmen are likely to share. Rather than collaborating so that a competitor may cut and polish the tiles, the owner of the first marble company will let the contract go to a foreign firm.

Lack of trust has meant extra cost and missed opportunities for the industry. Of course, it should be noted that trust is difficult to build among potential competitors at the best of times; in a conflict environment where competition for resources often results in violence, confidence is limited to a very small group of people with whom one shares close ties. Trust is easier when a mistake may cost profits; it is harder when it may cost you your life.

6. DEFENSIVENESS

At the beginning of this essay, I argue that the patterns of uncompetitive behavior in Afghanistan could be explained as survival strategies for a conflict environment. Actually, defensiveness is tough to justify under any circumstances. It is also one of the most common patterns of human behavior. In Afghanistan, as in most places, everyone blames some external force for his or her problems. There are numerous examples of this, and again here are a few of my favorites:

From the private sector side:

It is the government's fault; if the government would just reduce the levy on quarried stone, I could make money. I think we have already disproved this myth, but let me reiterate: the industry gets thirty dollars per ton for unprocessed marble blocks, while that same marble properly quarried and processed into slabs can sell for over four hundred dollars, suggesting that the real problem is the use of the Afghan method and the lack of processing.

It is the bank's fault; if I had money for working capital, I could start working and making money. This can be translated: "If I had money for working capital, I could return to blasting marble and sell it for a fraction of its value, which is what got me into this mess."

From the government side:

It is the private sector's fault; it does not know how to quarry. It is true that the private sector blasts the quarries (so does the government at the government-run quarries), but the government does not encourage proper investment because leasing policies are confusing (few businessmen understand them) and shortsighted (one to three years versus the ten years necessary to receive bank loans). If the government offered a secure, transparent process that granted long-term leases, it would find the private sector a better tenant of the quarries.

The real tragedy of defensiveness is that it paralyzes cooperation. It is well within Afghanistan's power to fix Afghanistan's marble industry. But any discussion quickly degenerates into a shouting match between traditionally "opposing" sides, the government and private sector. As anyone who has attended such a meeting can attest, when everyone is shouting, no one is listening.

7. PATERNALISM

In many cultures, paternalism takes the form of "breakfast with the minister." That is, if you want something done, you take the appropriate minister to breakfast in order to explain your problems. If you have proved yourself to be a good supporter of his, he pulls the appropriate strings to get you what you want. Such systems place a premium on investing in relationships with top officials rather than in investing in competitiveness. With Afghan warlords, it is best to have breakfast, lunch, and dinner.

In Afghanistan, people close to the power brokers prosper, while those without the right connections have little chance for success. Hence, should an entrepreneur encounter any problem on the road to profitability, the first place he looks is up. In fact, almost every businessman I have spoken to has boasted of his access to various ministers or to President Karzai himself. When businessmen spend their time maneuvering for favors rather than running their businesses, competitiveness suffers.

The government of Afghanistan cannot make Afghan marble competitive. It is the role of individual firms to compete. As long as the industry looks for help from the government, it will never take the necessary steps to enable itself to compete globally, and perhaps even locally.

One of the key investments needed for the marble industry to prosper is in institutions. Too much business is conducted in back rooms and dominated by a get-rich-quick mentality. Investors must have at least ten years' access to a quarry before banks are willing to provide loans. When businessmen tell me proudly, "I know the minister; I can get access to any quarry," I ask them if that same minister will be around for the next decade.

Maintaining the survival strategies of the past, though justifiable under certain circumstances, will only keep Afghanistan poor in the future. The scales today have tipped in favor of wealth creation rather than mere survival. Afghanistan is beginning to invest in areas that will allow it to unlock its competitiveness.

On July 4, 2005, a new mining law was passed that allows for ten-year leases with automatic five-year renewals. The law also introduced a new bidding process, and the Ministry of Mines and Industry is slowly bringing the regions to heel. Although the process will never be perfect, the groundwork is laid for secure investments to take place.

Afghanistan is also investing in its culture: mistrust must be replaced with dialogue between clans and ethnic groups. Prosperity in Afghanistan will not be sustainable if it is not widespread. The zero-sum game of the war years, where control of resources by any means necessary ensured the survival of the clan, serves only to limit investment and progress today. Businessmen have begun to see that their interests are best served by cooperation; and, most importantly, the Afghan people do not want to squander this valuable opportunity to rebuild their country.

I recently held a meeting attended by many of the key players in the in-dustry where we discussed the new mining law. For the first time in the history of Afghanistan, there is a clear procedure for getting long-term leases of quarries. The only question is whether the government can enforce the law. During the discussion, the issue of regional security was raised. General Amrullah Nazari spoke, emphasizing his points by thrusting a finger in the air: "Three things are required to quarry successfully: money, expertise, and security. We can get money and expertise." He paused and smiled, "And don't worry—I will guarantee the safety of anyone who wants to have access to Khogiani. After all, it will be good for Afghanistan."

15. Global Strategy in Old Kabul

ROBERT HENNING

KABUL, AFGHANISTAN

• • •

"**Y**OU UNDERSTAND this business very well," a shop owner said to me in the pre-monsoon heat of the bustling New Delhi Central Market. He was perhaps the twentieth person with whom I confirmed that to purchase dried fruits and nuts for retail sale in New Delhi, you had to go to Khari Baoli, a maze of wholesale stalls embedded in the oldest part of the city, accessible only by foot or bicycle rickshaw. Finally, I understood the key to how our clients, Afghan dried-fruits and nuts exporters, could make more money in the Indian market. In order to maximize profits and customer learning in India, Afghan exporters needed to establish a warehousing and wholesaling beachhead in this market.

A week earlier, deep in old Kabul, I had been sitting cross-legged as I sipped tea with a group of Afghan dried-fruits and nuts traders. They were led by Haji Hassan, the vice president of their association. I listened as the members complained about their dealings with Indian buyers. "We sell our products at good prices to the Indians here in Afghanistan, but we have no idea where the product goes from here." This is a conversation that I had also had in Mazar-e-Sharif, Herat, and Kandahar, the major dried-fruits and nuts centers in Afghanistan. These traders, our main clients, need to understand the final market to unleash opportunities to grow.

These insights did not come overnight; my education about Afghanistan began six months earlier when I arrived in Kabul for the first time. Amid the devastated ruins of the city and the American and NATO convoys

that patrolled the streets, I found it hard to believe that I could find businesspeople who would be receptive to new ideas. The idea that business
might actually happen in a country like Afghanistan, where remnants of
the Taliban still wage an insurgency and where bombings and kidnappings are commonplace—even in the capital—seemed outlandish. Over
these several months, the main mode of communication has changed
from seminars, where my colleagues and I preached competitiveness and
strategy in theory, to intimate, memorable meetings where Afghan businessmen tutored me on how to operate and make money in the Afghan
environment.

India and Afghanistan have a relationship filled with fierce conflict that
stretches back centuries. Moghuls such as Barbur made it their last wish to
be buried under the "bright blue skies of Kabul," where his tomb sits to this
day. At the same time, Indians have suffered horrible defeats at the hands
of the fierce Afghan tribes who inhabit the Hindu Kush (Hindu Killer in
Dari, a major Afghan language) mountains of eastern Afghanistan. As the
colonial powers learned centuries later, the Afghans will vigorously defend
their land at all costs.

However, in modern-day Afghanistan, relations between the two countries are cordial. Each maintains a large diplomatic presence in the other's country. More concretely, India is funding many development projects
in Afghanistan as part of the reconstruction effort, including connecting
Kabul and northern Afghanistan to mainline electricity in Uzbekistan
and building a highway to link southern Afghanistan with Iran to facilitate trade. Efforts such as these have won the hearts and minds of many
Afghans, from the poorest peasant all the way up to President Hamid
Karzai. In addition to these partnerships, India and Afghanistan have a
large and mutually beneficial trade relationship.

Indians adore Afghan dried fruits and nuts. India recently absorbed
forty million dollars or 19.5 percent of Afghanistan's total exports and
nearly 60 percent of the country's dried-fruits and nuts exports. For products such as raisins and figs, Afghanistan dominates India's import markets
with over a 90 percent market share of these two products.

In the case of raisins, Afghan raisins are positioned at the high end of the
market with wholesale and retail prices three to ten times that of Indian

raisins depending on the variety. For example, while Indian green raisins from Maharashtra State in India sell for $2.25 per kilogram, two jars down on the shelf, a remarkably similar-looking Afghan long, green raisin sells for $23 per kilogram. In a country whose per capita income is only $540 per year, it is amazing to think that there is a market for such an expensive consumable product. In subsequent conversations with importers in the United Kingdom and in other far-wealthier countries, I found that they could not believe that any consumer could be so discerning when it comes to dried fruit. The managing director of one of the largest European dried-fruits and nuts import houses told me, "The Afghans will never get those prices in London, so it is best they send those raisins to the Indians."

Sending premium products to the developing world is not an obvious strategy. However, thanks to India, Afghan exporters are also receiving among the highest prices in the world for their pistachios and shelled almonds. For almonds, India pays the second highest price in the world. For pistachios, India does not make the top five, but willingness to pay for Afghan pistachios is proven by prices that almost attain top-five status. In sharp contrast to this fortunate commercial relationship are current Afghan raisin exports to Russia. Approximately 65 percent of the volume of exports goes to Russia, where importers pay only seven hundred dollars per ton on average versus India's average import price of nearly twelve hundred dollars.

Although not the most attractive products on the market in terms of physical appearance, Afghan products are appreciated by Indians. They are willing to pay premiums for their unique taste vis-à-vis similar, more attractive, and better packaged products from more developed exporting countries such as the United States, Turkey, and Iran. Trade is further enhanced by many Indian importers and exporters who live in Afghanistan and who have developed an affinity for the country and its people.

While prices for the Afghan products are high in India, Afghani growers and exporters capture only a small fraction of the value. In order for the Afghanistan traders to take full advantage of this commercial relationship, they should examine one key question: how do Afghan dried fruits and nuts get from Afghan exporters to the end consumer? The simplest and most direct way is that an Afghan trader and exporter sells to Indian importers—wholesalers. These wholesalers then sell to a variety of institutional customers such as grocery stores, specialty dried-fruits and nuts shops, supermarkets, sweetshops, hotels, and bakeries. In many cases, there is a series of intermediaries involved—separate importers who act as intermediaries between the Afghan exporters and Indian wholesalers: these brokers, or "semi-wholesalers," will purchase relatively small, bulk quantities of dried fruits and nuts from the wholesalers and then sell them in smaller quantities to the same institutional customers in larger urban centers, such as New Delhi or Mumbai.

Figure 1 below illustrates the value chain of retained revenue for high-quality *shundukhani* raisins from Kandahar in southern Afghanistan to a wealthy consumer in either New Delhi or Mumbai. These long, fluorescent green raisins are shade dried in adobe drying sheds (*kishmish khana* in Dari) for one month. Their taste and appearance are highly prized by both Afghans and Indians.

There are two key insights from this chart. The first is that the Afghan exporters are capturing very little value from the sale of this product. The second is the *amount* of the value—as both wholesalers and retailers are

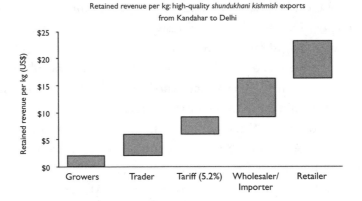

Figure 1. *Retained revenue for* shundukhani *raisins*

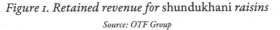

Source: OTF Group

able to mark up this product by 30 to 50 percent each, almost double the revenue retained by the Afghan exporters. In the final analysis, these raisins sell for up to twenty-three dollars per kilogram, while Afghan exporters earn around six dollars. *Shundukhani* raisins are the most expensive Afghan product sold in India, but the retained revenue distribution for the other products such as dried figs, dried apricots, pistachios, or almonds is similar.

Afghanistan's dried-fruits and nuts cluster members understand that they need to learn about new distribution channels and the needs of the different consumer-market segments in India in order to capture some of this value.[1] Often in the developing world, aid-funded development projects (or marketing efforts) treat market research as sales trips with the goal of signing new buyer contracts. Although sales are ultimately important, the cluster needs to understand the psychology and needs of its buyers to determine upgrades in product attributes and for relationship development. Armed with this information, firms can create immediate sales and reconfigure their organizations to build the long-term, profitable relationships that are key to building a competitive industry.

In the case of exporting Afghan dried fruits and nuts to India, there were two segments that the exporters wanted me to examine: wholesalers and the retail shops. Based on preliminary market research, wholesalers' needs are straightforward. The price to quality relationship is the most important. As noted above, the Indian market is willing to pay surprisingly high prices for dried fruits and nuts from Afghanistan, but suppliers must deliver high and consistent quality in order to remain long-term suppliers to these customers. This relationship is linear; there are no dramatic price increases for incremental improvements in quality, only steady rewards for better sorting in terms of size and color, removal of stems, and clean product.

A second major topic of conversation with the wholesalers was packaging. This segment explained that spending five cents per kilogram of dried

---

1. Editors' note: Economists since Marshall (agglomerations) and more recently Krugman (trade) and then Porter (business strategy) have acknowledged the concept of geographical centers for related and supporting industries.

fruits and nuts to have them in five-hundred-gram or one-kilogram bags is important, but that they would not pay much more for individual packaging. The explanation for this is simple. Once retailers purchase the product, they normally discard the wholesale packaging and sell the product loose. In their view, sophisticated packaging is money that is thrown away.

It appears that Afghanistan, as a "natural brand," could be the limit of developing a brand for dried fruits and nuts in India. The Afghan origin commands a premium, but other concepts do not seem to resonate with wholesalers. This important finding contradicted the hypothesis of many international advisors (including mine) that pushing branding would increase the value of Afghan dried-fruits and nuts exports.

Perhaps the most important learning of the Indian market research had nothing to do directly with products; it was the degree of trust that existed among the Indian importers toward Afghans. The head of the Mumbai dried-fruits and nuts importers association told me that he can trust 99 percent of the Afghan exporters with whom he deals. It appears that Afghanistan has a very strong position in the Indian market—it produces a high-quality product, and there is a high level of trust for the Afghan sellers among their current customers, the wholesalers.

Retailers are a new, daunting, and more sophisticated market segment for Afghan exporters. During my trip to India, I spent many hours speaking to a wide variety of retailers. From the sleek modern headquarters of India's largest retailer next to Bollywood, to screaming over a crowd in the center of Mumbai's Masjid Bunder market, the entire spectrum of retailers explained to me what they look for in suppliers and products and the needs of their customers. Based on these conversations, plus an extensive survey and focus group conducted by a local market-research firm, it became clear that, although the retail segment is also interested in the quality-price equation, there are other ways for wholesalers to differentiate themselves and win new customers.

Retailers expect surprisingly high levels of service from their suppliers, the wholesalers, in terms of logistical support and education. In a focus group of retailers, the participants agreed that wholesaler representatives should be visiting their shop at least two to three times a week to make new deliveries, take back spoiled products, and handle routine inquiries. Retail shopkeepers need their suppliers to be informed about the health benefits, shelf life, and other characteristics of existing products as well as to introduce completely new products and new varieties of existing products.

Retailers in New Delhi and Mumbai unanimously agreed that their wholesaler must be physically present in their local wholesale market. There are two reasons for this. First, retailers want to be able to compare prices and qualities of different products before deciding on a supplier. Second, they do not want to be burdened by import procedures and other bureaucratic hassles involved with dealing with an overseas supplier. Simply having a base overseas and attempting to serve this customer segment is not an option.

Instead of branding or packaging, the way to improve profitability in this market appears to be a forward-integration strategy. Typically, this strategy would include Afghan traders' establishing themselves as wholesalers in the large urban markets of India. This move will permit Afghan exporters to earn an extra 30 to 40 percent in revenues on every kilogram of product sold, understand the rapidly changing Indian retail market, and eliminate the bargaining power of Indian wholesalers and other middlemen.

Although at its heart a simple concept, moving forward into this market will be complicated by bureaucratic and competitive obstacles. First, Indian law may prohibit direct foreign investment into the sector. In order to solve this problem, Afghan exporters and the Afghan Embassy in India have contracted a local expert to advise them on how to best proceed, on whether these regulations apply to dried-fruits and nuts wholesalers from Afghanistan, and on whether the Afghan Embassy can intervene to facilitate this process. One Afghan exporter already has an Indian partner and is seeking to control the business and keep the profits. Another Afghan is married to an Indian and has a clear right to work in India. Both cases show that there are ways to circumvent the current regulations.

Predatory competition from the incumbent Indian wholesalers is also an issue. Afghan exporters report that there is a group of five to seven large Indian wholesalers—essentially a "mafia arrangement"—that colludes to control the market for Afghan dried fruits and nuts. The Afghans say that this group has already created a loss of one million dollars for one Afghan trader who tried to enter the market. However, the Afghans are optimistic that they can beat this mafia and win in this market *if* they work together and enlist the assistance of the Afghan Embassy and other government agencies to reduce the legal and administrative hassles.

A final piece of the solution could be to provide the Afghans with assistance in the form of a business start-up consultant. This person would help with staffing, systems implementation, distribution, and marketing and provide general business advice during the first twelve months of operations.

Working closely with this group of Afghan traders, an "export consortia" led by Haji Hassan, has been the latest stage of my education about doing business in Afghanistan. Contrary to what I believed, the traders did not need financial assistance to compete, just good advice. For the past few weeks, we have had lengthy discussions about the intricacies of setting up a foreign-owned business in India, new customers and new distribution channels that the traders will need to identify, and financial projections to seek additional working capital to extend to new buyers. The traders have humbled me with the sophistication of their thinking and their innovative solutions to both their new marketing strategy for India and how they deal with the brutal business environment of Afghanistan.

When I returned from India, the first question from many traders and partner organizations was, "So, did you meet any buyers who are interested in purchasing dried fruits from Afghanistan?" The answer to this question was "yes," but just talking to buyers is not the only way to build the competitiveness and increase the profitability of an industry. To build a successful cluster, you need to analyze where the most opportunities for increased profits are and then address these needs through careful planning. Simply increasing volume is one way to improve performance, but catering to customer needs and understanding and addressing market dynamics are the ways to create sustainable competitive advantage.

In the case of dried fruits and nuts from Afghanistan, weeks of visiting wholesalers and retailers helped me to gain a personal perspective on this market. That, together with an in-depth market-research study, helped to clearly determine what is important to segments of the market. Contacts made may help to generate sales in the short term, but, perhaps more importantly, cluster members are learning about new options that are galvanizing them to action. Armed with the knowledge and reinforced by good planning and inter-firm cooperation, Afghans such as Haji Hassan and his partners stand a much stronger chance of forward integrating and winning in the Indian dried-fruits and nuts market.

Afghan exporters will likely target obvious Western markets, such as Europe, the United States, and rich Asian countries, but they have both a unique opportunity to capitalize on excellent market positioning and a premium product in the Indian market to earn higher profits and capture more value for Afghanistan. The lesson that one cluster member recently reiterated is that "I guess that business strategy is not just for penetrating first-world markets, but it can also be applied in poor countries—and we might even make more money in the poor market."

The challenge for the private sector is to identify where the biggest opportunities are and to make productive and realistic requests to the government and the donor community for assistance where it is needed and appropriate. At the end of the day, after theory and strategy have been discussed and decided, the only true measure of success is increased profits for businesses. The sense of excitement and enthusiasm that I feel from the Afghan traders who are ready to work together to penetrate the Indian retail market indicates that they are on their way to a resounding success in their large neighbor. A win in this market will be the Afghan traders' first step in reestablishing themselves in the global marketplace. Armed with this knowledge, Haji Hassan and other like-minded traders will do their part to relaunch Afghanistan as a major supplier of dried fruits and nuts to the world.

As an imported expert from the United States, I thought the idea that business strategy might actually be happening in a country such as Afghanistan, where remnants of the Taliban still wage an insurgency and where bombings and kidnappings are commonplace, seemed outlandish. I learned a lot, however, and was humbled over these months, as the main mode of communication changed from presenting seminars and slide shows, where my colleagues and I preached the merits of competitiveness and strategy, to sitting cross-legged and sipping tea in old Kabul, sharing stories and ideas, and being tutored by Afghan businesspeople.

16. After God, It's Customer Relations

AREF ADAMALI

KABUL, AFGHANISTAN

♦ ♦ ♦

T HE FIRST MEETING of the Afghan carpet cluster took place in a newly built wedding hall in Kabul called *Sham-e-Paris*, meaning "Paris Nights." I was in a business suit, with a PowerPoint presentation projected behind me, introducing core competitiveness concepts to a group of fifty burly, turbaned men. I was speaking through an interpreter as the presentation was being translated into Farsi, the most commonly spoken language in Afghanistan. The entire group's attention would noticeably shift to the screen whenever I projected slides with photographs (or pictorial representations of ideas), with people leaning forward and even craning their necks to see. However, when I moved on to slides with text or graphs, few people were looking at the screen, and most of the attention was directed somewhere else altogether. It occurred to me that the majority of my audience was basically illiterate. I realized that I would have to change the format for the remainder of the meeting, cutting the written exercises and shifting instead to open group discussion. Communication would be a challenge.

Literacy is low in Afghanistan: at 43 percent literacy for men and an appalling 14 percent for women, Afghanistan ranks among the most illiterate nations of the world. Usually the business community is well above the national literacy average, but this is not the case with the carpet cluster. Despite being savvy and experienced businesspeople, most carpet producers in Afghanistan have had no formal education. And while they are quick on their calculators—all of them carry them in the breast pocket of their *shalwar kameez*—and can rapidly size up any given carpet deal, skills sufficient for operating in a local carpet bazaar, these businesspeople are not prepared for succeeding in a highly competitive global carpet market.

Today, Afghan producers have to compete head to head with aggressive and large-scale carpet manufacturers from Iran, India, and China, among other nations. Many global producers run sophisticated operations, actively shifting their production and product to keep up with— and even stay ahead of—constantly changing market trends. No longer is it enough to reproduce faithfully a traditional carpet design, regardless of its timeless beauty. Carpets need to be reinvented constantly to keep pace with design styles and cycles. This requires staying on top of consumer tastes and being able to rapidly adjust production in response.

Thus far, the Afghan carpet sector has been relatively successful. During the past twenty-five years of conflict, carpets provided a good livelihood for many Afghan families. In refugee camps in Pakistan and Iran, carpet production was often the only source of family income. For people who remained in Afghanistan, persistent traders arranged camel and mule caravans to cross over the formidable Hindu Kush mountain range, ensuring that producers maintained an access to markets. Therefore, when I arrived in Afghanistan three years after the conflict to oust the Taliban, I found carpets to be a stable and, at over fifty million dollars in export revenues, a comparatively large export sector.

Nonetheless, the stability of the sector is also fragile. Some years ago, producers started to face falling orders but were unable to understand why because most carpet producers have little contact with the buyers in end markets where their carpets are sold. The majority sells their carpets to traders in neighboring Pakistan, from whom they receive their orders. Having no contact with final consumers and no knowledge of the end markets where their carpets are sold, they are unable to develop effective responses to market shifts.

In Herat, a city in western Afghanistan, a lack of customer understanding is the overriding concern of carpet businesses. Sales for traditional Afghan carpets, the mainstay on the carpet cluster in Herat, have been declining over the past three years by as much as 50 percent a year. Despite low demand, supply has remained high, as many producers are unable to switch to other businesses: carpets are all that they know. This has led to high competition and aggressive price cutting. Things have gotten so bad that many industry members in Herat say that they cannot survive in this market for more than twelve to eighteen months.

The exodus of much of Herat's carpet producers from the trade would be a great loss for them as well as for Afghanistan. To prevent such an outcome, Herat's carpet producers realize they need to have a better understanding of their customers' shifting needs. But when asked how they planned to obtain this knowledge, they had no clear response other than "*Aref-jan*," *jan* being a commonly used Farsi term of endearment, "you will show us the way." As a newly appointed advisor to the industry, I was afraid of the outcome of such an exercise. I suspected that years of conflict and (as a result) sadly neglected education had taken Afghanistan out of the running.

These fears were compounded as I learned more about the global carpet market: particularly while conducting research in India, the largest handmade carpet exporter to the United States, the biggest market.

The Indian carpet industry was dynamic. Manufacturers talked of a competitive market where trends are constantly changing and where products' shelf lives are becoming increasingly shorter. Producers I met had full-time designers on staff in India, as well as in Europe and the United States. The Indians are constantly testing new ideas with buyers, churning out one new design every day. It seemed that every producer I visited was packing samples to send by courier for current or prospective buyers. When I asked one producer friend about the key to his success, he responded, "After luck, honesty, and God, it is relations with buyers."

While I doubted that India could have a competitive advantage over Afghanistan in luck, honesty, or even God (despite its many deities), it has a massive lead in buyer relations. Its producers are fluent in English and well traveled. They subscribe to a range of carpet journals and interior design magazines and are regular participants at global carpet fairs. I could not see how the good but unlettered Afghan carpet cluster would be able to develop effective ties with buyers from Europe and the United States. The leap seemed too far to make.

An idea of how Afghanistan could potentially make this leap occurred to me as I was driving through a relatively new and lively part of Kabul called *Share-Now*, the "New City." Share-Now is the main stomping ground of Kabul's trendy young men. Between the ages of eighteen and twenty-five years old, they are in the prime of youth: in good shape, strapped into tight jeans, and, judging by the number of faces peering at their reflection in the rearview mirrors of parked cars, extremely vain. I have always found image-obsessed young Kabuli men to be an oddity. They seem so different from their fathers—large, traditionally garbed, bearded men who care little for fashion.

But this was the point: the majority of today's Afghans—45 percent are under the age of fifteen—are very different from their parents. Many of them are increasingly online, speak English, and are plugged into fashion trends from other parts of the world (meaning, for the most part, Bollywood). Working every day with their parents, the business owners, I overlooked a great potential resource.

My shortsightedness was all the more embarrassing given that I have been surrounded by evidence of this young talent. I work with the future generation of Afghanistan every day. For example, my colleague Latifa is a smart, ambitious, and talented woman. She works with businesswomen to develop strategies and to write business plans, while in her spare time she designs clothes that merge modern fashion with traditional Afghan embroidery. She is the personification of business acumen and design flair. Young people like her can be brought into the carpet production and trade process to help bridge the cultural and educational gap between Afghan producers and buyers.

Also, I am one of them. I embody the idea of a new, more globally plugged-in generation with regard to my own family's business and its future potential to enter new markets. Started by my father almost thirty years ago, our company produces handmade, traditional furniture for a small niche of wealthy local and expatriate customers in Kenya. Recently, a friend who makes high-quality furniture in Thailand approached us about developing a partnership to export modern furniture to a variety of markets in Africa, merging his product with my father's market knowledge. But my father does not know markets outside Kenya, and the only product he is comfortable selling is traditional furniture. He is relying on the next generation to develop new products and to expand into new geographies. All along I had taken it as evident that the ability of a number of businesses to successfully develop new products and find new markets is dependent on the next generation of younger entrepreneurs, but I was slow to apply such an obvious truth to Afghanistan.

Latifa and I brought together a group of young and innovative Afghans (not all carpet producers), and began thinking about what kind of initiative was required to harness Afghanistan's youthful talent. The solution had to respond to two needs. First, we needed something resembling a learning institution, where complex market trends can be translated into actionable insight that carpet producers can incorporate. The emphasis would be on injecting knowledge upstream in the design or conception phase. Second, we needed to establish intermediaries to play a brokerage role between carpet buyers and producers, to act as conduits between both parties. The intermediaries would facilitate both linguistic and cultural barriers, translating from Farsi into the buyer's language, while also helping to bridge potentially divergent business cultures and norms.

So the Carpet Design Bazaar was conceived, a combination of a training institution and a marketplace. The main source of designs will come from independent designers who would come to the bazaar to take advantage of its resources, including market research generated by its staff. The bazaar will store these designs and make them available to producers for a fee. Designers will invest in market learning and, based on this knowledge, develop new designs. The more effectively they can translate customer needs to new designs, the better their products will sell and the wealthier they will become.

Producers do not have to turn into design aficionados overnight, but they will have to be smart in choosing their designers and their design wares. As with all bazaars, there will be a lot of junk on offer, and bad purchases will be made at unreasonable prices. The producers will, therefore, be bearing risk, but in such a marketplace, traditional business sense and wile will reap rewards. The risk will be reduced in time, as designers who imbue their products with customer knowledge come to develop strong reputations for quality and profitable designs and begin to rise above the fray. Some designers will develop strong enough industry contacts where they will no longer need to transact through the Design Bazaar but can deal with carpet producers directly. Others will forward integrate, acting not only as design agents but also as sales brokers between producers and buyers. Yet others will surely go into production as well.

The Design Bazaar is strongly market and competition oriented. It is not the kind of learning institution that benevolently bestows knowledge upon the needy. It is intended to be a knowledge brokerage, a place to kick-start a local design industry that will serve as a source of gainful and interesting employment for a young generation of Afghans, while also linking them to producers who lack their skills and need their services.

With the concept in place and approved by the leadership of the carpet cluster, Latifa and I prepared to pitch the idea of the Design Bazaar to the rest of the cluster. We started a thorough PowerPoint deck with market analysis on the strengths and weaknesses of the design sector in Afghanistan. As we discussed further, we shifted our approach away from formal management tools toward the core questions: why do design weaknesses lead to lower profits, and how can the Design Bazaar help?

The final product was more of an interesting but substantive show than the kind of formal presentation I had subjected the carpet cluster to in my first meeting with them. The atmosphere was distinctly different: the air was pensive. There were few interruptions (a rarity in any public dialogue in Afghanistan) as cluster members listened carefully while Latifa traced through the details of the Design Bazaar. One man's comments focused on the income that this initiative might bring to a budding generation of designers: "If we can support them through buying their designs, it would be a good thing." At that point, an older man whom I had not met before stood up and said simply, "Maybe we will support each other." That comment summed up the underlying vision of the Design Bazaar.

The discussion continued under Latifa's guidance and leadership. I realized that the Afghan carpet cluster, its customers, Latifa, and I (with some luck, honesty, God, and customer knowledge) would be able to communicate after all.

17. The Longest Roundabout in the World

DAVID I. RABKIN

PORT OF SPAIN, TRINIDAD

• • •

I MADE MY first visit to Trinidad in 2003. After living in Jamaica for more than a year, I was eager to see this important trading partner up close. The *Trinis*, I had been told, were "more aggressive" than Jamaican businesspeople. Sure, they have oil, but apparently it was more than that. What could I learn in this smaller but richer nation?

Upon emerging from the airport terminal, I met a courteous and knowledgeable taxi driver. As we drove into Port of Spain, Mickey told me a great many things about Trinidad. Our dialogue was as smooth as the expansive highway.

That is, until we hit the center of town. As it turns out, I arrived on the evening of Independence Day, and the Queen's Park Savannah, in the heart of town, was crowded with celebrants. The taxi slowed to a crawl as traffic became intense on the two-and-a-half-mile-long roundabout encircling the Savannah.

Yet even as the car slowed, Mickey kept up his pace. "This roundabout is the longest in the world," he informed me with obvious pride. An odd thing to be proud of, I thought, particularly as the qualifying criterion for a roundabout is that traffic moves in only one direction. As near as I could tell, allowing the traffic to flow in two directions would have quickly cleared up the current congestion.

The hotel I stayed in was located right off the roundabout, so every day I was on that roundabout at least twice, usually several times. Many

times I could have arrived at my destination more quickly had I been able
to turn right, but instead had to drive the roundabout and approach from
the other direction. This situation was clearly obvious to city planners, as
they have constructed small roundabouts abutting the main one, in order
to alleviate traffic congestion.

Why, I wondered, did they not change the direction of the second
lane?

Throughout the week, at least half a dozen people repeated Mickey's
proud statement that the Port of Spain roundabout was the longest in the
world. Eventually, I realized that the roundabout represented more than
just a fun fact: it was a quantifiable case of Trinidad's status as the global
leader . . . in something. The lanes have never been changed, I believe,
because their purpose is not just to facilitate transportation but also to
make the people proud.

There is nothing wrong with that, but it is essential to understand that
mixing secondary incentives (pride) with primary incentives (transportation) often diminishes the latter. This is a choice that can be made wisely
only if the incentives are made explicit.

This is just as true in Trinidad's dominant industry: oil and gas. It is no
secret that the country's location in the center of an enormous oil field has
produced significant income for the country and a standard of living currently far higher than Jamaica's.

It is important, though, to understand the difference between income
and wealth. Income is what you take home each year. Wealth is the capacity to generate income over a long period of time. Dubai has taken oil
income and invested it in projects that have led to long-term local industrial capacity. Dubai has taken income and created wealth.

Trinidad, however, has not moved beyond the income stage. It has taken
the first step by creating a stable and healthy economic climate with mostly
friendly rules and regulations for investment, both foreign and domestic.
So far, though, there is little business investment outside of the energy
industry.

There are some powerful Trinidadian banks, but that might be expected
with large pools of cash, relatively high interest rates, and a strong currency.
There are actually some very successful manufacturers, particularly in food

processing. Yet upon deeper analysis, it becomes clear that most of the successful manufactured products are essentially inexpensive alternatives to global brands, thriving largely in regional markets that are fragmented and often protected from international rivals. Among the most successful manufacturers, one is hard-pressed to find a uniquely Trinidadian ingredient, process, or brand.

Trinidad's government has provided a stable platform for wealth creation, and Trinidad's oil and gas have generated the income, but Trinidad's firms have not yet built the competitive advantages essential for long-term success. The government and fossil fuels may have actually hindered innovation. It is estimated that the government employs between 25 and 30 percent of the workforce, largely by turning taxes on energy production into income for citizens. Similarly, the availability of cheap energy makes the mass production of many commodity products, such as refurbished steel, more attractive than producing more complex and differentiated products for which fuel is a much less significant expense.

The precariousness of this situation is on the minds of many local businesspeople, as it is on the minds of the government and the donor community. Their response has been to encourage the "non-energy sector" to grow and thrive. Soft drinks and snack foods are a particular area of focus, with several local brands having achieved significant regional market share and consumer recognition. Agriculture, recently stung by the restructuring of the largest government-supported sugar company, Caroni, is the object of a surprising amount of optimism in a country with purchasing-power parity per capita of $10,500.

What I heard less about on my visit were sophisticated upstream and downstream energy-related businesses. In one meeting, an executive from a leading international energy company told me that his company planned to outsource $500 million dollars (U.S.) of business in 2004 *outside Trinidad*. At the moment, almost all of that goes to engineering, logistics, and software firms in Houston. The executive, however, would prefer that all of that money stay in Trinidad, not because of the good publicity but because it makes better business sense for his firm to be able to have its suppliers close by.

Unfortunately, the best Trinidadian efforts so far have risen only to the level of creating simple plastic products and smelting alumina with cheap natural gas. There is talk of call centers and data processing, but these conversations are focused around leveraging Trinidad's labor cost advantage relative to that of the United States. This talk disregards the fact that India, and even other Caribbean nations, have a dramatic cost advantage relative to that of Trinidad. More important, these basic call center plans ignore the market-driven opportunities to which the energy company executive refers, such as sophisticated geological modeling and web design.

By viewing rich foreign companies not just as sources of tax revenue but as customers, local companies can aspire to build wealth in much the same manner as their foreign counterparts. Trinidad as a nation and its firms collectively must do three things to move from a short-term value-capture mentality to a long-term wealth-building strategy:

1. Focus on building businesses that can be competitive in a truly global economy. Trinidad enjoys trading preferences with many of its Caribbean neighbors through the Caribbean Community and Common Market (CARICOM). The country enjoys other limited preferences with European and North American markets. These preferences are rapidly disappearing due to global trading systems such as the World Trade Organization (WTO) and decreasing costs of logistics and telecommunications. Many of the most lauded Trinidadian firms have succeeded based on artificial advantages, thus easily beating regional rivals, but are not cost or quality competitive with global peers. As a small island nation, this country has several cost *dis*advantages that make scale production particularly challenging.

2. Invest heavily in research and development, year after year. One of the most surprising gaps in Trinidad is a low rate of tertiary education and enrollment. Knowledge industries are the only logical manner for the majority of the workforce to advance beyond its current income levels. This will demand world-class research and applied education, both of which are lacking. Public-private partnerships, some of which are already established in Trinidad, can be instrumental in identifying and guiding research activities for maximum effect on enterprise development.

3. Pursue the most demanding customers. The international energy companies already based on the island are a logical place to start. These buyers will encourage local firms to supply world-class products, as opposed to settling for categories such as regionally advantaged consumer goods. The energy companies have management and political incentives to work with local companies, making them practical candidates as early customers. Yet even in consumer categories, seeking the most demanding, as opposed to the easiest, customers is essential. This does not mean that existing preferences should not be exploited; it means that the benchmark should be the toughest customers and competitors. Eventually, the world standard will arrive on local shores.

These three steps can lead Trinidad to great wealth, as they have for the overseas energy companies themselves and as they have for Dubai. One major barrier standing in Trinidad's way is mixed incentives: Trinidad is intent on replacing the income it knows it will eventually lose when the oil and gas fields slow down, but the difference between income and wealth is not yet clear to the government or to the majority of Trinidad's firms. The urgency to diversify away from energy has obscured some of the more obvious energy-services opportunities, many of which could be exported around the world; and the temporary cost advantage created by cheap oil and unsuccessful CARICOM neighbors has led many firms to focus on being low-cost providers, as opposed to offering differentiated products or services.

Macroeconomic price distortions also present a challenge. In economics, these distortions are referred to as "Dutch disease." They are so named for the suffering of many of Holland's industries when that country's booming natural gas exports inflated the local currency, making goods from other industries artificially expensive. In more recent decades, economists have understood that this syndrome can manifest itself in distortions from many classes of natural resources, from diamonds to timber.

Yet the macroeconomic symptoms of a disproportionately large amount of one type of natural asset are quantifiable and can be significantly mitigated by finance ministries and central banks. Perhaps more insidious are the psychological effects of these distortions: *attitudinal* Dutch disease. These symptoms include a belief that natural resource stocks are infinite and that the consequent income is a result of the home country's cleverness rather than its good fortune.

With new oil deposits being discovered, Trinidad has plenty of opportunity to follow Dubai's lead or even the more recent example of Holland. Too often, developing nations follow the path of Zambia, whose fortunes rose with the price of copper and then fell when prices fell. Fortunately, the Jamaican perception that Trinidadian firms are aggressive has some merit. As traders, many firms excel. This is an important asset with which to build.

What became clear to me on my first trip to the island and has since been confirmed on subsequent trips is that sustainable prosperity is within reach for Trinidad. What is less clear is whether that nation will choose to take a direct route or traverse a more circuitous one.

On the last day of my trip, Mickey was once again behind the wheel. As we approached the roundabout, I glanced to the right and saw the route to the airport only a few hundred yards away. Unfortunately, we were permitted to turn in only one direction.

Our left turn led us quickly into the afternoon traffic, and Mickey informed me that we were likely to be slightly delayed.

As Mickey was driving me to the airport, I reflected on how many times and in how many countries I felt stuck in an endless loop, always within sight but never being able to reach my destination. With a sigh, I turned to face Mickey, and I asked him what new stories he had to tell me.

"Did I ever tell you," he began, "that Trinidad has the longest roundabout in the world?"

18. Alexander the Great, Mother Teresa, and Arse

Michael Brennan

Skopje, Macedonia

• • •

Arse Janevski is an entrepreneur in Macedonia. He was a travel agent during the conflict period, with an office in Skopje. Arse provided regional travel excursions to locals and Kosovo and NATO soldiers looking for regional trips outside Macedonia. He made his living by identifying the needs of his customers and by creating tourism packages to address those needs. He is a small businessman, and he knows strategy. As the conflict subsided, Arse realized things needed to change for his business to grow.

Similar to millions of entrepreneurs in developing countries, Arse has not read World Bank studies that outline economic improvement strategies. For instance, he is not familiar with the studies of Paul Collier and Anke Hoeffler concerning aid impact and the absorptive capacities of a postconflict environment. Nor is he aware of the works of the economists Astri Surhke, Espen Villanger, and David Woodward that criticize Collier and Hoeffler and reach different conclusions. While scores of economists and technicians write reports that analyze and theorize how donors should approach development in a postconflict society, Arse and other entrepreneurs test these development strategies on a daily basis.

These entrepreneurs understand what succeeds and what fails in development. Ask Arse if he believes that Macedonia will be a safe and economically viable place to raise a family, and there will be a gleam in his eye when he says, "Of course," but he will later add, "We must do some things differently."

In order to understand what must be done differently, it is helpful to review the context of the tourism industry in Macedonia. In the late 1980s, according to the Macedonia statistics office, almost seven hundred thousand foreign tourists crossed the border into Macedonia, and most visited Ohrid, the World Heritage site that is a picturesque lake with mountains, ancient ruins, and over three hundred sixty monasteries. During that time, Macedonia was promoted abroad by Kompas, the Yugoslavian travel agency that had agents mostly in Europe, and was part of a destination package that often included Croatia, Montenegro, Serbia, and Greece.

As Yugoslavia dissolved with civil wars, travelers became wary of visiting this dangerous destination. Kompas closed offices and, in doing so, ended the international promotion of Macedonia as a travel destination. By 2001, foreign tourist numbers dropped below one hundred thousand. Many Macedonians in the industry stopped learning about tourists' needs, just as preferences for travel began to change rapidly. Tourists who were once content with basic outdoor activities began seeking "experiences" that focus on a particular culture or a specific outdoor activity and learning.

Arse is aware that the world is changing and understands that he must adjust. As a Macedonian entrepreneur, he is able to describe the challenges of building a business in a postconflict society: "My business will fail if I must promote Macedonia, create new tours, and find new customers on my own. I need to partner with people I never would have dreamed of as partners before. I'm talking about foreign travel agents and their customers, in addition to local hotels. The government? It should be our partner, but it shouldn't run promotions for Macedonia; it should help *me* promote Macedonia. It should not run hotels; it should promote investments in hotels. It should improve the visa process. It should provide incentives for training. It should enforce laws that keep Macedonia clean."

This is the nature of a critical issue in postconflict societies: the roles of the private sector and the public sector. The basis of this conflict is that the private sector must have the tools to understand both customers and competition and to use that knowledge to create and implement effective business plans. When the private sector lacks these business skills, neither the government nor the donor community should be overly responsible for creating or protecting firm-level strategies. Rather, the government and the civic sector need to support and enable the private sector to develop better strategies on its own.

The government should provide basic infrastructure and education, develop appropriate regulations, and enforce the rule of law to enable private sector innovation. The private sector must simply innovate to meet the needs of demanding customers. Unfortunately, all this needs to be done quickly.

Some postconflict societies often require skill building in key business areas such as marketing, research and segmentation strategies, operations, finance, and accounting. In others, progress may be dependent on the revitalization of the entire education system. This is the case in Afghanistan where the literacy rate is less than 50 percent and curricula has not been updated in thirty years. In Macedonia, where there is a highly educated workforce, the focus should be on understanding competitiveness principles. Years under a command-based economy makes learning to make strategic choices to serve the demands of global customers a critical skill to win against savvy regional and global competitors.

Upgrading the skills of the entire private sector is not easy in a country, but the goal is crystal clear: provide entrepreneurs with the tools to implement effective strategic choices. These choices must involve a research-based approach to answer questions such as the following: Which group of consumers will purchase your product? Will your customer be a supplier, retailer, end user, etc.? What is the industry you are joining and the product you are creating?

Arse made choices in each one of these categories to run his business effectively. His geographic target was northern Macedonia and Kosovo. His segment was the wealthiest Macedonians that had a history of traveling, as well as foreign soldiers who wanted experiences in the region. Concerning his vertical market, he targeted the end user, and his business was an informal partnership that focused on outbound tourism. He provided sales, and his partners provided the experiences for his customers.

Arse's next choice was how to differentiate his business. The objective of a differentiation strategy is to develop a unique position as compared to that of the competition, where potential customers might be willing to pay a premium for a product or service given the unique value it provides. If the target market perceives that a product or service more effectively matches its needs compared to the services of the competition, providers will have more flexibility in setting prices. An efficiency strategy focuses on providing outputs that are usually similar to those of the competition, with fewer inputs or less expensive inputs than the competition's. In economics, this is also known as "x-efficiency."

Here, Arse was a particularly adept strategist and understood that, in order for clients to trust him and become repeat business, he must offer premium and difficult-to-replicate services. In order to provide that, he would visit destinations and ensure that his partners treated his customers royally. He would also search for extra perks or be certain that an excursion would visit the best restaurants. However, he also understood that with a differentiation strategy, customers might still be price sensitive. As a result, he would organize tours just in the off-season, which would provide him bargaining power in rate negotiations. This made it easier for him to offer a premium package while keeping prices reasonably low, which was difficult for his competitors to replicate.

The problem with Arse's strategy was that it depended on an ongoing regional conflict. When the conflict subsided, the customer base of NATO soldiers left the region.

However, it was also at this time that economic development organizations, such as the United States Agency for International Development (USAID) and the European Union, decided to support Macedonia. This included a Competitiveness Project, intended to speed up the process of improving firm-level strategies through industry-wide collaboration. With the aid of this project, the tourism industry began to evolve into a functioning cluster in a period of a few years. As a seasoned and inquisitive member of the industry, Arse became the leader of this nascent cluster and played a central role in many cluster activities.

The cluster group, made up of hoteliers, tour operators, and other members of the industry, began with three initiatives to improve the industry's prospects. It assessed Macedonia's nature adventure tourism strengths and weaknesses, based on surveying local expatriates who travel in Macedonia. It surveyed international travel agents to learn about their customers' needs. This included understanding the customer's view of competitive destinations. And it created a leadership council and work teams to institutionalize these activities.

The research suggested that the industry should focus on developing inbound tourism and targeting international tour operators. The market segments are nature-adventure and history-tour operators in Europe and the United States. Key buyer criteria for this group are safety, interesting historical itineraries, great nature, and a pristine environment. The cluster members must also address the problems of a lack of information and customer service, litter, and a dearth of themes or experiences, all of which were problems identified by local expatriate travelers.

In order to win with their chosen segment of nature-adventure travelers, cluster members now realize that they need to innovate continuously. They need to address problems, create experiences for a targeted group of nature- and culture-seeking travelers, and compete by being a unique location and not just an inexpensive destination. They also need to promote the destination continuously to the nature-adventure segment.

The group responded with specific action steps as part of their new strategy. Over fifty cluster members, including local tour operators, guides, hoteliers, restaurateurs, entertainers, and transportation executives collaborated to host the first of what should be many familiarization (FAM) trips for specialty foreign tour operators and journalists. In addition to targeting customers and building and testing experiences, several cluster members were involved with cleaning up litter in parks as part of an anti-litter campaign. The result was that seven of the thirteen foreign operators who visited Macedonia in this first cluster-hosted FAM trip have developed itineraries with local partners.

Cluster members also built "tour experiences" that are being presented at trade shows, during FAM trips, and on web sites. These resulted in mountain biking trips, trips to monasteries and heritage sites, and an excursion to see Rock Art, which is an ancient writing form that is found carved into rocks in central Macedonia.

A key finding from the research was that the number one attraction that foreign operators would promote in Macedonia to their clients is Alexander the Great. That learning inspired the development of horseback riding or hiking tours to follow in the footsteps of Alexander. Another cluster member wants to respond to the growth in religious excursions by developing a tour that focuses on the hundreds of churches in Macedonia, including several that have entire walls of intricate wood carving, which is known as *iconoclastie*. He wants to culminate this itinerary with a visit to the birthplace of Mother Teresa. What is most important about this activity is that the cluster members are learning about and responding to customer needs.

The local tour operators made strategic choices along the dimensions of scope, advantage, and technology. They began to work together to shift the tourism strategy to create experiences for a foreign tourist segment and, in doing so, realized the need for collaboration both inside and outside Macedonia. They were aware that, to succeed with their strategy, they needed to develop partnerships in Macedonia outside the private sector.

This cluster strategy also led to improved relations between the tourism industry and the government. First, the newly developed leadership council met to prioritize the cluster's issues. The group approached Macedonia's national competitiveness council with a prioritized list of obstacles and suggested solutions. The request included obtaining more support for FAM trips and related promotions, expediting visa approvals, and supporting a web portal for the tourism industry. In addition, cluster members approached the Ministry of the Environment to support and develop a campaign to address the litter issue. In response, the government reduced the time to issue visas, allocated some funding for tour operator and journalist trips, supported the web portal, and collaborated on a cleanup campaign.

The cluster also approached the civic sector and donor organizations. For instance, in collaboration with the Macedonia-based Dutch Chamber of Commerce (DCC), the cluster has received positive press in one of Macedonia's former major markets, Holland, after a small-trade mission visit organized by the DCC. Members are also focusing on training programs through local organizations. Some members are considering innovative ways to improve service levels, such as by working with

Association Internationale des Étudiants en Sciences Économiques et Commerciales (AIESEC), a foreign student volunteer group that brings in foreign students to work at hotels. They received support from the "E-Biz" project, the USAID-funded program that focuses on using technology to help in Macedonia industry development and from Geekcorps to develop their web portal.

Why are these seemingly small collaborative activities important? The primary reason is that they are led by private sector knowledge of customer and competitive markets. The government is not taking the role of an over-protective parent trying to help the private sector by doing the work of the private sector. The public sector is listening to the needs of the private sector and responding by creating a competitive, enabling environment. Much more collaboration is needed. However, these steps, albeit small, are steps in the right direction.

The role of a modern government in developing nations is to maintain and enforce stable policies, improve infrastructure and institutions, invest in people, remove obstacles that inhibit competition—such as corruption—and create a platform that encourages productivity and innovation. The government (and the donor community as well) should focus more on an enabling, competitive environment and focus less on export promotion strategies that favor one firm. For some, the distinction between the two may seem nominal, but ignoring that difference can significantly delay development.

There are five subtle distinctions between enabling competition and supporting export promotion strategies. The underlying principle behind enabling competition is that the public and civic sectors should not become over-responsible for basic firm-level activity but should determine ways to support innovation:

1. Rather than picking one firm as a winner, enable entire clusters of firms with a platform that encourages industry-wide innovation. Helping the cluster position itself in world markets encourages rather than prevents competition and is more likely to occur when industry leaders discuss issues with the government as a group, as when the tourism cluster leadership council met with the national council.

2. The focus of any government strategy should not be simply to try to "sell 'em what we got" (and call it a strategy) but to migrate to the best customers. An example in Macedonia's tourism industry would be to attract better customers by developing "experiences," such as following the footsteps of Alexander or praying in the home of Mother Teresa.

3. Encourage clusters and the partnering that ensues in such initiatives. For instance, act as a fair broker to encourage firms to engage in joint training or procurement or promotion in foreign markets. In Macedonia tourism, for instance, in order to create an experience where tourists participate in an archeological dig, several cluster members need to partner with the Ministry of Culture, well-respected local and international archeologists, and specialty tour organizations such as Earthwatch to start the program.

4. Take a long-term view. In this step, current government revenue is used to invest in the migration to an improved strategy, as opposed to a short-term view where a sale is simply the goal. Investing in long-term initiatives that support human capital and encourage trust within a cluster framework will have the higher payback.

5. Create a learning environment for all members, show the importance of analysis and differentiated sales, and create programs that will provide relevant training. The central economic goal for a postconflict region should be to rapidly attain a high and rising standard of living for *all* its citizens. This is reflected in high per capita income and higher paying, satisfying jobs for a large proportion of those who are able to work. In order for development to achieve these goals, a few things must be done differently. In Macedonia and to a greater extent in other postconflict societies, the government should not be *over-responsible* for individual firm success, and the private sector must focus on market learning and innovation in order to meet the needs of demanding customers.

As Arse targets travelers in foreign markets, he is receiving moderate support from the government to address visas and some promotional issues. Still he adds, "This is a good start, but it is not enough. This process must continue, and the government must really talk with us." So, the *real conflict* in a postconflict society must be addressed by beginning with an action-oriented private and public sector dialogue. The result must enable small-scale entrepreneurs to make timely actions with informed choices that meet the needs of demanding customers. In Macedonia's tourism industry, this will be creating memories of Alexander the Great and Mother Teresa as unique and enjoyable experiences.

In Macedonia, entrepreneurs will ultimately create the innovative environment to achieve this creativity, which will help to bring prosperity and stability back to the region. They will do so only by understanding customer needs and by creating unique advantages for Macedonia, with partnerships in the public and civic sectors. These joint efforts that address specific customer issues and enable entrepreneurs to innovate will not only address the real conflict in a postconflict society but may ultimately help to maintain its status as a postconflict society.

19. Archimedes' Formidable Dare

ERIC KACOU

SUB-SAHARAN AFRICA

• • •

AROUND 200 BCE, Archimedes made a formidable dare: "Give me a lever long enough and a fulcrum on which to place it, and I shall move the world." Two thousand years later, an end to poverty has become Africa and the world's most formidable dare. The world still is searching for the lever and the fulcrum to lift Africa out of poverty.

Any person who looks at Africa will see a bounty of natural resources, a rich cultural heritage, and a vibrant, young population. The same person would undoubtedly observe the scourge of HIV/AIDS, weak institutions, and low purchasing power. The litany of Africa's woes can seem interminable.

Consider the following facts on poverty in Africa. One in two people in sub-Saharan Africa survives on less than one dollar per day. A third of the African population suffers from malnutrition. Less than half of Africa's population has access to hospitals or safe waters. One in six children dies before the age of five. This number is twenty-five times higher in sub-Saharan Africa than in Organisation for Economic Co-operation and Development (OECD) countries.

Yet these chilling statistics fail to capture the ongoing human tragedy. For most Africans, poverty is a daily experience that robs them of their dignity and freedom. I have witnessed this pain throughout rural Africa. I once shared a meal with a family that, for lack of money, used water with Maggi seasoning cubes as their meal for the evening, instead of meat and fish. Beyond serving as a nagging reminder of the plight of my continent, such situations fuel my passion for development in Africa.

I have never doubted Africa's potential, and it is personal experience that motivates my optimism. When I was born, my country was the poster child of development. I not only witnessed but also benefited from this growth boom. It translated into prosperity for most, and hope for me. I enjoyed full-board scholarships up to my high-school graduation.

It is the same personal experience that now makes me skeptical of much of the development advice for Africa. Such advice often recommends top-down, capital-intensive, government-focused reforms. While such reforms are paramount, their sustainability leaves me searching for more. Such reforms are necessary, but they do not feel sufficient. My worry is that, as poverty worsens in much of the continent, the impact of such narrowly focused advice becomes increasingly futile.

The fulcrum to lift Africa out of poverty, however, may already exist. A new breed of African entrepreneurs is emerging. I have witnessed their impact on the ground. These Archimedean entrepreneurs epitomize the crucial role of business in the Africa of tomorrow. Africa's new economic agenda should focus on finding and unleashing these forces for creating prosperity.

What sets this group of innovators apart? The answer lies in how they conceive of four stakeholders in their businesses: customers, owners, workers, and the future (COW-F).[1]

To comprehend fully the power of the COW-F paradigm, one must reflect on the current discourse on Africa's development. Africa and its development partners have recognized the limitations of the prevailing "solutions" that often focus on poverty alleviation at the expense of growth. Development partners have worked with African leaders to articulate poverty-reduction plans where health care, education, and rural development take the center stage. This is logical considering the ongoing humanitarian crisis.

---

1. COW-F is a framework developed by Michael Fairbanks. He first wrote about it in "Prosperity, Competitiveness, and Natural Capitalism—The Ultimate Integration" in *The Natural Advantage of Nations: Business Opportunities, Innovations and Goverance in the 21st century*, ed. K. Hargroves and M. H. Smith (London: Earthscan Publications Ltd., 2006), xxxv.

But there is one important area where poverty alleviation plans fall short: economic growth. While addressing the humanitarian crisis is necessary, it is not sufficient to create prosperity in Africa. Africa's growth imperative is to raise the standard of living of hundreds of millions of Africans, simultaneously. In 2005, Africa registered a record growth rate of 4.5 percent, thanks to the commodity boom and the dividends of macroeconomic reforms. Yet, in real terms, such growth is still not enough to lift Africa out of poverty, given an average population growth rate of 2.5 percent.

Africa must achieve what Harvard Business School professor Clayton Christensen has described as a discontinuous leap in productivity. Archimedean entrepreneurs can be powerful actors in achieving this leap. This new breed of entrepreneurs is mastering the trade-offs between serving customers, owners, and workers while respecting Africa's future.

Customers: Archimedean entrepreneurs strive to create sophisticated products for high-paying and demanding customers. These business leaders innovate by embedding customer knowledge into their products. In doing so, they transform Africa's natural resources into competitive products.

Owners: The primary motive of business is to create shareholder value. Archimedean entrepreneurs are economically motivated. Often, they open their circle of shareholders to include their workers and community. This explains why some of them choose to operate within cooperatives.

Workers: Archimedean entrepreneurs have graduated from the paradigm where workers are considered mere operating costs and have embraced workers as their companies' foremost assets. They understand that the key to continuous innovation is paying high and rising wages and constantly upgrading the skills of their workers.

The future: The concern of Archimedean entrepreneurs for the future begins with their community. They are often contributors to the social well-being of their employees and the wider communities in which they live. This concern goes beyond their immediate communities. These business leaders adopt business practices that responsibly leverage our common natural capital endowment, which includes the environment.

Archimedean entrepreneurs intuitively grasp an important reality.

Traditional firms often make the wrong trade-offs, which disadvantage the weak or the silent, namely, workers and future generations. The often-publicized conflict with the diamond industry is an illustration where both population and environment lose. Although customers and owners may realize a quick win, their situation is not sustainable, and prosperity remains elusive for the majority of those involved in this business.

Where most of the continent often chooses to work cheaper and harder, Archimedean entrepreneurs understand that the world provides sustainable economic rewards only for smart work.

Although I have met Archimedean entrepreneurs throughout Africa, they are the exception rather than the norm. Most businesses still look to make the quick win. Unfortunately, no obvious traits, physical or otherwise, distinguish the entrepreneurs from the masses. It is more an art than a science to identify these business leaders. The best way to identify them is to observe the decisions these entrepreneurs make.

Identifying Archimedean entrepreneurs is crucial for one important but often overlooked reason. Archimedean entrepreneurs are living testimony to the role that business can play in Africa's development. As such, they can help change mindsets toward enterprise as the solution to poverty in Africa.

First, such successful business leaders are the best inspiration for the next generation of entrepreneurs in Africa. Second, Archimedean entrepreneurs provide a strong impetus for shifting capital investments from top-down, state-focused programs toward a more optimal competitive allocation of resources that empowers the private sector. Finally, Archimedean entrepreneurs break Africa's monopoly on bad news. Such entrepreneurs show the rest of the world that success stories abound on the continent. These entrepreneurs provide an example that helps in shifting the development conversation toward enterprise as the solution to poverty in Africa.

In the summer of 2007, I helped launch a unique competition to identify, reward, and promote Archimedean entrepreneurs in Africa. In its inaugural year, the Pioneers of Prosperity Africa Award attracted over 450 applicant firms from five countries in East Africa. This competition's six winners were revealed by an international jury at an award ceremony attended by His Excellency President Paul Kagame in Kigali on November 30, 2007.[2]

Reflecting on the role of entrepreneurship in Africa during the 2007 Pioneers of Prosperity Africa Award gala, President Kagame noted, "It is becoming increasingly clear that entrepreneurship is the surest way to development. Government activities should hinge on entrepreneurship because entrepreneurship unlocks people's minds, allows innovation to take place, and allows people to implement and to exercise their talents."

Archimedean entrepreneurs are certainly talented, innovative, and creative. But what is so unique about Africa's Archimedean entrepreneurs?

Consider Ariff, who is the founder and CEO of AAA Growers, a horticultural company based in Nairobi, Kenya, that grows, processes, and exports vegetables to the United Kingdom and other European countries. Ariff's first words to me were about the promising investment banking career he left in New York to start a business in arguably what is one of the toughest sectors—horticulture. Besides the unusual spark in his eyes, Ariff combines an obsession to succeed with a moral purpose.

Customers are clearly AAA Growers' obsession. In a quiet voice, Ariff told me, "Our customers love us because we are smaller, and we are able to give attention to detail. We do not sell huge volumes, but we sell for higher prices." Ariff's humility is in direct contrast with AAA Growers' success. Seven years after its inception, AAA Growers supplies 60 percent of the U.K. broccoli market. This small firm also has leading positions in other markets for specialized vegetables in the United Kingdom, Scandinavia, and now Japan.

AAA Growers' customer list reads like a "who's who" in world retailing, including Tesco and Marks & Spencer. The company's customer focus is evident throughout the value chain. Farm managers painstakingly monitor the many steps required to produce ready-to-eat vegetables of the highest quality. The focus on standards has resulted in a reputation for quality

2. The Pioneers of Prosperity Africa Award was conceived by the SEVEN Fund, sponsored by Legatum Global Development and the John Templeton Foundation and implemented by the OTF Group.

in the unforgiving world of horticulture importers. AAA Growers has implemented a customer-feedback system that allows for continuous customer contact. During our due-diligence process, one customer told us, "They are willing to do what it takes to get it right."

Ariff does not think only of his customers: he ensures that the *owners* and *workers* of AAA prosper. When asked, Ariff will be the first to point out that his primary motive in starting the business was to make money, and he has achieved that goal, given the profitability of the business. His next aim is to list his company on the Nairobi Stock Exchange. Such a listing would accrue benefits to other AAA Growers' stakeholders. In fact, AAA Growers' employee option plan ensures that both the management and employees have shares in the business.

AAA Growers has created two thousand permanent jobs in the areas where it operates. In the highly competitive Kenyan horticultural industry, the company has successfully retained its staff, thanks to its human-capital development policies. For instance, AAA Growers is well regarded for its training and for promoting from within, and the company has also taken the HIV/AIDS scourge seriously with a well-funded program. Former AAA Growers' employees have gone on to set up their own farms with management support.

A better *future* for his community is an important factor in Ariff's intrinsic motivation. He adds, "Investing in the community is good for business." This moral purpose shines through AAA Growers' operations. AAA Growers has built dispensaries, police stations, and schools. The firm also purifies water and distributes it free to the community. Environmental concern is embedded in the operations. AAA Growers recycles water, uses drip irrigation, and employs solar power. It uses integrated pest management to reduce insecticides and environmentally friendly packaging.

Ariff is not an isolated case. Gerard Sina, the CEO and founder of Entreprise Urwibutso, is fast becoming Rwanda's most celebrated Archimedean entrepreneur. Visiting the village of Nyarangarama provides insight into Gerard's impact. This once sleepy little village is now at the heart of Rwanda's agribusiness industry. Previously seen as a mere rest stop en route to Rwanda's famed mountain gorillas, Nyarangarama has become a bustling town. The one constant landmark at the heart of this town is a shop complex that sells Gerard's products, all made in Nyarangarama.

Entreprise Urwibutso has recently built a new fully integrated fresh juice plant. When he started his business fifteen ago, Gerard named it *Urwibutso*, meaning "memories," but the innovativeness of this business has looked more to the future than the past. From a simple bakery, Gerard has grown his business into Rwanda's largest integrated food manufacturer.

The company has built its success on its symbiotic relationship with Nyarangarama, contributing to the town's growth through thousands of direct jobs, buyer-supplier relationships with local farmers, the building of schools, and even public infrastructure such as street lighting.

Besides Ariff and Gerard, the 2007 Pioneers of Prosperity Africa Award identified four other winners: Good African Coffee, a roasted and packed specialty coffee exporter from Uganda; KenCall, a call center serving global corporations from Nairobi, Kenya; Tele-10, a regional entertainment and media firm based in Kigali; and, Virtual City, an IT solution development based in Nairobi, Kenya. The competition and all finalists are profiled in the documentary *Unlocking Africa* by award-winning filmmaker Jeff Zimbalist.

Most African countries have yet to mainstream entrepreneurship development in their prosperity-creation agendas. The current paradigm for private sector development often errs on the side of laissez-faire. The underlying assumption is that if the business environment is right, African entrepreneurs will just mushroom. Yet experience suggests that a sound business environment is not enough for entrepreneurship development. Africa must go beyond legal or institutional reforms to foster entrepreneurship.

How can Africa unleash its Archimedean entrepreneurs? Strategy, capital, and support are required ingredients.

First, Archimedean entrepreneurs must articulate a winning *strategy*. More specifically, they must make informed choices about which product(s) to compete in and how to win. A sound strategic approach is what allows these innovators to work smarter and better where most businesses work harder and cheaper. Most entrepreneurs often find it difficult to garner the customer knowledge required to make the right decisions. This is particularly true when they target customers in export markets.

Such business leaders often lack the time, skills, and financial resources to develop a sound strategy. Collaborative approaches, whereby competitiveness strategies are developed for a whole industry or cluster, can facilitate such entrepreneurs to make the informed choices necessary to succeed. Archimedean entrepreneurs are also more successful when their individual strategies are part of upgrade efforts for the industries or cluster they are involved in.

Second, for much-needed *capital*, African countries must co-invest with Archimedean entrepreneurs. The average African entrepreneur faces abnormally high operating and transaction costs mostly because of poor infrastructure, weak institutions, and a poorly educated pool of human resources. Under such difficult conditions, entrepreneurs need co-investors in the form of government and development partners to build specialized infrastructure, provide business development services, and help with the development of skilled human capital.

Lastly, African countries must *support* their Archimedean entrepreneurs. A prerequisite for this is a change in the mindsets of African civil servants and government leaders who feel they cannot help entrepreneurs who make more money than they do. Private sector rights to speedy answers or timely payments from government are construed as favors, resulting in red tape and corruption. An important aspect of any civil service agenda must be instilling a culture of service toward the private sector.

Development partners' mindsets must also change; this sector often perceives assistance to entrepreneurs as helping the rich of Africa who should be able to fend for themselves. The development donors believe this goes against their primary role of channeling resources for poverty alleviation. Archimedean entrepreneurs are better placed to help the poor of Africa in a sustainable fashion, and they can also help development partners by increasing the absorption capacity for incoming resources.

The rewards are great for nations able to unleash their Archimedean entrepreneurs. These leaders can help generate economic growth and become outstanding social transformation agents.

While most of Africa is busy complaining about globalization, Archimedean entrepreneurs are busy seizing opportunities. The only promise globalization holds for the continent is that competitive African products will find attractive markets. These businesspeople play a crucial role as innovators. They understand how to transform Africa's bountiful natural resources into superior products, and they are duty-bound to manage their businesses in a socially responsible way.

Rwanda is a compelling case of this theory in action, a country whose exported goods reached two hundred ten million dollars in 2007, triple the 2003 exports. Gerard, Ariff, Tele-10, and others are the invisible artisans behind this transformation. Their collaboration with government and development partners is paying off. Some of Rwandan bourbon coffee from cooperatives fetches forty-eight dollars per kilogram at Starbucks. Rwanda's peace baskets are sold at Macy's in New York.

Rwanda owes an important part of its current stability to the silent work of Archimedean entrepreneurs. In the aftermath of the 1994 genocide, reconciliation has become a major imperative to rebuild the very fabric of Rwandese society. In Rwanda and other African nations, Archimedean entrepreneurs not only provide jobs but also restore a sense of pride, thus becoming important actors for reconciliation.

Archimedean entrepreneurs are the fulcrum needed to lift Africa out of poverty. These innovators have discovered the holy grail of economics: simultaneous wealth creation and redistribution. Watching them in action has finally begun to satiate my need for sustainable home-grown solutions to Africa's development. I now know that change is more subtle and best when it is indigenous. As a change agent, I am learning to create opportunities for these entrepreneurs to express their talent fully.

What is the way forward? First, African businesspeople must strive to join the ranks of Archimedean entrepreneurs. Adopting the COW-F business model means doing good while doing well. Second, African leaders and development partners must unleash these entrepreneurs by providing them with the strategy, capital, and support required.

Though we have much more to accomplish, our way is clear. We have role models who are emerging, resolute, and strong. They have decided to create new business models based on a new optimization of customers, workers, and the future. They are unafraid to respond to Archimedes' formidable dare.

PART III: GLOBALIZATION

· · ·

"This is an era of total global competition for resources."
Michael Fairbanks reluctantly accepts an escort outside Kabul.

20. On Presidents

MICHAEL FAIRBANKS

• • •

No ONE, outside the small group of men and women who have done
it, can comprehend the experience of leading a nation: the pressure
to create frameworks for justice and prosperity; to improve that society's
stock of progressive human values such as trust, civic-mindedness, and tolerance for those unlike oneself; to position that society in the community
of nations and in history.

Still, sometimes we forget that these are men and women who have
more in common with the rest of us than not. They sleep badly, own pets,
laugh at off-color jokes, squeeze their toothpaste mid-tube, like to learn,
and worry. They worry a lot.

I watch each of them carefully and wonder if the small things, an unfin-
ished anecdote, a throwaway comment, the way a beard is scratched, a
seemingly casual observation, might presage something bigger: a policy
change, a historical trend, the fate of a nation.

They invite me to speak to them about how to use enterprises to solve
poverty. The settings differ from conference rooms to pickup trucks, and
the conversations meander from world market share through demographics to parental woes. In that process of sharing and conversing, of getting
me to be willing to be guided by them, of helping me to help them, some
have disappointed me, some have surprised me, and some have inspired
me. All of them have taught me something, though, about the low odds
of accomplishing great things, about fortitude with and without grace,

and about maintaining goals and objectives that are outside myself so that others might be willing to be guided by me.

It is perhaps trite to say they are people like us, but they are people like us who run hundred-billion-dollar economies, people like us who have fought for justice and sometimes lost, people like us who have embodied the values consistent with great promises. However, they are also the people who will be judged by history as to how they keep those promises.

I present to you five vignettes of such leaders. They are action oriented, see speeding up their failures as part of learning, and are deeply introspective. History will not regard all of them as successful, and each of them has sometimes failed. There are those for whom the challenge is too great, perhaps too great for anyone; those who had the right intention but the wrong process; those who are on the wrong side of history; and one— despite presiding over the smallest nation and in the most desperate of circumstances, possessing the least amount of basic advantages, receiving the least assistance from other nations—who may have the best chance to improve the lives of his country's citizens, and with a chance not only to be regarded well by history but to make history.

HAVANA

My head swam when the Cuban ambassador to the United Nations invited me to Havana to address the *comandante* and his entire cabinet.

I flew through Venezuela, spent British pounds, and entered Cuba on my Irish passport. I was asked to deplane first, and an official met me on a red carpet. The comandante called meetings when it suited him. I waited for two days at a guesthouse, which was formerly a mansion of the owners of a sugar plantation.

My hosts guided me around Havana, which was like a fallen and decrepit Florence. I went for a run each morning around a lake in front of the house. I ran with an affable man who came to Cuba for medical care. His bodyguards viewed me contemptuously. I thought it was better if we did not exchange names and occupations. He spoke softly. He was overweight. He was under pressure, he said. He had a heart problem.

He told me that the Cuban medical system was the best in Latin America. The Cubans understand education, medicine, and community, he said. He added that any country could learn from the Cubans. I liked this jogger's capacity for warm admiration.

The comandante's office called me to meet in the middle of the night. Perhaps unsurprisingly for the hour, few cabinet members arrived. The vice president informed President Castro of this, and the president called them on their cell phones. All sixteen arrived within thirty minutes.

The comandante's office suite was like that of the dean of an economics department of a state university, spare. The furniture was metal, topped with Formica. There were chalkboards and overhead projectors that needed repair.

I lectured. I spoke about building a private sector, inviting foreign investment. The night went on; my audience stared as blankly as schoolboys. Some took notes.

The old man rubbed his beard like a Jesuit.

My listeners were receptive, which encouraged me. I explained that democracy supported economic growth and vise versa. I told them that globalization would punish them for mediocrity, and it would reward them for doing one thing just a little better than anyone else. I told them globalization was a tsunami wave that would wash over the island one day. They would learn to surf it, or they would be crushed.

We were there for a long time. They wrote down what I said, and I added, "The problem with classic socialism is that governments are over-responsible for the welfare of their citizens; those that provide everything—employment, houses, and leisure activities—will dampen the spark of their own peoples' innovation."

Then I thought, "What am I doing?"

My heart pounded against my chest. I am in Cuba. I am in Fidel Castro's office in the middle of the night.

My mouth was parched.

I arrived with another passport, no one knows I am here, and I am telling the entire leadership of the world's most pristine example of Marxism what is wrong with its ideology.

A gentleman at the back of the room raised his hand politely. He was the minister of finance. I called on him. He stood and said, "*Ud. tiene toda la razón*" ("You are exactly right").

I breathed.

We spoke for some more hours. The men asked questions earnestly. I left the building with the minister of foreign relations and the vice president of Cuba. The minister took my hand in both of his and shook it warmly.

The vice president said to me, "Today, you have imparted much to us. And you told us the truth." He added, "Today, you have made eleven million new friends."

I walked with the minister of foreign affairs who said that he would like me to do him a favor: speak to Daniel Ortega, the leader of the Sandinista revolutionaries. Give him the same message.

I said, "I am sure that my government would approve even less of my going to Nicaragua." He laughed and said, "You needn't go that far. Each morning at the lake, he is your running partner."

LIMA

The helicopter whirred. We traveled together to where the Shining Path guerrillas lived. It was still dangerous, even though, or perhaps because, President Alberto Fujimori had captured their founder and killed their leaders.

The helicopter screamed low over anonymous villages. I asked my neighbor if he was scared of the Shining Path. He said no.

The president was exhausted. He did his thinking throughout the night, at the butler's table, in the back of the gold-gilded *palacio*. The politics of Peru were fragmented, and the economy was a shambles. His wife Susanna had just left him. She ran for president against him. Hell hath no fury . . .

He fell asleep and leaned on my shoulder, and we descended into the valley. Its main crop was coca. He awakened with a start, grabbed his green duffle, and reached into it to find an indigenous knitted hat and poncho.

We alighted to cheers of "El Chino!" from those who mistook his Japanese heritage. He grinned and walked into the crowds. He dug into his duffle and handed t-shirts to the children.

He promised the mayor a paved road. His military attaché handed him an army radio, and Fujimori commanded that the bulldozers start tomorrow. He built two schools a day that way.

We arrived back in Lima. He asked if I wanted to ride with him through the city's poorest barrio. He commandeered a pickup truck from someone in the security detail and gestured for me to get in.

He drove away fast and left his bodyguards behind. The president and I coasted through the streets of Lima. Adults on the side of the road never looked into the vehicle. Children did, though. They had no expectation of who was in the truck or who was not, and so they noticed and yelled *"Presidente!,"* which made their parents look.

He stopped reverently at a red light. I laughed, and he turned his eyes on me.

"Mr. President," I said, "I have to ask. You fired your Supreme Court and told the congressmen to return to their homes. You rewrote the entire constitution, and you gave yourself another term in office. Yet you are the only man in Lima that stops at a red light."

I thought he would smile, but he did not. He said, "That was the time for action; now is the time for law." He looked straight ahead at the traffic.

His words moved me. He was focused, fastidious; he possessed a powerful will. Graffiti on the streets of Bogotá, Caracas, and La Paz said *"Necesitamos a Fujimori"* ("We need Fujimori"). We thought he was the answer for all Latin America.

His words would have made the perfect end to a wonderful story, if Fujimori did not so consistently believe his own sloganeering and if he had not run through the next several red lights.

JOHANNESBURG

A prince of Swaziland married Nelson Mandela's daughter and moved to Boston, where I met him. He arranged a meeting for me with President-elect Nelson Mandela and instructed me to call him *"Matiba."*

I met Mandela in his office in the old Shell Oil building in Johannesburg. He was taller than I expected, gentle, and ran an efficient meeting. He looked for opportunities to smile and laugh.

I had my small camera in my pocket but did not take it out.

He spoke of his problems. The African National Congress was good at freedom fighting, but now it had to run a hundred-billion-dollar economy.

Walter Sisulu came in. He was once regarded as a terrorist but enters history as a freedom fighter. He shared a cellblock with Mandela for twenty-five years. I told him I was from Boston, and he told me that his daughter and grandchildren lived there. I asked how his grandchildren liked America; he laughed and said, "Oh, they like it fine. They are a group of little terrorists, though," which made Mandela and the prince laugh.

Mandela explained that the seven corporate conglomerates had too much economic power, there was insufficient housing, and the regulatory regime had fourteen thousand outdated statutes. He emphasized that the government and the private sector had no shared vision of the future.

The populace did not know entirely what to expect from their new leaders, either. The day after Mandela won the election, an old woman walked day and night from a remote region to meet him in the capital, to receive her refrigerator. She had misunderstood something he said and thought that if he won the election, the government would provide refrigerators to all the old women.

I went to Mandela's home in Soweto. It was new and brick and had a swimming pool. The prince gave me a tour. The living room was modern and filled with mementos of Mandela's recent trip around the world. There were busts of Mandela and scores of plaques and paintings of him in all styles: European impressionistic, Russian industrial, Latin magical, Asian spiritual, American realistic.

His kitchen was suburban. Mandela had a toaster. His bedroom was spare. His bathroom was undistinguished. Mandela squeezed Colgate at mid-tube.

I am in Mandela's bathroom!

Later, when it was time to part, I was not sure if we would meet again. I knew that I would always remember Mandela, but I was not sure that he would always remember me. I thought to say something useful about the problems he described to me.

I explained that Rudyard Kipling had described the problem of a shared vision when he wrote about the blindfolded men's feeling opposite ends of the elephant.

One man is feeling the tail of the elephant and describing the entire elephant as thin like a snake. Another man feels the tusks and says the elephant is hard and sharp. "Both hold only a piece of the truth, and believe they understand everything."

Mandela was impassive.

I thought I had said something useless or, worse, offensive. Who was I to use metaphors of Africa with *Matiba*?

Mandela said, "Your story makes me uncomfortable." My throat constricted. "It makes me uncomfortable," he smiled mischievously, "to think what is it that I am used to feeling under that elephant." He laughed.

Two days later, President-elect Mandela, *Matiba*, used Kipling's metaphor in an address to the entire nation.

La Paz

This president slept badly.

We met late at night at an ornate table of black tropical hardwood in a ballroom with a gold-leaf ceiling, sad drapes, and dust.

Gonzalo Sanchez de Lozada told me that Bolivian politics was like "two bald men fighting over a toothless comb." "Goni" was raised in Chicago.

He explained that his presidency was like "an author in search of a play." Goni spoke Spanish badly.

He wondered out loud to me, late at night in the dilapidating palace, if Bolivia deserved to be a nation. Goni had studied philosophy at the University of Chicago.

"Maybe some countries don't deserve to be a nation. We have no port, our navy is one boat, and our best talent lives in Miami and Chicago. Our government is organized around obtaining foreign aid. Our private sector extracts the assets of the land. Our miners numb themselves each morning with the coca leaf before they sink into the caves." Goni was a scion of a rich mining family.

It was a dark hour, late at the palace. "Maybe, Bolivia can merge with

Peru to create one nation: maybe then I can create the vision and get some sleep, and Fujimori can run the place."

KIGALI

President Paul Kagame stood on the veranda of his home and told me, "There haven't been dogs for a long time in Rwanda. You don't notice it but are aware something is not right. Then someone tells you. The dogs fed on the cadavers and had to be killed."

Rwanda is poor, isolated, small, crowded, and clean. There is not a mango peel on the roads. The president has made the importation of plastic bags illegal; he wants clean streets, and the bags are not biodegradable. There are thousands of green hills—everywhere you stand in Kigali provides a long view. But the view is of a peripatetic group of Africans, cooking fires, farm animals, and small expertly cultivated farming plots.

Rwandans are called the Germans of Africa, not because of the genocide but because of their efficiency at whatever they do, good or bad. The Hutus killed one million people in one hundred days with machetes: a gruesome accomplishment.

The president explains to me, "When economic scarcity occurs, human values deteriorate: with poverty comes mistrust, impatience, and intolerance for those unlike yourself."

The economy shrunk for five years before the genocide. There was famine in the south. The government, which was supported by the French, had an official policy of division among the ethnic groups. That prime minister is now in jail in Mali for life, put there by a French court.

I am haunted by the complicity of the Catholic bishop and his priests. I am haunted by the Rwandan nationals who worked for the American embassy and were left behind and murdered. I am haunted by the image of a girl walking on the road, wounded on the neck by a machete, holding her head so it would not fall off her shoulders.

Thousands of bodies sprinkled with lime and stacked, as if by woodsmen. Visitors can see them preserved in the genocide "camps."

Bill Clinton apologized. President Kagame told me, "Clinton apologizes each time he sees me. He is really in pain." World leaders did not help when they could. They explained their reasons afterward, reasons that were inadequate. They promised the horror would never happen again. Kofi Annan won the Nobel Peace Prize, and Rwanda, alone again among all nations, protested.

Nongovernmental organizations dominate the country's economy. Each morning Toyota Land Cruisers with expatriates and nationals roll up to these headquarters like piglets to their mothers' teet.

In a casual moment after dinner, I say to the president, "You are tall and thin like the great East African runners. Tell me, have you ever competed?" He says, "I had to run up to 250 miles at a time, away from the enemy who tried to kill me." Paul Kagame was raised in a refugee camp in Uganda and fought in two of the wars of independence in East Africa.

The president points into the darkness off his veranda and says, "You see that tree there?" I nod. "I used to climb that tree as a twenty-year-old and look into the then-president's yard. I didn't know why I was obsessed with entering the country unnoticed, sleeping during the day and wandering at night, to make mental maps of the yard, the neighborhood, and all of Kigali." I asked him, "Did you know that one day you would come back and fight a revolution?" He took a sip, paused, and said, "I knew there was something in my mind. I had a hazy idea."

Intrepid tourists come to see the gorillas. There are no amenities. They crawl under the brush, in the mud, to get close. The silverback grooms one of his wives, who in turn grooms an adolescent, who playfully prevents a smiling infant from approaching a homo sapiens. Another adolescent climbs a tree, pounds his chest, and falls comically.

I wake up one morning to go for a run on the streets and see the well-dressed children of this prosperous suburb. They braid their hair and attend school with backpacks and packed lunches. The neighborhood has satellite dishes and birthday parties. The university announced six hundred new graduates. The press is proliferating. Some of the Rwandan diaspora is returning. The French offer no assistance and the Americans very little.

President Kagame has asked people to keep their neighborhoods clean and to forgive one another. Some say they will because he has asked them to do so; others say they will because God would not have spared them to do otherwise. He tells them not to expect favors from anyone.

Rwanda was the first country to send peacekeepers to Darfur. Working side by side, many of the soldiers are children of either perpetrators or victims of the genocide. Kagame spends more on education than on the military, and Rwanda is the only country in Africa that does that.

Kagame was democratically elected and rewrote the constitution such that his party cannot have more than 50 percent of the seats in parliament. Though Kagame is a Tutsi, his prime minister and 70 percent of his cabinet are Hutu. Thirty percent of elected officials at the level of municipality, parliament, and cabinet are required to be women; in reality, more than 50 percent are. The country is secure. Wages are growing, but the economy is not yet self-sustaining. It could all happen again, and everyone knows it.

But I have to write this, my reflections on mundane moments with leaders, because maybe the small things presage something bigger. Maybe, looking back, I can now see the comment that meant so much more, the veiled mannerism, the poker player's tell. Maybe, if I improved my ability to see these things in the leaders and their countries, I could find that sign of things to come, the thing that portends the future.

I have to write this because this morning I ran the clean, bustling streets of Kigali as the sun rose, and somewhere up on the hills that surround the promise of a new Africa, above the smoke of small breakfast fires and below the cool mountain mists, I heard a dog bark.

Umuganda: President Kagame participates in a monthly community tradition of cleaning streets, picking up litter, and clearing brush around water sources.

21. The Risk of Dreams

DAVID I. RABKIN

SOMEWHERE IN CENTRAL AMERICA

· · ·

I ALWAYS SEEM TO meet the optimists first.[1] Each country I visit has "so much potential." The people are filled with enthusiasm over industries that once were, one day could be, or just need this or that to be successful. I admit that I get caught up in these daydreams every time, imagining what kind of future the country in question might have. Perhaps I will never learn.

Sometimes I work with these countries for a few months but more often for a few years. No matter the length of time, the daydreams never seem to come true. Occasionally, I visit the same countries years later and find new people with the same imaginings. Their plans seem so possible, so realistic, and yet their dreams remain just that.

Luis Sandoval owns a small coffee plantation in Central America. He employs three local workers to help him manage his trees and an additional ten during picking time. Each year Luis takes his unprocessed harvest to the local Coffee Board station. There someone weighs his crop, sorts through it quickly to determine an average product grade, and offers a price. The price for each grade is predetermined, and there is no haggling.

The amount Luis receives each year for his coffee fluctuates, but not based on factors he can control. The biggest variables are the quality and the volume of his harvest. "Sometimes they give me more than the year

1. This essay is a composite of several characters.

before, but I think it's basically getting to be less and less." He is right: the average price that the Coffee Board pays has, in fact, been declining for nearly twenty years. The local price is still somewhat higher than the world market price for Arabica coffee, but the price in real terms, for undifferentiated green beans produced in Luis' home country, has been dropping steadily. This stands in stark contrast to rapidly rising prices for specialty coffees, driven by booming demand in wealthy consuming markets.

Processing and marketing account for the difference between specialty Arabica coffees and basic Arabica beans. The specialty beans are painstakingly separated, washed, and dried. Bulk beans are indifferently sorted, then fed through large, low-quality separating machines. These machines are rarely cleaned; as a result, fermented skins frequently fall in with the beans, marring the quality of the finished product.

"The old law requiring coffee growers to sell their entire harvest to the Coffee Board was overturned years ago, but it's just too hard to do it all on your own." One of Luis' neighbors attempted to export directly to the United States, through a friend in Miami. "The shipping costs too much, and my goods were delayed at the port, so I lost a lot of money that year." The next year Luis' neighbor went back to the Coffee Board.

Three years ago, a consultant for an international development agency told Luis about some successful Costa Rican coffee farmers who had dramatically improved their quality and pricing. The consultant explained that Luis' trees produced the same quality bean; he then left detailed marketing plans and encouraged Luis to attempt to emulate the Costa Rican model.

"He gave me a picture of a second-hand roaster that cost only three thousand dollars, and I really wanted to believe what he said was possible." However, when too few farmers followed the consultant's recommendations, the development agency canceled his contract, and the consultant left. One year later a new consultant visited Luis and asked if he would join a project sponsored by a different overseas development institution to assist farmers to improve yields and take on more of the processing steps themselves. Luis agreed, but the program did not begin for eighteen months. "By then we all lost interest. Those consultants were just like all the rest: nothing but ideas behind their fancy reports. If they have such good ideas, why don't they invest in my business?"

What is wrong with Luis and other farmers like him? They know what the successful firms are doing and aspire to be like them, yet they never seem to follow through. With seemingly all the necessary tools and knowledge at their disposal to reverse their fortunes, they repeat the same hopeless patterns year in and year out.

Countless businesspeople in developing countries around the world are caught in the same routine. The result is that business simply does not get done in many developing economies. When transactions are completed, and progress does occur, it is often at an agonizingly slow pace.

There are many commonly cited reasons for this lack of follow-through: limited access to capital, poor infrastructure, unfair trade regimes, and so forth. These factors are daunting and clearly make doing business difficult. It is possible, however, to find examples of companies overcoming each, and at times, all, of these obstacles.

Culture is often invoked as the cause of this lethargy. Indeed, culture is an important part of the equation. Beliefs and attitudes certainly affect the way that businesspeople in developing countries perceive opportunities. But culture cannot explain it all.

There is something far simpler inhibiting business development. Ask yourself: if you had three thousand dollars to invest, where would you put it? Into the U.S. stock market? A global bond fund? An overdue repair on your home? Would you risk even this small amount on Luis' coffee roaster?

Every transaction, whether it is a purchase, a loan, or an investment, is the result of a calculation of risks and rewards. Behavior in poor economies that seems irrational is often actually the rational result of a series of unaligned incentives. Luis does not improve his business because, deep in his gut, he does not believe there are enough benefits to justify the additional efforts and risks he would have to undertake.

The goal of a nation is to encourage and to harness business growth in order to build more prosperous societies. The goal of the firm is much narrower: to increase profits for its owners. In pursuit of this goal, company leaders spend their time seeking rewards and mitigating risks.

The gasoline you buy is likely to have originated in a relatively high-risk business environment, such as Saudi Arabia or Nigeria. These are environments that lower-margin businesses such as manufacturing or consumer goods shun. The reward that comes from selling the oil compensates for the enormous risk. The leaders of companies such as Exxon spend a vast amount of time and money evaluating those risks. Others are spending fortunes in search of alternative energy sources. These are great risks *balanced* by great rewards.

This equation is not fixed. When risks are removed, competitors require lesser rewards to be enticed into a given transaction. In such scenarios, prices are eventually bid downward. One of the reasons powerful Western governments are concerned with stability in the Middle East is that greater stability in the region would likely translate into lower oil prices.

The balance between risks and rewards continually changes. Successful individual businesses maintain balance or exploit imbalances in their favor. Unsuccessful businesses fail to balance risk or become victims of a slight imbalance in the wrong direction.

When the risks dwarf the potential rewards, transactions slow; sometimes they virtually cease. When rewards exceed risks, transactions occur frequently and rapidly. In many developing countries, this potential risk is multiplied across an entire industry or economy, resulting in stagnation.

The most successful programs for economic growth recognize this. These efforts seek to identify and improve the few factors that can tip the balance in a nation's favor, so that local and foreign investors are enticed by rewards commensurate with the risks they must be prepared to take—and rush to take advantage of the resulting opportunities.

The pursuit of reward precedes the mitigation of risk. Companies exist to find rewards, and while they may conduct many transactions to mitigate risks, it is the reward itself that is the goal. Three essential factors determine the reward side of an economy's business platform: underlying value, market opportunity, and financial context. The total available return of any product or service is a function of these three variables.

Underlying Value

Historically, wealth was what could be pulled from the ground, off of a tree, or out of the water. Wealth was subsoil assets, a favorable location, or sunshine. Columbus went searching for spices and Pizarro went searching for gold. These are examples of *found wealth*.

For all of human history, until approximately 250 years ago, the productivity of human beings was based on the sweat of their brows and the luck of the tasks at which they toiled. With the onset of industrialization, the prices paid for found wealth began to decline, while those paid to designers of factories and managers of finances began to rise. Found wealth still had value, but *created wealth* became more valuable.

By encouraging innovation, created wealth can generate even more created wealth. Found wealth, by definition, can only be found. Found wealth can make individuals rich and, in some cases, can even alter the trajectory of nations. Yet, it is ever decreasing as a percentage of total wealth; and it is finite in even its most abundant instances. Nevertheless, both types compel transactions.

MARKET OPPORTUNITY

There are two compelling market reasons to enter an economy or to do business there: pursuit of the local customer base and access to nearby markets.

General Motors (GM) has made Brazil a center of enormous investment. It manufactures, markets, and sells automobiles to Brazil's 184 million consumers. GM also uses Brazil as a hub for purchasing, producing, and servicing other South American markets. It is clear, however, that the sheer size of Brazil is the key driver in the company's choice to locate there.

Barbados, with fewer than three hundred thousand inhabitants, is tiny. But Barbados has skilled labor, advantageous tax laws, and an excellent location quite near the United States. Many international companies choose to operate in Barbados; few do so to sell their goods on the island.

Trading preferences and quotas have begun to obscure the relevance of geography. Some European software providers have chosen Israel's high-tech corridor near Tel Aviv as a site. One important factor is Israel's excellent access to the U.S. high-tech market. This access is not just characterized by positive trading terms, but more importantly it is about the relationships between the Israeli and U.S. industries, and the insider status that having a presence in Israel can bestow.

FINANCIAL CONTEXT

The most common challenge that CEOs in developing countries cite is lack of "access to capital." Not coincidentally, these private sector bosses often lack a compelling vision for their companies (a clear strategy for turning capital into wealth). The first problem for many of these businesspeople is a lack of good ideas, not a lack of capital. The best firms can survive in the worst markets, and the worst firms fail in the best markets. Fundamentally, however, these frustrated businesspeople are right. The cost of capital in most developing markets is extremely high.

While individual companies generally can do little to affect interest rates, taxes, and other transaction costs, the government—either through effective or misguided policies—can have an enormous impact on these expenses. When considering policy decisions, governments must keep in mind how these decisions affect the balance between reward and risk.

There is a common misperception that entrepreneurs are businesspeople who love risk: gamblers with suits. Nothing could be further from the truth. Successful entrepreneurs are frequently those who are better at managing risks or those who envision ways to generate returns that outweigh great risks. But the best entrepreneurs do not roll the dice; they find ways to tip the risk-reward balance in their favor.

There are three essential elements of risk: institutional, market, and informational.

Institutional Risk

When people have no confidence in the security of an agreement, they will not enter into it. This basic fact underpins the paramount importance of property rights and begins to explain why rule of law is such a powerful indicator of economic growth.

People rarely trust other people enough to enter into transactions without contractual assurances. Not surprisingly, transactions not backed by some systemic guarantee occur at a much lower rate than those that are secure. Relative security is the result of two types of institutional risks: explicit structures and norms of behavior.

Explicit structures include legal and institutional constructs, traditionally provided through governments. Contracts and contract enforcement, the relative effectiveness of the judiciary process, and the extent of participation in international agreements are prominent examples. Explicit structures also include the provision of physical security.

Norms of behavior can be just as powerful but tend to be socially or culturally determined. Examples include the powerful Chinese hongs that allow for community lending of money to members who reside thousands of miles away.

Norms of behavior and governmental structures have the characteristics of *clarity* and *consequence* in common. To qualify as a norm, a structure must be understood by all parties and carry punishment for aberrant behavior. The degree to which norms mitigate risk is the degree to which they are understood and enforced by the community.

Collaborative processes, such as the formation of cluster working groups and competitiveness councils[2] can do much to build institutional capital. On the surface, they may appear simply to build trust between individuals; however, when they are most successful, they achieve new codes of conduct. Cluster processes can create communities of interest that have the structure to provide clarity to their members and the power to punish through exclusion.

Market Risk

One of the surest marks of a developing economy is the concentration of wealth into large conglomerates of unrelated businesses, controlled by small family groups. Korea has Chaebol; Japan has Keiretsu; and Latin America has Grupos.

---

2. Editors' note: In 1987 Ronald Reagan started the first competitiveness council, and Michael Porter was a member. In 1992, Colombia established the first competitiveness council in a developing country. Since then, dozens have sprouted up around the world with mixes of governmental and private sector participation, different levels of influence, and varying levels of success.

The agglomeration of unrelated businesses arises from an insufficient pool of skilled managers, lack of capital, and government favors. Such concentration increases the risks of doing business for all but those with special access. The CEO of a particularly diverse conglomerate in a small country reports that his company has a competence for competing in developing markets. However, this CEO's company struggles to compete in many of its neighboring markets. The competence of this company, it turns out, is not in a certain type of economy but is in managing the specific environment in its home economy. This competence is owed to the deep and preferential relationships it has fostered in its own market over many decades.

The presence or lack of clusters is a salient feature of risk inherent in market dynamics. This is easy to observe in the case of Macedonian versus Greek or Czech tourism. Macedonia has cultural, historic, and geographic characteristics that are in many ways similar to those of its neighbors, but it lacked the breadth of restaurants, theaters, tour guides, and restored historic sites as it reopened its doors after its conflict. This weakness in the overall tourism cluster means that it is more difficult for each of the players in the Macedonian tourism industry to be successful without working together. Firms in a cluster depend on each other; the more robust the related and supporting organizations are, the lower the risk of an individual firm's failure.

Developed economies possess more complex, complete, and varied clusters. It is, therefore, not surprising that identifying and filling crucial gaps in a given industrial cluster can cause radical improvements for all firms involved.

Informational Risk

The third component of risk is the easiest one to alter. Traditionally, there has been a gap in knowledge between rich and poor markets. Exploiting this gap allows savvy traders to uncover undervalued opportunities in emerging economies across the globe. Allowing this gap to persist means that millions of firms follow antiquated business practices that their global competitors have long since abandoned.

One common type of information asymmetry is that between economies. It can be seen in the extent to which local firms appreciate international best practices. It is also measured by their degree of familiarity with international customers and competitors. This does not only apply to exporting firms who must deal directly with foreign actors but to every local firm since the global environment ultimately impacts the terms of trade of even the most remote localities. The more accurately and rapidly companies in a local market adjust to international market changes, the lower the informational risk.

The pricing of a local opportunity may also reflect a second kind of information asymmetry. International investors may not be able to accurately assess the value of local goods or services or the risk of doing business. This lack of knowledge can be seen in the pricing of developing country sovereign bonds, which often carry very high coupons in order to attract investors. This pattern repeats itself, though, manyfold. The international perception of Colombia's security situation leads to foreign investment levels that are low, relative to the size and strength of the Colombian economy. Colombian businesspeople complain that the perception is worse than the reality, which, they claim, leads to undervaluation of local opportunities.

These risks can be mitigated. Every firm can now survey its customers electronically at an extremely low cost of both time and money. Export promotion agencies can communicate the opportunities of their markets and the rewards of dealing with their country's firms. Increasing the flow of good information in both directions is inevitable, but quickening the pace can yield incredibly cost-effective benefits to firms in developing countries.

Luis Sandoval's decision not to change the way he runs his farm becomes quite understandable when one examines it in light of his risk-reward profile. He can only increase the *underlying value* of his product by innovating in some way. Accessing a broader set of customers and changing his *market opportunity* will require an investment that is very large by Luis' standards. When he then considers the *financial context* of his business, such as the cost of capital required to purchase the roaster or the transaction costs associated with slow customs procedures, the rewards seem limited.

On the other side of the balance, the risks are high. Luis finds consid-

The Case of Luis Sandoval

Figure 1: The case of Luis Sandoval
Source: OTF Group

erable *institutional risk* when he considers the norms of behavior, which result in his temporary workers stealing his coffee beans. Having suffered as a result of favoritism in the past, he concludes that his *market risk* is high relative to well-connected local businesspeople. Not having a consistent link to the global market represents an important informational risk relative to those foreign investors that compete against Luis. The risks are simply too great. With all this in mind, his decision to continue doing business in the traditional way is perfectly rational.

Firms, groups of firms, civil society, donors, and governments can each alter the risk-reward balance to make transactions more attractive. This is particularly true when these actors join together to focus on a given industry. The most successful private sector development projects, like the most successful firms, are those that find situations where slight imbalances can be corrected. These little changes unlock the powerful force of market dynamics.

Understanding the risk-reward profile and how to change it is critical to anyone who is serious about pursuing economic development, not just those focused on the private sector. No matter how well intentioned and committed the government official, the nongovernmental organization, or the donor, unless the risk-reward profile is altered, the transactions that drive economic growth will not occur rapidly enough to increase prosperity.

It is tempting for those in the development community to look at the most advanced economies and ask what elements make them different from their poorer counterparts. We use corruption indices, institutional strength, and macroeconomic statistics as answers. This method would simply be inefficient if we had the resources to tackle every factor independently. In practice, this approach frequently causes us to miss the easy and right answers that can be found in every single, small-market economy.

There is a simpler test: would you put your money in this economy and in this business? If the answer is no, ask why not. Then fix those things.

Three years later, Luis Sandoval continues to farm his coffee the way he was taught by his father. Little has changed since he first met the development consultants. The Central American Free Trade Agreement (CAFTA) has inspired some of his countrymen, but Luis is skeptical that it will bring the investment he needs to buy his roaster. There is a new road project, but better access will not really change his business much.

"Each day I take out the picture of the roasting machine and wonder whether I should throw it away. The picture is old now, but the roaster continues to be beautiful to me." Perhaps one day the balance will be tipped in his favor. Until then, Luis and I will continue to dream.

22. Praying to the Virgin of Guadalupe

MARCELA ESCOBARI-ROSE

MEXICO CITY, MEXICO

• • •

ASK A TYPICAL Mexican businessman about the state of his country, and he will tell you he is worried. Leading causes of his concern are China's low labor costs, Mexico's increasingly unprotected markets, and the U.S. assertiveness in trade negotiations. Mexicans joke that even the little printed stamps they use to send promises to the Virgin of Guadalupe are "Made in China." No wonder, they say, the Chinese are the ones getting favors from her, growing at 8 percent, while Mexico has stagnated.

Mexico is not alone. A similar concern sweeps all of Latin America and the Caribbean as their free-trade zones are thinning and no fiscal incentive will keep foreign firms from fleeing to the land of cheap labor. Every conference I go to, I get asked the dreaded China question: how can we compete when we are one-hundredth the size and have ten times China's labor costs? It is a question framed by hopelessness, a hopelessness that is intimately familiar. Growing up in a poor developing country, competing successfully with China seemed not only difficult but impossible. The truth is that the more I study China, the scarier it becomes. It is moving from low cost to high tech, buying renowned brands and getting enough foreign investment to solve problems as they appear. Visiting China confirms it. In between the frantic pace, there is an unapologetic ambition and sense of possibility.

After years working in development, I now have an answer, but the answer I provide is not satisfying. These countries are right to be worried. But they are not worried for the right reasons. China is a force to be reckoned with, but the true threat to Latin American and Caribbean economies is the persistent focus that their firms have placed on trying to compete on price. It is a historic prevalence, rewarded by short memories and volatile commodity prices. We are like the anecdotal frogs that will jump out of a boiling pot of water but will unwittingly boil themselves to death if the water heats up slowly.[1] The hope is that China will provide the boiling water or the tension necessary for a radical change in the way we compete. Not only is success amid the Chinas of the world possible for Latin America, it is imperative.

The Mexican economy can provide an illustrative case as an economy that feels particularly threatened.[2] Mexico is also a country that most would have expected to be prepared. It has what it takes to be globally competitive: first-class firms, an experienced managerial class, a large and rich market of sophisticated consumers sitting just across the border, excellent climates, and sufficient natural resources. However, the promise of prosperity has yet to become a reality for Mexico.

Mexico has not shown the necessary will to turn these advantages into prosperity for its citizens. Mexico's political and industrial leaders are stuck in an old model of competition that no longer works, for them or the country in general. Right now, Mexico has a choice: it can draft a new way forward or continue to be left behind and drift into recession.

Mexico is currently focused on the old model of competing in global markets. This model dictates that, in order to prosper, you must focus on your comparative advantages. Success in this old model depends on things like natural capital, economies of scale, and a government acting paternalistically as the "master strategist." It is a formula that used to work. But it turns out that these advantages are easily imitated. In fact, they are the most easily imitated advantages a nation can possess.

There is a new model for global competitiveness, one that embraces

---

1. Editors' note: Recently, a group of curious MIT students did an experiment and proved this to be a myth.
2. The data and insights for this essay were published by *PODER Y NEGOCIOS* magazine in Spanish in its Mexico edition. Marcela Escobari-Rose, "Un Gigante Dormido," *PODER Y NEGOCIOS* (April 15, 2005): 38–42.

innovation and differentiation as a strategy for creating wealth. Mexico should be worried, but what should worry it most is that it competes on the wrong principles.

MACROECONOMIC VERSUS MICROECONOMICS

Stable macroeconomic indicators are imperative for growth, but they are not deterministic. The last ten years of the Latin American experience confirm that. There is a critical role for the Finance Ministry: to maintain consistent exchange rates and inflation, be fiscally responsible to achieve that goal, and eliminate the hidden costs of doing business for firms. For the most part, the ministry has done that, including moving a difficult reform forward to broaden and simplify taxation. Inflation is low, the debt to gross domestic product (GDP) ratio has remained stable, and the exchange rate has undergone only a slight devaluation.

Competitiveness, however, is not about the macro levers. Attempts to create growth and jobs by devaluing the currency or subsidizing producers only generate short-term gains and impoverished workers. *Competitiveness is a firm's ability to export complex, differentiated products that add unique value to increasingly demanding consumers.* These consumers will reward a nation's companies by paying higher prices, which translates into higher income. That income is distributed in the form of high and rising salaries and investment in training. This virtuous cycle creates competitive environments and stronger societies.

Mexico's firms are now exporting basic products to sophisticated consumers and producing more complex products for less sophisticated, local consumers. This choice creates no incentive for upgrading. It also explains the lack of new businesses created in Mexico. According to the Instituto Nacional de Estadistica y Geografia (INEGI), the Mexican statistics agency, the total number of firms has actually decreased since 2002.

PROTECTED MARKETS VERSUS COMPETITION

The "old model" pushes for protected markets where—under the pretense of leveling "the playing field"—governments end up limiting firms' ability to compete globally. In the "new model," competition and globalization are embraced. The North American Free Trade Agreement (NAFTA) has indeed been an unprecedented push toward an open economy, and, despite a debilitating financial crisis, Mexico has been able to adapt and reap some key benefits.

Surprisingly, this competitive push from the international markets has only entrenched the economic elites within domestic monopolies. Mexico is the only country that does not allow foreign participation in the oil industry. Electricity costs almost twice as much as in the United States, Canada, and Europe. In telecoms, the privatized Telmex is also a de facto monopoly in private hands, and it has used every political and legal tactic to maintain its dominant position. This reality burdens almost every industry in cost and efficiency gains. Particularly worrisome is that the country's elite lawyers and businesspeople are spending most of their energy and talent exploiting loopholes in the archaic government legal system rather than in creating new businesses. While there are renewed rumors around strengthening competition laws and attracting new investment in some industries, most analysts see these promises as another political ploy.

Natural Capital versus Human Capital and Knowledge

Studies by my colleagues and others show that countries that possess some of the world's most abundant resources (in hydroelectric potential, minerals, oil, sugar, unskilled labor, and sunshine) have become poorer, on average. The problem is that these advantages are also possessed by other countries and thus are easy to imitate. Countries that invest in using knowledge and insight to differentiate their products and services, in contrast, are becoming richer.

This is not an easy transition. True competitive advantages are hard to create and hard to imitate. They involve deep insight into customer needs and demands, fast and flexible operations, and real interfirm cooperation to deliver products and services to the standards of sophisticated consumers.

Where does Mexico lie on this spectrum of sophistication? One important metric is Mexico's exports. A quarter of Mexico's exports are in upstream industries (inputs into other industries such as natural resources in oil, timber, gold, etc., usually sold unprocessed) and compete on the basis of low cost and environmental degradation. Final consumption goods (processed foods and beverages, clothes, furniture) represent 28 percent of total exports and compete on the basis of economies of scale and low cost of labor. Exports in industrial and supporting functions (such as power generation and motor vehicles) are characterized by innovation and upgrading. These exports account for a staggering 47 percent of total Mexican exports. This distribution is similar to the United States's export base, implying that Mexico is exporting highly innovative products.

Unfortunately, imports in the same category account for 43 percent of total imports, and Mexico has a slight trade imbalance, which means that Mexico is importing most or all of the sophistication in these exports. These numbers represent the *maquila* industry, which has had very healthy growth through NAFTA. While much of the *maquila* is based on complex products, Mexico adds a mere 2.9 percent value to what it imports, probably in assembly and labor.

Under the *maquila* model, Mexico is competing on its low cost of labor, scale, and proximity to the United States, and thus there is little incentive to improve the condition, skill, and knowledge base of Mexican workers.

Fortunately for Mexico, China and India have become more cost competitive, meaning that the worst jobs are moving elsewhere. While this movement of basic *maquila*, particularly in textiles, is being witnessed in horror, it might not be such a bad thing. But Mexico must react the right way and do it quickly.

Trade has given Mexico the keys to the East Asian success: new equipment acquisition, increased foreign investment, technology licensing, transfer of proprietary technology, and customer learning. Now Mexico needs to have the internal environment and level of skill to apply those advantages to its own industries. Investing in research and development, education in science and technology, reinforcing protection of intellectual property, and encouraging links between the *maquila* industry and the rest of the economy are necessary to encourage innovation among Mexican firms.

Mexico needs to reduce investors' interest in low-cost labor and raw materials and to increase their attraction to a uniquely Mexican economic, political, and social platform that offers advantages that cannot be found, or imitated, elsewhere. These include sophisticated demand for products, specialized human resources, excellent suppliers, and industry structures that are both competitive and cooperative—all of which spurs innovation. The fact that 47 percent of Mexico's exports are complex products is an advantage that Mexico must take to the next level, before it dissipates.

ECONOMIES OF SCALE VERSUS AGILITY AND FOCUS

Although viewed with great concern right now, the recent end of the Agreement on Textiles and Clothing (ATC), which imposed limits on textile exports from China and other low-cost garment producers, may actually create more long-term prosperity for Mexico. If textile producers become convinced to move away from trying to compete on price and scale and to start competing on a combination of superior manufacturing flexibility, innovative design, expert workmanship, and extraordinary customer service, many (albeit not all) of the company owners and their workers can become more prosperous.

Mexico is currently "stuck in the middle"—without significant scale to compete with China and India and with antiquated and costly logistics, it has yet to turn its proximity to the United States into a competitive advantage. Most exports are burdened with poorly maintained and expensive roads, all-time-high fuel prices, and bureaucratic procedures. Mexico should not be competing in the same markets and for the same consumers that are interested in China, and while it will be a painful transition, the government and the private sector should rapidly embrace a new winning strategy.

REDISTRIBUTING WEALTH "VERSUS" CREATING WEALTH FOR ALL CITIZENS

Under the new model of competitiveness, governments and the private sector focus aggressively on creating wealth. Under the old model, most of the political discourse focuses on how to redistribute existing wealth.

In Mexico, it is difficult to avoid talking about redistribution of wealth with the immense disparities in the country. With a Gini Coefficient of 0.55, Mexico lags some of its Central American neighbors. Regions such as Chiapas, Oaxaca, and Guerreros are so poor—even compared to their northern neighbors—that if redistribution is not accompanied with a growth agenda, some people question whether these regions will stay inside the same borders for much longer.

The growth versus redistribution discourse presents a false dichotomy. As Felipe Gonzalez, the famous Spanish socialist president, said in a recent speech in Colombia, you need wealth before you can redistribute it. If the reforms in Mexico take growth as paramount, they would dissolve monopolies that inflict costs on local and foreign consumers. They would encourage the *maquila* industries to create productive links with the rest of the country. They would provide citizens with the education and skills to build innovative products and services to sell to sophisticated consumers for a premium. Leaders who understand that wealth lies in firm-level productivity organize their institutions so that they are nimble and designed for learning, guided by focused strategies that create wealth in a sustainable way.

You can continue to judge Mexico's report card. In almost every category, Mexico is trying to compete with the old model of comparative advantage in a global environment that increasingly demands a new model to succeed.

For most of Latin America and the Caribbean, it is time to look internally at their own report cards. Globalization is the tsunami wave for Latin America; it is not controlled by anyone, and it is powerful. This wave will disproportionately benefit those who are ready and disproportionately punish those who are least prepared. Mexico has led the region in opening its borders, but the Central American Free Trade Agreement (CAFTA) and other new agreements will put the rest of the region on an equal footing. The faster our countries learn to compete in this new model, the faster they will be able to reap the benefits of prosperity for all their citizens.

My dream for the region is that I stop dreading the "China question" and that I stop being asked how *can* we compete and start being asked how *will* we compete. It is a slight change in word choice but a dramatic shift in outlook. It means that hopelessness has been replaced by possibility. This possibility is ours to create.

If all else fails, and Latin American firms cannot learn to understand customers just over the border, they need only look to the Virgin of Guadalupe.

23. Our Greatest Fear

MICHAEL FAIRBANKS AND DAVID RABKIN

AIRPORT DEPARTURE LOUNGES

• • •

O NE OF THE great fears a man can have is becoming the kind of person that he used to, as a younger man, make fun of. It can happen easily. The norms and values of an industry are powerful, subtle, and wash over you and change you slowly, incrementally, until one day you wake up and are like everything you promised you would never be. You entered the industry to change it, not have it change you, but you failed.

You have your reasons, the rationale. Things are not as easy as you thought. Change takes longer. No one else plays by the rules. The really insidious part is that no one expects you to behave any better, anyway. If you play it the way you want to, you will lose. No one rewards the righteous man. At least, you say to yourself, you are not as bad as some.

Then real world needs come into play. You have a mortgage, certain needs of occupational status. You need to take care of your own family. And, finally, the last refuge of the defeated: one man (in this case two), you say, cannot change anything.

But before we wallow any further in self-pity and develop our lament, we need to catch the reader up on the industry, its players, and the economics.

A growing body of research demonstrates that rising incomes, up to about five thousand dollars of purchasing power parity per year, lead to a greater satisfaction with one's life, self-esteem, and a sense of personal competence. Alex Inkeles of Stanford University also shows a correlation between incomes and tolerance for others, productive attitudes toward authority, support for civil liberties, and a disposition to participate in community and national affairs. Prosperity, it seems, not only supports happiness, but it also fosters positive human values.

Late night session: David Rabkin, Michael Fairbanks, President Alvaro Uribe of Colombia, and former President Felipe González of Spain en route to Medellín

We have traveled to more than fifty countries in the name of building more prosperous companies in the developing world. We have seen some astonishing successes and much grinding poverty. Largely it is the kind of poverty that is the most common state of humankind on the planet today. The two billion people trapped in this kind of poverty do not starve, but they are malnourished. They often go to school but lack the advanced skills needed to compete in today's global economy. They sometimes have access to emergency medical care but routinely succumb to maladies that are easily treatable. Increasingly, they are allowed to vote, but their leaders lack the competence to govern effectively. This is the poverty found in the slums of São Paulo, not the rural communities of Mali.

Poverty, not just extreme but also relative, erodes human values and retards human progress. It is vivid in postconflict societies such as Serbia and Macedonia, once more prosperous and now filled with corrupt practices and poor results. The horrors of genocide in Rwanda and suicide bombings in Afghanistan would not have been possible without poverty.

Deng Xiaoping was right when he exhorted his countrymen to become rich. Hundreds of millions of Chinese have been lifted out of poverty in the decade and a half since his speech. Analogous, although not quite as striking, numbers have come out of India for an even longer period of time.

Yet, particularly in Latin America and Africa, the numbers are getting worse, not better. While it is encouraging that enormous gains are being made in a few countries, the economic gap is still growing between the northern and southern hemispheres. As human beings, we are failing to live up to our potential. As citizens of rich nations, we are shirking our moral commitment to our fellow man. As capitalists, we are incurring significant costs due to lost opportunities.

There are many areas in which the developed world can do better. In the area of foreign aid, we are squandering a historic opportunity to foster new markets and build prosperous societies around the world. Doing so is not just a moral obligation; it is in our enlightened self-interest. And we are getting it wrong.

One particularly glaring missed opportunity is trade. For example, Europe and the United States have long protected their local farmers through tariffs and the use of massive agricultural subsidies. These subsidies, driven by special interests within rich countries and by competition among them, render the very farmers they are meant to protect uncompetitive. In the process, they disadvantage developing world farmers, for whom agriculture might otherwise be the first step in an economic progression. Ironically, the more economically successful our neighbors become, the more benefit can be derived by the developed world through trade. Europe, Japan, and the United States owe some of their greatest successes to embracing competition, yet such subsidies impede it.

The rich world's future prosperity and security are dependent on embracing a new paradigm in international trade and foreign aid. This paradigm is one familiar to citizens of free democracies: create a world in which opportunities are universal, markets are efficient, and free commerce is encouraged.

We believe that helping poorer nations develop is squarely within U.S. foreign policy interests: it yields new markets, new sources of innovation, and broader competition, which increases total productivity. The steady march forward of global trade and the emergence of ever-stronger trading partners are at the heart of the expansion of the world economy over the past two centuries. Trade and aid, designed to genuinely improve the lot of other peoples, should be a pillar of the rich world's foreign policies.

Our worldview fits well with the espoused goals of U.S. foreign policy, but in practice our nation often defines our self-interest more narrowly. In so doing, we undermine those loftier objectives and ultimately perpetuate a global trading system that entrenches poverty, while it fails to provide the meaningful development assistance so many programs intend.

The most glaring U.S. illustration of this narrow focus is the destination of our foreign aid, the vast majority of which goes to military allies such as Israel, Egypt, and Jordan or to military zones such as Iraq, Afghanistan, and Colombia.

Less visible but insidious are the reams of regulations forbidding U.S. aid funds to be spent assisting firms that compete with U.S. firms, even if indirectly. If we believe in competition as the source of innovation and promote it at home, why do we stifle it abroad?

We often worked with, and our projects were occasionally funded by, bilateral and multilateral agencies representing these rich nations. In one recent instance, our competitiveness project underwent an annual review by one of our international donor sponsors. This project was conducted on behalf of a local developing country government and its private sector association and partially funded by the donor agency. The project sought to bring producers in several industries together to compete in international export markets. To do so, we often search for areas in which local entrepreneurs can gain advantage through cooperation, while maintaining their economic independence.

One of the signature accomplishments of this particular project was coordinating the agro-processors in an industry to jointly purchase the glass bottles in which they package their product. In so doing, the members of the industry were able to shave over 10 percent off packaging costs, resulting in savings of approximately 5 percent of total costs or about one million dollars per year. These processors are small and operate in a market that has no local glass manufacturer. They were paying a premium because their glass was purchased in small, infrequent lots and because no one processor had enough volume to be significant to the glass manufacturers (who are large, multinational corporations). This was a smart example of "co-opetition": competitors working together to eliminate a competitive disadvantage in a non-differentiating but significant part of their business.

The review committee criticized the program as having established a "monopsony." We were bewildered. A monopsony, the inverse of a monopoly, occurs when there is only one buyer for a particular product and prices are forced unfairly down. In some sense, we had created a single buyer for a narrow range of goods in that one small country. However, the glass industry is global, its products are myriad, and the companies from whom the industry purchases literally have thousands of other buyers. In fact, the industry's two to three million dollars per year of purchases could hardly be claimed to impede opportunity in the multibillion-dollar glass market. The final proof is the price itself: the local industry now receives prices closer to world standard, but lower price tiers still exist for larger customers in other countries, and the overall international price floor did not budge at all.

This story is relevant for three reasons. First, it is a too common example of an advisor hired to monitor a program on behalf of a donor, who himself lacks the requisite local knowledge to place the economic issues in context. Second, it highlights an adherence to broad economic rules of thumb with too little regard to practical applications; in this case, the fact that the "market" is actually the planet, not one small country. Third, it is striking that there was such concern about the impact our program would have on a particular multinational conglomerate. In negotiating with the glass suppliers, we found them eager for the new business, which while it lowered their total price in this market, also lowered their coordination costs significantly and raised their profits. Yet the donor's representative appeared more concerned with their potential loss of a comparatively insignificant dollar volume than the enormous impact that volume was having on the small, previously disadvantaged developing world producers.

There are relevant monopsonies in this equation, and they are the donors themselves. Each donor attracts dozens of contractors whose business consists almost entirely of contracts funded by them. The United States Agency for International Development, or USAID, has one set; the European Union, another; and regional development banks such as the Inter-American Development Bank or IDB have their own. It is revealing that each contractor tends to configure to serve one donor almost exclusively because of its country of origin and because the various regulations and procedures heavily favor firms that invest an enormous amount in learning the systems of one particular agency.

In competitive industries, the best performers make above average returns, there is entry into and exit out of the industry, and innovation occurs at a high rate, represented by trademarks, patents, peer-reviewed publications, and research and development spending. In the industries serving donors such as USAID, all competitors make exactly the same returns, the same players exist in an oligopoly for decades at a time, and research and development (R&D) is almost nonexistent. Instead of R&D budgets, contractors invest large sums in intelligence gathering to anticipate which procurements will be forthcoming and when, and then spend long hours attempting to anticipate what their client wants to see in a proposal. When the donor requests changes, contractors frequently make them without first understanding the underlying motivations for the request or doing their own analysis as to whether the change in question would indeed be in the best interest of the ultimate program client. Donors demand rapid turnaround for both proposals and refinements, while they themselves routinely miss self-published deadlines by months and years. In one recent case, we waited almost a year before being asked to submit a proposal document *after* prequalifying under an exhaustive process that required us to submit several hundred pages of text and forms. The entire project was only budgeted at one million dollars and one year in duration.

Expectations are equally out of proportion. To work in economic development, the first requirement is a humility borne of the knowledge that, collectively, we still do not clearly understand what works and what does not. Successes are identifiable, and results in certain areas have certainly been achieved. But for every success, there is usually a failure. Practitioners from William Easterly to Joseph Stiglitz lament the low return on the world's foreign aid "investment." Ironically, programs often contain goals such as "ten thousand new jobs created," sometimes for projects with total funding of ten million dollars. One donor requested an increase in national exports equivalent to about $1.4 billion, with a project budget of eighteen million.

We do believe in seeking real returns and measuring program impact. But such astronomical rates of return would dwarf those of the highest priced hedge-fund managers. Nonetheless, professional service rates are predetermined by agencies at levels typically far below private sector alternatives. The *maximum* allowable salary, barring special exemptions, is roughly equivalent to the average *starting* salary of a newly minted MBA from a top school. Capitalism is the system the developed world practices and espouses that we will preach to our less developed neighbors, yet our donor agencies create memoranda suggesting that underpaid contractors can generate 7,000 percent returns on investment. Surely, this qualifies as *voodoo economics*.

In addition to being underpaid, personnel featured as staff proposals must commit many months in advance to being available on the chance that their team's proposal is selected. This system inadvertently rewards those contractors that do not invest in their own people and instead build enormous databases of consultants for hire. Shortages of available and qualified candidates can also lead to an ethical laxness, in which contractors and consultants alike over-represent the extent to which they can deliver on their promises, including the availability of their personnel. While a contractor may promise that its proposed management team will be available at an unspecified future date when an award is ultimately granted, both the donor and the contractor often know that these same team members simultaneously appear in several proposals for several different contractors in several different countries.

The system is inefficient at its best and anticompetitive at its worst. We are all winking and nodding at each other, gradually slipping down the slope of bad business practices. The result is high transaction costs and low service quality.

The most compelling illustration in private sector development is that the world's most successful private sector consulting firms, McKinsey & Company and the Boston Consulting Group (BCG), virtually never choose to compete for the projects offered by donors. While the developed world's most successful corporations hire McKinsey and BCG to advise them on strategy, their governments' aid agencies are rarely willing to pay their fees. In the end, instead of the world's best knowledge-based firms tackling the world's most intractable private sector issues, we have a network of procurement specialists and headhunters choreographing a play that rarely has a happy ending.

We can do better. And we can do it in a few simple steps:

Contractors must themselves be competitive firms. They need to invest in their own human capital, promise only what they believe they can deliver, and refuse to succumb to the pressure of their donor clients. Contractors should avoid concentrating on one customer alone, thus allowing ourselves to become entrenched in a system we all believe is suboptimal.

Donors must hold themselves accountable for project failures. Their role in monitoring contractors is only part of their responsibility. They must also examine their own roles in why failed projects fail and better understand the gap between objectives requested and objectives met. Donors must set reasonable goals for themselves and their contractors, and they must stick to them. This includes internal deadlines as well as overall results.

Governments in the rich world must understand that prosperity in the developing world will increase prosperity at home and that the inverse is true. What is good for the goose is truly good for the gander, and the agents of our foreign policies should reflect that. Governments in these same countries must commit to dedicating the necessary resources to confront the enormity of the challenges we face, just as we would in an armed conflict or natural disaster.

Recipient country leaders must demand reasonable programs, not simply dollars. Whether they feel that the developed world is obligated to them or not, they must act as partners instead of victims if they want to leverage aid to become prosperous.

We have met thousands of people involved in the economic development community. The great majority of them are good people who start out trying to "do good." We make small sacrifices along the way in pursuit of these ideals and because the alternative is simply too hard. Eventually, we lose not only our ability to accomplish positive change but, we would argue, our integrity. As a result, we have all ended up in a collective hypocrisy, leaving us short of our ideals, missing historic opportunity, and leaving poverty safely intact.

In the era of total global competition for scare resources, where ethnic groups are at war and the rich are getting richer, where values are being transformed by technology faster than we may reflect upon them, indeed, overwhelming the sensibility of humankind, the development industry represents one of the last, best hopes for positive transformation. Instead, its values and actions are, perhaps, destroying value for the world and turning, at least a few of us, into the kind of people we used to make fun of.

24. Changing Mindsets

DONALD KABERUKA

TUNIS, TUNISIA

• • •

I HAVE BEEN privileged in the last decades to have been closely involved in Africa's quest for prosperity. I have done so from many angles: as a young commodity analyst, as a worker for international organizations, as a cabinet minister working with colleagues in rebuilding the Rwandan economy after 1994, and most recently, as president of the African Development Bank (AfDB).

Throughout my career, like many others in my position, I have faced many problems that appeared intractable, only to realize that, with determination and the right mindsets, change is possible.

At 5 percent annual average gross domestic product (GDP) growth over the last five years, Africa is making steady progress, but these strides are largely about geology and its spin-off effects, where raw material needs of Asian growing economies have outstripped supplies around the world, not necessarily changes in the structure of the economies.

While we now have a wealth of experience in managing commodity booms, we still have lessons to learn on how to transform such sudden receipts into sustainable and equitable growth; how to take the rents from subsoil assets and reinvest them in institutions that matter; how to increase skills and abilities; how to devise winning strategies; and, ultimately, how to achieve a higher standard of living for the poor in our societies. Much of our growth is yet to be based on indigenous innovation, on companies that produce great products for demanding consumers around the world.

While growth is back on the agenda and we are all now advocates of the "Monterrey Consensus," it is clear that each African country will take a different path depending on its endowment, history, and vision of the future. In my recent travels throughout Africa, I have seen some African firms able to compete with, and win against, the world's greatest enterprises. Regardless of the exact growth path each country takes, I now believe that businesses from Africa can lead our continent into its new growth era.

Where African businesses succeed, lives, communities, and countries are transformed. Our challenge is to ensure that the leaders of these enterprises continue to succeed and that their success encourages more of our young and talented populations to take up the challenge of entrepreneurship. Creating the conditions for such success for our businesses to compete requires many changes, including less reliance on natural endowment and more focusing on innovation and catalyzing private capital flows to augment what is often fragmented official public money.

While I was still a serving member of the cabinet, the Rwandan government adopted Vision 2020, which aims to transform Rwanda from an agrarian-based to a middle-income, knowledge-driven economy. We embraced competitiveness as the driving force behind our growth agenda. We identified specific interventions to rebuild our private sector, while laying the foundations for a sound macroeconomic framework, making key social investments, articulating business strategies that were explicit in finding new target market segments abroad, understanding that consumers the world over choose products from companies that suit their needs, irrespective of origin. As one expert put it, "It is companies that compete, not nations."

In doing so, we often faced incomprehension from donors who misunderstood our commitment to growth and competitiveness as a disregard for the poor of Rwanda. Often, my colleagues and I had to point out the contradictions in the advice of our friends in the development community who, though meaning well, had not yet fully internalized our commitment to own our development agenda. Much water has since gone under the bridge. Alignment behind government strategies has since worked faster in Rwanda than anyone thought possible as a result of this strong early direction from and ownership by the government.

In Rwanda, government did not have to wait for outsiders to point out the importance of strong macrofoundations, fiscal discipline, monetary stability, zero tolerance for abuse of office, and mobilizing stakeholders around a longer term national vision. The whole nation was inspired to keep its feet on the ground while focusing eyes on the ultimate prize: prosperity creation, instead of a narrow agenda of poverty reduction alone. In the process, the mind of the nation began to change.

Public servants became assertive, not jumping at any project submitted by donors but only considering those that fit coherently developed national plans. While capacity was always an issue, we also knew that the capacity would not be built while decisions are taken by donors and then rubber-stamped by civil servants. Such assistance, though well intended, could not be a replacement for building local talent.

Change of mindsets has its place especially in African classrooms and amphitheaters, where the next generation of leaders is being trained and where local talent must be groomed for business and government alike. Such local talent can come only from an education system that fully challenges and develops talent to lead and not fear embracing new paths to wealth creation.

When I worked in the coffee industry, I interacted on a continuous basis with businesspeople, large and small, traders and dealers, major roasting companies and hedge-fund managers. The City of London fascinated me, people so bursting with entrepreneurial spirit, imagination, and the thirst for competition. I also saw firsthand the profound difficulties faced by countries relying on a narrow range of raw-material exports. This was a stark contrast to the capital flows that poured out of London into new businesses and new technologies across the emerging markets. Commodity crises in the late 1980s saw many countries fail to repay external debts as their export receipts tumbled, while small farmers faced ruin. At the time, I traveled for a month to Southeast Asia on behalf of my principals to assess the emerging competition from the region. They were producing up to two tons of coffee per hectare against an average of five hundred kilograms in Africa. But producers in this region were not only having higher yields per hectare, they were diversifying into other agricultural and nonagricultural products and moving fast up the value chain.

When I was appointed to the Rwandan cabinet, our country faced many challenges, the legacy of genocide, security threats, a hostile environment, and a destroyed economy. As we set out on the reconstruction path, these were daunting enough. But there was another obstacle of a different type. Years of dependence on aid had generated an excessive mentality of reliance on government, donors, and nongovernmental organizations (NGO). This had not, surprisingly, stifled Rwanda's ability to take risks. It took time for mindsets to begin to shift. Several years down the road, Rwanda is slowly bearing the fruit. Foreign direct investment is flowing in, but, most interestingly, local businesses, large and small, are beginning to chart new domains.

Across the continent, significant investments are needed, especially in infrastructure and in building our human capital—a skilled workforce able to innovate and take risks, a new generation of entrepreneurs leading world-class firms. These, in turn, will be underpinned by business strategy and actions, the sum total of which will raise world export market share, increase profits and wages, and change a nation.

At the African Development Bank, we are investing in infrastructure, knowledge capital, regional integration, building institutions, and managing emerging threats such as skyrocketing food prices, water systems' stress, climate change, and the energy gaps. I have made it my personal goal to ensure that the AfDB plays the strongest possible role in creating the conditions for the young business leaders of tomorrow to succeed in this new paradigm of business-led growth for all the citizens of Africa.

25. Entire, unto Himself

ELIZABETH HOOPER

HAMILTON, BERMUDA

• • •

I ASPIRE TO BE an integrator. As a young professional not yet overly invested in either pursuing anthropology or business, I want to turn my limited experience into a strength.

I have found there is some tension between the values and goals of these two spheres of knowledge. Most anthropologists think businesspeople are greedy, self-centered, and obsessed with getting rich. Most businesspeople think anthropologists sit in ivory towers, obsessed with obscure cultural details, devoid of insights relevant to the real world. The most interesting thing about these stubbornly held ideas is that both groups engage in self-sealing logic, are largely uninterested in each other's domains, and are unwilling to test the limits of their own frames of reference. The tragedy is that the cultural insights of anthropology, coupled with the action orientation of business, are uniquely positioned to inspire discontinuous leaps in economic growth.

A few anthropologists have already found a place for their perspective in business. Consider this example: an anthropologist visits a suburban home in Anytown, America. It is dinnertime. Mom fields a post 6 p.m. conference call from the office; Dad zips around the kitchen unpacking Thai take-out for four. A ten-year-old boy zones out in front of a zombie-shooter video game; a teenage girl hides in her room, chatting on the Internet. The anthropologist will participate in this family's microcosm over the course of dinner. She will observe interactions, uncover underlying assumptions about their lives and environment, and identify cultural patterns that will later inform her firm's business decisions.

Ethnography already enriches the product development processes of some major corporations including Intel, Kodak, and Nokia. Anthropological research techniques provide deeper insight into how people live and consume. But the contributions anthropology can make to business go way beyond using ethnographic techniques to create better products. By the very nature of their work, anthropologists observe culture and human behavior while recognizing broad patterns and the underlying beliefs and ideas that inform them. Armed with this knowledge, businesses and development workers can cocreate effective local plans for a country's economic growth.

I did not always know this. As a student, I attended lectures on Yanomamo religious practices and Maori warfare tactics. I studied how "pure" cultural traditions were destroyed, altered, and exploited by colonialists and the subsequent emissary of the West, the Evil Multinational Corporation (EMC). At the time, I bought the argument as presented. I would not have believed then that ten years later I would write that I have learned more about observing, analyzing, and influencing culture while working in the private sector than I have learned anywhere else.

The problem is not that anthropologists do not research poverty or work with disenfranchised populations. They do, but anthropology's insights about poverty are largely unknown outside academic circles. At the same time, the vast body of anthropological knowledge is not directed toward action. The main line consists of endless debates on whether culture influences development and to what degree or on the sacredness of culture and the importance of an absolute relativism. There is little actionable information that demonstrates useful connections with other domains.

And yet, a key differentiator in the successful development work I have seen firsthand occurs at the nexus of anthropology and business. Linkages between these disciplines increase our understanding of the power of mindset and the impact of culture on the way a firm does business; of how individual leaders make decisions; and ultimately of how countries position themselves on the path toward prosperity. The approach is a mix of market research, facilitation, business strategy, and another element that I call *actionable human insights*.

Culture has three levels. The first level is the physical and tangible expressions of culture such as institutions, architecture, food, and dress. The second level is more intangible and includes music, artwork, and rituals. The third level is psychological or spiritual and focuses on the way in which people attach meaning to their lives. These thoughts, beliefs, and ideas held by people on every subject are called Mental Models.[1]

How people think about business, competitiveness, and trade has a direct impact on their level of prosperity. A high and rising income correlates with trust, tolerance, self-esteem, and overall satisfaction with one's life. These Mental Models can be defined, informed, and tested around a specific, well-defined objective. For example, we might ask the question, "Whose responsibility is it to create wealth for a nation, the government or the private sector?" Countries where large segments believe the responsibility for prosperity lies with the government face more challenges in creating a vibrant private sector to drive growth. The most important thing about Mental Models is that, once they have been identified, they can also be discussed and changed. The real power of Mental Models is to make the implicit *explicit*.

Is one set of Mental Models "better" or "worse" than another? Anthropologists are immersed in cultural relativism. Cultural relativism is the idea that, within the context of its own culture, each idea is valid and acceptable and should not be judged as good or bad. This leads to ambiguity over even the most contentious practices. Some have suggested that, when dealing with difficult problems such as poverty, it is appropriate to distinguish between cultural relativism and ethical relativism and consider adopting a universal humanitarian standard. When confronted firsthand with the devastating poverty that affects much of Africa, Latin America, and the Middle East, I find it hard to remain relative about any contributing factor.

1. Editors' note: "Mental Models," a concept developed by Kenneth Craik in 1948, was brought into management literature in the 1980s by Chris Argyris and then Peter Senge. It was originally brought into the development literature and developed by Michael Fairbanks and further refined by his colleagues, including Phil Cooper, Jonathan Donner, Jeffrey Glueck, Kaia Miller, and Elizabeth Hooper.

Ensuring that people are able to meet their fundamental needs for shelter, food, and medical care strikes me as both an audacious and attainable "universal humanitarian standard."

Relative to that aspiration, there are sets of beliefs that are either pro-innovation or anti-innovation. As a tool in development programs, Mental Models allow us to facilitate productive dialogues about where a people's belief system lies. By understanding Mental Models and therefore elements of culture, we can respond more effectively to the mindsets that reinforce poverty and limit growth.

Getting to Mental Models can be a messy process. Some time ago, I collaborated on a competitiveness study on the impact of information communication technologies (ICT) in the Caribbean, comparing the levels of integration of ICT in fifteen different countries in the region. By far, I had more exposure to Jamaica than to any of its neighbors. Jamaica's rich, vibrant culture deeply affects the business climate, just as it creates some of the world's most expressive music. By contrast, Trinidad and Tobago, at the other corner of the Caribbean, has a more restrained and conservative feel. One perfectly rational economic answer for this is oil wealth: Trinidadian culture has evolved in contrast to Jamaica's history of struggle and lack of sustainable resources. Traveling between the islands, our team could not help but note the difference.

There was one pervasive story told again and again. The first time we heard it was while sitting in the office of a Trinidad and Tobago ministerial-level official. We asked, "So what do you think causes the cultural differences between Jamaica and Trinidad?"

In the dying afternoon light of the government office, the minister paused and gave the question some thought. Leaning forward slightly in his seat, his voice lilting with that melodious Caribbean accent, he said, "Think about it this way. The slave ships coming from Africa would arrive to the Caribbean. Their first stop would be Jamaica. Who do you think they would want off the ship first? The ornery ones, the troublemakers. Well, by the time the ships got to Trinidad, only the nice and calm ones were left on board." While this explanation seems wrong, its dimensions tell us much about how people identify themselves and frame their own experience. Of course, the truth is much deeper than the convention.

Perhaps the real story is that the businessmen were left on Jamaica, while the anthropologists were sent to Trinidad.

There are as many different ways to think about competitiveness and prosperity as there are to explain the cultural differences between Trinidad and Jamaica. One fundamental mindset difference occurs between individuals who equate competitiveness with cheap labor, the promotion of easily imitated products, and the presence of natural resources and those who equate competitiveness with the opportunity to bring a sophisticated product to a demanding consumer in an attractive market. This basic understanding of how wealth is created is crucial. The first assumes that the economy is a zero-sum game and that development's goal is to alleviate poverty by reallocating the pieces of a limited pie. The second understands that development is about wealth creation and that economic growth is not a limited proposition. The first set of beliefs holds countries back from creating a high and rising standard of living for their citizens.

To assess Mental Models as part of our projects, we conduct nationwide surveys of public and private sector leaders in which we ask a battery of questions. The answers help us understand perspectives at the individual level and along social cleavages such as age or income level and, most importantly, help us segment clients into different groups with well-defined beliefs on competition. Through more than ten years of implementing this technology in twenty-five countries, five distinct segments have emerged.

The *basic factor focus* segment believes natural resources, access to cheap labor, and imitating main competitors are the most important sources of strength for countries and firms. Those who fell into the *market threatens social justice* segment fear that open competition threatens national solidarity and believe that the government should redistribute wealth. The segment that focuses too strongly on *short-term wins* give short shrift to long-term planning. The *government leads economy* segment holds that it is the government's responsibility to "fix" the economy. The *innovation creates wealth* segment recognizes competition, change, and risk as things to be embraced because the potential rewards are boundless.

Understanding attitudes toward competitiveness and innovation and the composition of the different segments in a country is like understanding exactly where the starting line is in a race. As advisors, once we know where to begin, we can help local leadership focus on the key issues they need to understand to get to the finish line. In practical terms, it also helps to refine the strategies and proposals given to persuade and mobilize the local private sector. The importance of a localized solution to a development problem cannot be overemphasized. The cultural insights provided by Mental Models better enable development professionals to offer tailored solutions with a higher potential for positive returns.

Pairing a global perspective with local insight is a powerful combination. Hence, the essential question is what data inputs are needed for an advisor to develop a tailored strategy that will both work in the global marketplace and resonate with the businesspeople of a particular country. Three factors must be taken into consideration.

The first factor is mindset, or understanding the composition of the "Mental Model landscape," and how these perspectives determine audience receptivity to proposed solutions. The second factor is cultural context or answering the following questions: What are the cultural nuances that must be taken into account when looking at prospective strategies? How do people attach meaning to relevant concepts? The third factor is simply being realistic about the nature of the problem; good business practices are universal, but business problems, although easy to diagnose with good pattern-recognition skills, vary from industry to industry and from country to country. Each scenario must be analyzed within its own context.

Armed with this information, the task of advising a client country on its own specific challenges with a strategy designed to maximize existing potential becomes manageable. It is worth noting that the insights from the above categories are directly gleaned from people or from the cultural context in which a situation occurs.

An example of where understanding local culture and context greatly enriched our impact was on the sandy shores of Bermuda. This beautiful island country in the middle of the Atlantic Ocean is just a short flight from the eastern seaboard of the United States. It offers an impressive history in addition to its famed rose-hued beaches, grand resorts, and world-class food. Yet the island's most vital industry was not performing. We were asked to help tourism leaders address declining revenues. We brought the standard consulting tools to the case as we studied the economics of hospitality, addressed the importance of service, built complex costing models, and performed detailed customer segmentations of who travels to Bermuda and why. Everyone said that the problem was a forty-year labor dispute and that if we could resolve a few paramount contract clauses, things would be on track. Everyone was wrong.

The key to solving the problems facing the hoteliers and their workers was identifying, discussing, and ultimately resolving a critical culture difference. Hoteliers and service staff had fundamentally different perceptions of specific issues. Tourism executives felt, for example, that if maids could complete their daily allocated room cleanings in five hours, the maids could take on more responsibility. The maids, in turn, felt they were being punished for their efficiency. Over the forty years of disagreement, trust between management and line staff had been eroded. Without understanding this core problem and how it was preventing the tourism industry from a truly productive conversation, we could never have achieved what successive premiers (prime ministers) from different political parties consistently hailed as a development that ended up "changing the course of history in Bermuda."

Understanding the complexity of underlying human behavior and the way that drives action in the business arena creates a true competitive advantage. Anthropologists can bring that knowledge to the economic development task. For a discipline so skilled at the art of segmenting people along complex lines (language groups, kinship systems, types of religious ritual, to name just a fraction of the innovations that happen in the science of anthropology every year), its practitioners have grossly underestimated the intentions and ability of businesspeople to use human insights to create a better world. Some of the best businesspeople are far more concerned with creating market opportunities for poor countries, creating sustainable social equity, and developing products that serve people's needs than they are with their own wealth, comfort, or prestige. I have spent my career looking for the EMC among the firms I have worked with, and I have yet to find one.

Using the human and cultural insights of anthropology to create under-standing, shared vision, and localized solutions through the action and results-driven mechanisms of business, we can create far more compelling results than either discipline can achieve alone. Business welcomes any-one that can make a contribution; this call to action is to anthropologists. There are several ways in which anthropologists can immediately contrib-ute to economic development programs.

Anthropologists can help the people doing business and development work to create solutions, products, and programs that are both sensitive to the needs of the people they serve and likely to be adopted by them. Ultimately, the goal of improved prosperity and all that comes with it will be best served by a localized solution.

We can do further research to understand how culturally perpetuated mindsets promote or inhibit growth. Each group of people holds a set of beliefs, ideas, and thoughts that will, to some degree, determine its des-tiny. We need to point out when cultural relativism hinders growth and identify the specific beliefs that are holding people back from achieving prosperity.

Use anthropology's unique tools to allow for richer, more meaningful segmentations of groups of people. As our Mental Models segmentations demonstrate, there are powerful ways to look at different groups of people that help refine approaches to development. Use the highly effective qual-itative research techniques of anthropology to help businesses understand and segment their clients.

Help people doing meaningful work; use cultural cues to construct messages that truly motivate people to action. Create messages that inspire people by using deep, specific knowledge of a culture to appeal to their deepest needs, fears, and beliefs. Show tension, create hope, and propose solutions that will create the need to act.

And, lastly, use knowledge to have a tangible impact on the lives of peo-ple. In whatever way you choose to get involved, take action. Study top-ics that have relevance to improving the lives of people living in the world today. Do not be afraid to frame ideas in ways that are accessible to the average person and that address real problems. This only enhances the last-ing value and insight of the work.

Anthropologists, as academics, bring valuable insights into the workings of human organizations; businesspeople are perfectly positioned as practitioners to put these insights to use in mobilizing new opportunities for developing countries. I am reminded every day of how little I know, how much I have to learn, and how big the gap is between these two fields. And yet I am optimistic about the possibilities and energized by much of what I see.

Perhaps it is my perspective as a young professional, not yet overly invested in either discipline, that allows me to see the potential in both, together.

26. "When Are You Coming Back?"

DIEGO GARCIA ETCHETO
CARACAS, VENEZUELA

• • •

LIVING IN AFGHANISTAN, you get used to a lot of things. You get used to not walking after dark. You get used to living behind high walls topped with razor wire, under the watchful eye of men with guns. You get used to getting run off the road by fast-moving armored personnel carriers. And you get used to conversations with friends and family centered on the sentiments "You're crazy for being there" and "When are you coming back?"

Anyone with a TV can tell you that Afghanistan is a dangerous country, second only to Iraq in headline-grabbing violence. Though far from safe, reports of Afghanistan's unrest are greatly exaggerated. As one journalist told me over drinks at a Kabul watering hole, "The 'things-are-getting-better' story only sells once, and we ran it a few months back." Meanwhile, half a world away, in a country that does not grab headlines, a real tragedy continues to unfold. This is not a famine or a war that CNN would bother to beam into our living rooms. There are no gripping images of starvation and bloodshed. It is the lazy death spiral of a resource-rich nation as it treads a road to poverty and ignores a tougher but ultimately more rewarding road to prosperity.

This is actually a story of two nations: how they have come to be and what the future may hold. The first, as you may have guessed, is Afghanistan, where I have been living and working for the past eighteen months. The second is Venezuela, my mother's homeland and a place I remember fondly from the Christmas and summer holidays of my childhood. Venezuela was rich and vibrant in the 1960s and 1970s, while Afghanistan, though perhaps vibrant, has never been truly wealthy. Both countries have seen their fair share of conflict, though only Afghanistan saw open warfare. Venezuela's conflict grows worse by the day, while Afghanistan, though scarred, is moving on. Where these two countries are today is a result of history, location, and resources. Where they are headed is a result of choice.

For me, it is especially painful to watch Venezuela disintegrate. I have nine cousins who come from Venezuela, all in their teens and early twenties. Five of them are currently living in Europe. The four who remain also have plans to leave. My grandfather's family, originally from Germany, fled the Nazis in the 1930s. One of my uncles left Italy as a child in the aftermath of World War II. Venezuela was the country that opened its doors to them. For over sixty years, they called Caracas home; now, in his ninth decade of life, my grandfather is forced to watch as his grandchildren leave to find better opportunities in the countries his family once fled.

Military coups, corruption, and dictatorships are Latin American clichés, and Venezuela has more than done its part to uphold that image.

Stepping out of the terminal at Maiquetia Airport on a recent trip to Venezuela, the first thing that hit me, as always, was the humidity. The second thing was the realization that, though I am now thirty-one years old, most of the cars at the curb are the same models I remember from my childhood. Graffiti supporting Hugo Chavez, the current president, cover a wall in lieu of a welcome sign. As I climb into my uncle's car, one of the first questions he asks is, "How bad is Afghanistan?" I tell him about the continued fighting along the border with Pakistan, the fears of the country's becoming a narcostate, the threats against foreign workers. Driving past the *ranchos*, the slums that spread inexorably over the hills surrounding Caracas, on a freeway built fifty years ago—now decrepit due to a lack of maintenance—I say, "Maybe it's worse than here, but at least there things are getting better."

Venezuela is a rich country that is full of poor people. Despite sitting on seventy-eight billion barrels of oil and with oil prices at an all-time high, over half the population lives below the poverty line. Caracas is a city full of areas where no one travels during the day. Common nocturnal precautions, like rolling up the windows and locking the doors, are supplemented with more aggressive techniques such as not stopping for traffic lights and driving at excessive speeds. In this city of just over 3.5 million, an average weekend will see anywhere from twenty to twenty-five murders, mostly in the *ranchos*. During the holiday season, from Christmas to New Year, the city can easily rack up over one hundred murders. The violence extends beyond crime—into the political arena. I can recall vividly two different coup attempts—there have been three since 1992. My uncle keeps a spent machine-gun round in a jar at home by the window it traversed.

By contrast and despite its reputation in the media, Kabul, an overcrowded city of three million, sees relatively little violence. Violence has claimed fewer than twenty lives in the city over the past year. And while most nongovernmental organizations (NGOs) have strict security guidelines for their foreign personnel, most expatriates routinely ignore them to no ill effect. Locals can move around the city at all hours with little risk. It is true that many regions of the country are no-go areas due to insurgent activity, but equally dangerous are Venezuela's border with Colombia and the interior where illegal gold miners hold sway.

Venezuela made a choice long ago. It chose to live off oil revenues. Oil exploration began in the early 1900s, and today petroleum contributes about half of central government revenue, 82 percent of export revenue, and a quarter of gross domestic product. In the words of *El Universal*, Venezuela's leading daily, with regard to the state-run oil company, "The policy [of the government] has always been that Petróleos de Venezuela should produce economic rents that the state will distribute, through programs and projects, for the people."

It is no surprise, then, that the Venezuelan economy lives and dies by the price of oil and that the careers of Venezuelan's politicians—closely tied to the performance of the economy—do the same. The current president of Venezuela, Chavez, swept into office in 1999 with 56 percent of the vote and promptly founded the "Bolivarian Revolution," a socialist movement meant to mimic what Chavez considers the successful socialist experiment of his idol Fidel Castro. His party has won six elections since and is steadily taking control of all branches of government. In what is a signature move of strongmen the world over, he is amending the constitution so that he can run for president again. Not bad for a man who could not get promoted past lieutenant colonel in an army that suffers from an excess of generalship and who was jailed for leading a failed coup in 1992 (the one responsible for putting a bullet through my uncle's window). The price of oil when Chavez took the presidency was at seven dollars per barrel. As the price has risen—reaching sixty-three dollars per barrel in 2005—so did his approval rating (at 70 percent). Surprisingly to many, the economy continues to slip despite oil's peaking at nearly one hundred fifty dollars per barrel in 2008.

Venezuela's reliance on oil has come at the expense of the nation's competitiveness. Everyone familiar with "Dutch disease" is aware how petroleum exports can appreciate the exchange rate and hurt traditional export industries. Ideally, a nation will counteract this problem by investing the revenues in ways that foster innovation and diversify exports. Unfortunately, rather than supporting economic development, Venezuelan oil has acted as the fertilizer for the growth of corruption and cronyism. Populist politics are the order of the day as groups vie with each other for a slice of the oil revenues. Debates center on which social programs should be funded, and revenues are invested in gaining short-term political capital instead of long-term knowledge and institutional capital.

In Venezuela, years of mismanagement have produced industries that do not know how to compete. How many people can name one Venezuelan export apart from oil? Not even most Venezuelans can do so. Industry exists only because of protectionist tariffs and only in sectors where regional presence lends it a comparative advantage. Firms compete globally at the most basic level, by leveraging natural factors, proximity to markets, and friendly government policies.

Things are unlikely to change and, in fact, are getting worse. In 1992, President Carlos Andres Perez took steps to liberalize the petroleum industry. He was impeached soon after for corruption, and the experiment came to an end. Chavez, correctly sensing the surge of redistributive sentiment in the population, has increased taxes on many of the downstream functions open to private investment and has taken a more active role in the operations of Petróleos de Venezuela. His government is firmly in control of oil receipts—which, of course, are doled out to supporters of the Bolivarian Revolution. The political groundswell has also moved more generally against the private sector (and the so-called "rich elites"—actually the middle class), whom the poor, now the majority of the population, feels has usurped the country's resources.

New laws that allow the government to seize and redistribute "under-utilized" farms have been expanded to allow the seizure of "idle" firms. In the words of President Chavez, "It's against our constitution. . . . as we cannot permit good land to lie uncultivated, so we cannot allow perfectly productive factories to stay closed." Over seven hundred factories are currently classified as idle, and, hence, candidates for expropriation. Opposition groups are not taking these policies lying down; recent years have been marked by protests and violent clashes between the two sides. The latest wrinkle involves the formation of citizen militias to defend the "fatherland," ostensibly against an invasion by the United States, but they are much more likely to see action against the internal enemies of the revolution.

In the fight over expropriation, no one has thought to ask why so many firms are shutting down or how it is possible that a country whose economy is so dependent on oil revenues should face a rapid increase in poverty just when oil prices were at their highest. And few are debating the most critical question: what happens to Venezuela once oil prices drop?

Although Venezuela has so far chosen to squander its natural resources, it can just as easily choose to invest them. One of the country's greatest advantages is its democratic institutions. Venezuela has been a democracy for fifty years and has invested so strongly in its institutions over that time that even the current attempts to erode them have not been entirely successful. And if the current government would rather subvert the country's institutions than invest in them, there are millions of Venezuelans whose daily investment—writing newspaper columns, taking part in protests, or voting in elections—continues to shore them up.

While some institutions remain strong, years of oil revenues have entrenched a culture of dependence in the polity. This is exacerbated by the socialist, jingoist rhetoric of its leaders, which focuses on the victim-ization of the country at the hands of Western imperialist powers (a theory that conveniently ignores the heavy dependence of Venezuela on Western countries for 60 percent of its exports and 40 percent of its imports). Venezuelans have always been keener on dividing the spoils than making the pie bigger. This needs to change.

Venezuela must create a system that enables the private sector to take the lead in providing the country's wealth and prosperity. Among other things, it had better build institutions that protect private property and cut the bureaucracy that stifles entrepreneurship; a national dialogue on the need for fostering competitiveness and innovation should commence. The government, despite the abundance of resources at its disposal, has failed, and now it is up to the private sector to improve the standard of living of the citizenry. But the only way these changes can be made is if the Venezuelan people acknowledge the need for themselves. That will require a drastic cultural shift.

Cultural investments may be the most difficult of all to make. The Mental Models in effect throughout the world are hallowed by usage and time, regardless of the benefit they provide. People do not like to change until catastrophe is staring them in the face—and it may be that Venezuela is now going through the catastrophe that will shift its Mental Models. The long-held tradition of socialist rhetoric among the educated elite is not as popular now as it was decades ago—now that they finally have the socialist government of which they had always dreamed. My cousin Marco studied in Italy for a year when he was nineteen. There he gleefully took part in antiglobalization protests and dabbled in the communist and anarchist movements. Now twenty-one years old and living under President Chavez, he has become disillusioned by what he considers the hypocritical rhetoric of the Left: he finds little in common with his old friends. He has even stopped wearing his Che Guevara t-shirt.

While empirical data showing a shift in Mental Models do not exist, my cousin's case is not unique. When Chavez first came to power, he had many supporters among all levels of society. Now his support comes mainly from those who are more easily influenced by social spending programs—that is to say, the poor—while the rest of society seems to pull away from his policies. It is not clear if this will be enough to effect a change in the nation's course in the near term, but at least a new generation of leaders is being raised who have had a front-row seat at what my aunt refers to as, "a very interesting experiment—if you don't have to live through it."

Afghanistan, by rights, should be headed in a worse direction than Venezuela. Where Venezuela is embarking on a socialist path, Afghanistan walked it for twenty years under Soviet rule. Where Venezuela's polity is polarized and increasingly violent, Afghanistan is emerging from a decade of vicious, multipartisan civil war. But while Venezuela focuses on redistribution, Afghanistan focuses on wealth creation: taking the road less traveled, which will make all the difference.

Chavez pounds his lectern and frames the choice as "either capitalism, which is the road to hell, or socialism for those who want to build the kingdom of God here on earth." Curiously enough, the last people who tried to create the kingdom of God here on earth were the Taliban; judging from their results and those of the Bolivarian Revolution so far, heaven is a very poor place. In contrast, Hamid Karzai's vision for the future is for the private sector to act as the engine of growth of the Afghan economy.

At its heart, the issue is about providing opportunities for prosperity to the citizenry. Both Afghans and Venezuelans are voting with their feet. While Venezuelans leave for Miami or Europe, Afghan returnees are streaming back across the borders by the millions, eager to take part in their homeland's reconstruction. I personally work with about a dozen businessmen who left Iran, Pakistan, and even Europe and America in order to come back to study, work, and live in Afghanistan.

It is especially poignant that many young, well-educated Afghans are returning to their homeland. Many who not long ago would have left to study in Pakistan or Iran are choosing to stay and study in Afghanistan instead. Abid Akbary, one of my colleagues in Kabul, is a great example. His family fled to Pakistan during the worst of the civil war and Abid did his high-school studies there. He now plans to get a degree from Kabul University and is currently enrolled in evening classes in accounting and finance. Smart and dynamic, Abid is in Afghanistan for the long haul.

Since one of the best measures of expected prosperity is the migration of a nation's youth, the large number of young Afghans who feel that theirs is a land of opportunity is a telling indicator of Afghanistan's trajectory toward a more prosperous future. Likewise, that Venezuela's youth are willing to leave behind friends and family to seek their fortunes elsewhere speaks volumes about the perceived future of Venezuela.

Afghanistan has been able to provide a better vision of the future because it has managed a drastic cultural change. Afghanistan survived its catastrophe. After twenty-five years of war, it has managed a cultural shift away from the zero-sum mentality of feudal warlords where resources are finite, expansion means encroaching on someone else, and trust is reserved for people in your own clan. It is shifting toward a culture that acknowledges national unity and that leaves open the possibility of working with disparate peoples. It is the opposite of Venezuelan culture, which is still based on redistributive, zero-sum economics and which is increasingly more exclusive—based on class and politics.

That cultural change has helped fuel investment across the entire spectrum of Afghanistan's capital. As I write this, Afghans are going to the polls to elect their first parliament in forty years. New laws give control of natural resources to the private sector. Corrupt courts are being purged. Businessmen are forming associations to improve cooperation and to better engage the public sector in dialogue. Bureaucracy is slashed to allow entrepreneurship to flourish. Universities are forming partnerships with foreign organizations in order to fill the gaps in their curricula, while students eagerly take advantage of every opportunity. From the carpet industry's setting up cutting and washing facilities, to raisin exporters' setting up retail outlets in India, and marble processors' exporting slabs and tiles rather than unprocessed stone, the Afghan private sector is investing in knowledge and equipment to forward integrate along the value chain and enhance its ability to compete. All of this should be emulated in Venezuela.

Take, for example, the agricultural sector. Despite the years of conflict, Afghanistan's agriculture is rebounding strongly and exports are growing. Afghans are pushing the government to rebuild roads and to sign agreements with neighboring countries to facilitate trade. Processors are keenly aware of the industry's shortcomings in areas such as marketing and packaging and are actively searching for solutions in an effort to better compete internationally. Venezuela's agricultural sector, despite benefiting from heavy subsidies and preferential tariff treatment, is so grossly inefficient and unproductive that two-thirds of Venezuela's foodstuffs must be imported.

Both sectors suffer from lack of capital and outdated production. Afghanistan at least has an excuse. The war destroyed many factories, and many vineyards and orchards need to be cleared of land mines and rehabilitated. However, where Afghanistan is trying to fix the deficiencies by investments in equipment and knowledge, Venezuela stagnates with farm-expropriation policies that give long-time city dwellers tiny plots of farm land on which they must try to subsist.

My mother was born and raised in Caracas. Until recently, all of her family lived there. That I can find work in Afghanistan and not in my mother's homeland is a sad tribute to Venezuela's declining fortunes and to the mindset that outsiders have little to offer.

Afghanistan is a welcoming country, seeking to tap not just funds but expertise from around the world in order to build prosperity. Chavez, on the other hand, feels no need for expertise beyond that of Fidel Castro. Venezuela today is firmly entrenched in a socialist system that largely ignores the role of the private sector. For things to change, the polity will have to exercise its democratic option to choose a different course. And that means the people will have to realize that a different course is necessary.

Afghanistan has managed it, and although the road ahead is not devoid of pitfalls, the hope of prosperity has been introduced. If that happens in Venezuela—if prosperity is at least a possibility—then maybe my cousins will return someday to study, work, and live.

27. "That's My Duck!" (The Case for Integration)

MICHAEL FAIRBANKS

TIPPERARY, IRELAND

• • •

M Y MATERNAL great-grandfather, Grandpa John Fahey, provided a comfortable home for his wife Brigid, and he considered it the most important of the three things in his life in which he took the most pride.

He still possessed both his thumbs, which was the second point of pride for him and a rare thing among his peers who, as young men, switched trains in the yards at Dublin. It seems few were fast enough, over a long period of time, to fix the grips that connected the moving trains and still get their hands out of the way without losing at least one thumb.

The third thing Grandpa prided himself on was that he could tell stories. Others asked him how so many interesting things in life could happen to just one man. He said, with an Irishman's fondness for rejecting the linear, chronological aspects of Greco-Roman logic, "Good stories happened to those who can tell them."

Grandpa Fahey's home was located on the border of Tipperary and Limerick in a town with a granite church, two pastures, and a dozen cottages, called Monahela. The home was made of stone from the pasture and whitewashed. The roof was thatched. There were just two rooms: a front room with just enough space for a table for two and a rocking chair, and an even smaller room with a single bed that he and his wife shared without complaint.

Grandpa possessed the only rifle for miles. The English had successfully kept firearms out of the hands of most rural people. He walked out one morning and shot a duck that passed over the house, and the duck flew awkwardly for a while, like a flung-open book, and plummeted dead into the neighbor's yard.

Grandpa climbed over the mossy, dry-stacked stone wall that separated the two properties and went to collect the duck; but the neighbor, whose name is lost in the mist of history, garbled up in the scores of dinnertime stories that must have taken place before I finally learned it, grabbed it and started to reenter his own stone cottage.

Grandpa Fahey yelled, "That's my duck!"

"Not really," the old man said, not even turning.

"You give me my duck. I shot it."

"It flew in my yard. It's my duck."

Grandpa liked those who told stories, and he did not like those who would not talk. He used to say, "The *second* last thing I can endure is a quiet man; the last thing I can endure is when a quiet man steals from me."

"Tell you what," he said to his neighbor.

"What?"

"Let the duck go to the best man."

"Bah!" The neighbor waved his hand and dismissed the offer.

Grandpa shouted, "We face each other, three paces away. I kick you in your manhood, and then you kick me, likewise. Whoever takes the pain best is the best man of Monahela and keeps the duck."

The neighbor was receptive to my great-grandfather's challenge. This was, perhaps, just the opportunity to get even for implied threats, petty condescensions, and slurs that went back years. He set down the duck and, with some anticipation, walked over to Grandpa. "I got you this time, Fahey."

Grandpa wasted no time and kicked the man below the belt. The old man fell to the ground and rolled over onto his stomach, gripping himself, wincing in pain. He started to get up, got so far as onto his knees, and still holding himself with both hands, fell back on the ground again. Long minutes passed. Grandpa stood ready, in a fighter's stance.

The neighbor finally stood up and wiped the dirt and sweat from his brow. He was resolute, buttressed by the pain and humiliation. He said, "My turn, ya' old crank."

Grandpa said, "That's all right. You keep the duck."

Practitioners in different domains of human understanding tell their own stories too, attempting to illuminate and edify the human condition. They use specific tools to do so, ones agreed upon by the priestly caste of, usually, older, white North American males trained at the approximately six universities "that matter." They shape their narrow kind of discourse, promote like-minded acolytes, reinforce each other's values, and reciprocate with awards for their age-mates.

Practitioners are often rewarded by the elders in their domain with the able use of accepted tools to push the prevailing paradigms. They rarely borrow tools from other domains, perhaps out of a not-invented-here mindset, though some are better than others. E. O. Wilson states in his book *Consilience* that the thought leaders in the soft sciences, ones in which outputs and results are hard to quantify, are worse at collaboration than those in the hard sciences. Sometimes even, it is the use of these specific tools that place practitioners in a domain and provide to them their identity rather than the practical end value of their work.

Tools are often segmented into quantitative and not quantitative, but one can double-click on this simple distinction and find a richer ecosystem of tools and representative practitioners: multivariate analyses (sociologist), pile sorting (anthropologist), meta-analyses (philosopher), model building (economist), mechanisms (chemist), plot lines (novelist/screenwriter), and metaphors (poet).

My experience over the last three decades (read: middle-aged, white North American male) in economic development suggests that a small number of experts with a narrow scope of tools rarely look kindly into the backyard of their neighbors with a view toward finding out what are other possibilities for understanding, edification, and communication.

All knowledge workers, including practitioners in economic development, rely upon data, information, knowledge, and insight. Pictured another way, data are like the individual letters of the alphabet, information is like a word, and knowledge is like a sentence. Insight, then, is how we attach meaning to the sentences.

Paul Krugman reminds us that "broad insights that are not expressed

in model form may attract attention, but they do not endure unless codified in a reproducible and teachable form."[1] He says a good model represents an "improved insight into why the vastly more complex real system
behaves the way it does."[2]

I define a model as consisting of a small number of determinants, each
of which is embedded with data, information, and knowledge. This model
provides a range of options, informs a specific choice, and, if it is a good
model, compels one to action. It is obvious then, but still must be said, that
the quality of the choices are only as good as the chosen model and the
least precise data that are available and correct.

It follows that when professionals in economic development obtain bad
outcomes measured by low purchasing power in society's poorest people
over a long period of time, they either had the wrong model, employed bad
data, or lacked the decision rights or moral capacity (courage) to deal with
unavoidable competing tensions and to make the correct choices.

But there is another, different, kind of brain: the kind that uses metaphor, musical language, anecdote, and morality tale. A morality tale is an
anecdote with emotional content, a point of view. It seeks to edify all who
read it but leaves slight room for interpretation.

Different people get to insight and action in different ways, and many
people find it hard to see how others assimilate information, process it,
learn, and take action.

There is the old Irish joke where a foreigner walks into a train station
and sees the ticket salesman sitting under two clocks. One clock says 10
a.m., and the other says 10:10 a.m. The foreigner, schooled in linear logic
and chronological thinking, asks, "Why do you have two clocks that say
two different times on them?" The Irishman looks up and says, "Since I
have two clocks, why would I need both to say the same time?"

The few that do try to comprehend another's way of thinking, to work
with ideas outside of their domains, can be called *integrators*. Those that
open their hearts and minds to all possibilities while retaining the ability
to make hard choices, those who are able to use such diverse things as met-

1. Paul Krugman, *Development, Geography, and Economic Theory* (Cambridge: MIT Press,
1997), 27.
2. Ibid., 71.

aphors and data, anecdotes and models, might be called *master integrators* and are as hard to find as the *wee small faeries* of Monahela.

I have found the Eight Domains of experts in economic development, whose members opine about what is prosperity and how best to achieve it. All are informed, righteous, and valid in their beliefs. They use different models, which inform the data they seek and the way they make inferences and cause action. The descriptions below are, by necessity, brief. Denizens of each will no doubt see them as reductionist.

1. Basic factor. These people believe that the existence of raw materials, location, sunshine, and cheap labor to sell is critical to trade and prosperity. They are supported by the theories of "absolute advantage" (Adam Smith) and "comparative advantage." They also tend to put great belief in basic things like mosquito nets, clean water, and fertilizer. They think that most problems can, at least, begin to be solved with a massive infusion of financial capital. Later on, they say, markets will take over.

Government bureaucrats and nongovernmental-organization (NGO) leaders are the main proponents, though some Hollywood celebrities and a few economists buttress them. Their tools are budgets, moral suasion, and public relations.

The weakness in this domain lies with how linear its arguments are, how many times the strategies have been tried and failed, how the proponents *parentalize* the poor, and how uninterested they are in working with those who do not share their views.

2. Microeconomic. These experts believe that technological and business innovation will solve most problems. They believe in the power of markets—local demand and supply, segmented markets, distribution channels, specialized infrastructure, and the rate of new business formation—to fulfill most human needs. The nature of microeconomic changes is bottom-up, slow to take, and cognitive in that it requires changing many minds.

Their tools are those of an MBA. Proponents include CEOs and some social entrepreneurs. They are suspicious of government competence and the motivations of NGO staff, whom they regard as mediocre. When they explain the material prosperity they personally enjoy, sometimes, they confuse their own competence with luck.

3. Macroeconomic. These changes are top-down, structural, fast to act, but very painful. They require, normally, only three people to enact them: the head of government, the finance minister, and the Central Bank governor. They fall into four categories: stabilize the economy, privatize firm-level actors, liberalize trade, and democratize political institutions. This is the domain occupied by the Washington consensus of the late 1980s and 1990s.

Proponents include most PhD economists, leaders of multi- and bilateral aid organizations, specifically the International Monetary Fund (IMF), and the editors of the *Economist* magazine.

They see these changes as the first step, which will lead to many other changes in sequence. They explain the often-poor results of this domain, when it is used exclusively, as due to the lack of courage of the leaders of poor countries to do the right thing.

4. Institutional. This domain exhibits both codified and uncodified norms of behavior. Examples abound: rule of law, specifically, the protection of tangible and intangible property; democracy; business associations like chambers of commerce; and efficient government procedures (fast, low-cost, good guides of behavior).

Douglas North and Hernando De Soto brought this domain into the dialogue of development with their groundbreaking writing in the 1980s; North won the Nobel Prize in Economics in 1993. Political scientists, lawyers, and government managers thought the recognition was overdue. Like so many domains, it was regarded as a magic salve to develop nations all through the 1990s.

5. Knowledge. This domain consists of research and development, archives of information (data sets and libraries), and international patents. There are some direct correlations between patents, innovation, and prosperity. Causality is less clear because sometimes the types of people who codify knowledge are the ones to improve economic productivity at the same time.

Proponents include professors, chief information officers (CIOs), Internet pioneers, and authors. Famous scholars that support this with their research would be Nobel laureate Joe Stiglitz for his ideas on "information asymmetry" and Paul Roemer with his work on the "idea gap" between nations.

The problem here is that, when I asked these thought leaders what types of knowledge anticipate prosperity, their answers were not very resolute. It seems that identifying the gap is easier than filling it.

6. Human science. This is a broad category that entails theories behind migrations (Thomas Sowell and Jared Diamond) and biology, the fact that humans are bipedal and possess stereoscopic vision, opposable thumbs (read: Grandpa Fahey), and a modular brain to create economic activity as we know it.

This domain, up until recently, explains the past more than anything else. Diamond, for example, uses topography to explain human movement and prosperity up to the thirteenth century in his book *Guns, Germs, and Steel.*

Now, there are new thinkers, like Juan Enriquez. His book *As the Future Catches You: How Genomics & Other Forces Are Changing Your Life, Work, Health & Wealth* explores how genomics will be to the economy of the next few decades, the way the microchip was to the last few decades.

I have even seen research that correlates prosperity with trust and trust with specific molecules and the location of certain receptors in the human brain. It is marvelous to think of a society's prosperity linked to molecules in our brains.

7. Human capital. The single best line in economic development lies in this domain. It is a quote frequently attributed to Nobel laureate Gary Becker: "The only investment with the possibility of infinite return is the investment in children." Human capital is knowledge capital with legs.

Teachers, politicians, and parents are the obvious proponents of this domain, though their strategies are more espoused than demonstrated. Thomas Friedman's thesis in his new book *The World Is Flat* is that it used to be better to be a B-student in America than an A-student in India, but that situation is now reversed. The argument is overstated but illustrates an important ideal. The world is becoming fairer to people who learn. Meritocracy is, increasingly, a possibility in the global economy. Amartya Sen, Nobel laureate and humanitarian, is being proved right: the important thing in economic development is not the redistribution of wealth but the redistribution of opportunity.

8. Culture. Culture, according to Clifford Gertz, is how individuals who are recognized both within and outside their group attach meaning to life. It is not just the culture we can see, hear, or feel—language, food, clothes, music, oral traditions; it is how we think. All people look at certain things like human relations, time, risks, self-determination, and material prosperity in ways that identify them. If the way they look at these things promotes prosperity with the group, then they can be said to be pro-innovation (see for example, Edward Banfield's *The Moral Basis of a Backward Society* and Lawrence Harrison's *Culture Matters*). Likewise, if their views retard the accumulation of prosperity, then they can be viewed as anti-innovation.

For example, if a group of people believes that strangers cannot be trusted, the past will always be better than the future, life is inherently risky, what will be will be, and wealth consists of subsoil assets, location, and government advantages—this group is going to be poor. The obverse is true also.

Of course, culture is the third rail of economic development. It is not discussible in the conference rooms of the aid agencies; nor will government leaders or outside advisors take this area on. Perhaps not ironically, but sadly, another aspect of the anti-innovation mindset is not to learn from outsiders and not to tolerate the views of people unlike yourself. Even innovative people with good intentions do not want to be called racists. So the argument stalls, and the cultural domain becomes the least discussed— though, perhaps, most important—aspect of human development.

Unfortunately, we rarely see the practitioners of one domain learning from the practitioners of another. They are like members of their own cultures. They attach meaning to their lives with their own symbols, and as long as their explanations are internally consistent and plausible and have some (intermittent) power of prediction, they do not have to tolerate, let alone learn, from those unlike themselves.

The way the story of my great-grandpa Fahey ends is that he wanted that duck for its feathers, soft and warm, to withstand the North Atlantic weather to make a pillow on the bed for his wife Brigid. The neighbor, who earned the duck the hard way, cooked that duck. It must have tasted good. The protein and fat helped to nourish his large family. He threw the feathers and guts out their shuddered window. By the time Grandpa came across them, they were of no use.

Grandpa never spoke to or looked into the eyes of that neighbor or any member of his family again, not even in church, which was a few hundred yards away from their homes, not even on the holiest day of the year, Easter Sunday, for the several decades until he died.

If the two neighbors had spoken and understood each other's needs, they could have apportioned the duck. Trust was destroyed. There was no longer an opportunity for collaboration, to share knowledge, to help make each other's life better. My great-grandfather could have had the feathers as an input for pillows. The neighbor could have cooked the duck and nourished his family. They could, perhaps, have shared the gun and the duty to watch out for other low-flying birds. They might have gained food and comfort for both over a period of time. The story around the dinner table would have been less funny, maybe lost earlier, but lives would have been better. The neighbor's name, however, might still be known to us, the descendents of John Fahey.

Prosperity is the material goods that define a standard of living, but it is also the hope and aspiration of a better life. It can be understood at the level of metaphors and anecdotes, and it may be understood through any number of abstractions placed across the Eight Domains.

The challenge is not just for us to develop *good enough* explanations so that we might be masters in our own academic disciplines, our domains, to be intellectually self-sufficient, with all the awards and prestige that come from that. We must become master integrators across domains, to start with appreciating one another's experience, to view anomalies in our understanding as possible stepping-stones into another's model, to learn to use each other's tools, to make inferences together, and to collaborate with and honor other experts, not just those on our side of an old stone wall.

28. "Mr. President, Tear Down the Walls!"

KWANG W. KIM

DIGITAL HARBOR, BRAZIL

• • •

EVERYTHING was going well, I thought, as I closed my laptop at twenty thousand feet in the air. I asked the flight attendant for another cup of coconut water to keep hydrated. This was my third month of nonstop traveling around Brazil's poorest states—thirteen states in nine weeks, including two in the Amazon region. Even for a development professional accustomed to grueling travel, this was a stretch. The day before, I had met with the president of a burgeoning software association, a key decision maker on technology policy, and a cabinet member close to the state's governor. Now I just needed to prepare a presentation to international aid officials on my findings. I thought these meetings represented the best and the worst in Brazil and in the development world. Why is Brazil's northeast still poor, and what explains the exceptional "pockets of excellence" such as Pernambuco's *Porto Digital* (Digital Harbor), which I visited just a day ago? I sipped the coconut water and imagined listening again to Alberto Magalhães, the cluster leader whose energy reminded me of an evangelical on steroids. He was an odd character in a region notorious for its relaxed view of time.

In an almost exact remake of the legendary tale of Stanford professor Frank Telman; his two most famous students, David Hewlett and William Packard; and the birth of California's Silicon Valley, Recife's *Porto Digital* moved from a student project to become one of Brazil's most dynamic technology regions. "We didn't wait for the government to make this happen," said Alberto, although some revenue was available for information technology (IT) infrastructure development through contracts with state-owned agencies. "Instead, we [business and academic entrepreneurs] created the cluster ourselves, with the government playing an important but secondary role," willing to be guided by the private sector rather than assuming the lead role as master planner.

The Digital Harbor is actually a building, housing several dozen IT firms and even a venture-capital firm within a beautifully restored colonial house. Recife's port and downtown, the home of the Digital Harbor, has been revitalized thanks to the rising prosperity of local firms. In just five years, the number of local software companies jumped from a few dozen to several hundred. Alberto's enthusiasm and optimism still echo in my mind, as he proudly mentioned that Motorola's president visited the Digital Harbor. Today, Motorola has an office there, and it is also a major customer of several local firms. He continued, "Firms in the Digital Harbor love competition, . . . and we work together to export our software to Europe and Asia. Now we're trying to sell banking and wireless software to U.S. clients." Hyperinflation has given Brazilian financial software firms the needed pressure to adapt to their customers and become among the most sophisticated in the world, pioneering e-banking, for example. They were willing to compete with the very best, not just with India or their Latin American counterparts. Alberto admitted, however, that, although it had the right business instincts, the cluster did not have the world-class tools needed to create a strategic plan to break into a sophisticated new market such as the United States. So he asked for our help.

"Good stuff," I thought, as I took another sip of my drink. I opened *O Estado de São Paulo*, one of Brazil's major dailies. The headline read, "Industrial Policy Nearly Approved." I sighed. The Brazilian federal government was flirting with sectoral subsidies, not surprising given the generation of the self-labeled neo-Keynesians nostalgic for Brazil's development years (early 1970s) who represented about one-half of key decision makers in the new economic cabinet. As predicted, the "industrial policy" became a bizarre combination of "picking winners" based on credit and tax incentives, import substitution combined with upgrading national trade, and macroeconomic stability. It seemed like the making of an economic Frankenstein. At least some people in Brazil's northeast, of all the unlikely places, are getting it right.

I put the paper down and thought about my own approaching deadlines. I needed to make a presentation to our client, an influential global aid organization, with recommendations on which clusters to support in the next few years. Besides software, tourism seemed extremely promising. Cashew nuts was interesting too, but there was little doubt in my mind which top two clusters could potentially create lasting prosperity through rising wages and linkages to other clusters in the region.

Then I heard the pilot buzz, "Ladies and gentlemen, we are approaching our landing in the state of Piauí. Please fasten your seatbelts. The temperature outside is thirty-five degrees (Celsius)." I cringed. That is ninety-five degrees Fahrenheit. And it was evening, about 9 p.m.

I checked into a local hotel. I was pleased to find that my São Paulo–based free Internet provider worked beautifully even in the most remote places of Brazil, while my United States–based colleagues were struggling with expensive online providers. I received an e-mail from my colleague in Rio de Janeiro, which made me turn pale: ". . . given that we will no longer support software and tourism, we will be allocating Carla to work on honey and cashew nuts with you. Cheers, Andre."

What on earth?! Shortly after, the electricity went out, shutting off the air-conditioner. My laptop screen was the only bright spot in the room. The bugs noticed it, too. It was going to be a long evening.

Days later, I found that our contact client, the local representative, was under intense pressure from his superiors and other key decision makers to back down on his initial support for the software and tourism clusters. Their main argument was that this was a "poverty-reduction" trade development project and that they could not justify the use of their resources to make the "big companies" within these clusters wealthier. Never mind that these two clusters would be key economic engines for the whole region, impacting more small businesses than all other poverty-reduction-qualifying clusters combined (we had the data to prove it). No amount of argument could change their minds. This was a closed matter.

This experience helped me confirm an important insight. The world's greatest development challenges are not primarily about money, lack of good will, or even the absence of technical knowledge. They are mainly about "mental walls" by key decision makers and opinion shapers in government, business, academia, industry associations, the media, and civic and international aid organizations on how they view wealth, prosperity, trust, distribution, the role of government, competitiveness, and business strategy. The results of these mental barriers are that, rather than making things better, these leaders create economic barriers with very visible effects on the poor.

The following illustrates some key "mental walls" I found in developing countries. I refer as *gate keepers* all those with significant freedom to decide whether a region will choose prosperity or unintentionally (and tragically) perpetuate poverty. Though this has been written with current Brazilian realities in mind, non-Brazilian readers familiar with developing countries will find these mental walls disturbingly familiar.

The First Mental Wall

People see the government as the master planner, responsible for creating the right business environment; as a result, academic, business, and other nongovernmental leaders do not take proactive roles in driving change and building new institutions.

What is interesting to note in the most prosperous and competitive regions, such as in Pernambuco's *Porto Digital* and California's Silicon Valley, is what the federal and regional governments *did not* do. They did not create a master plan in industrial strategy, they did not pick winning or losing sectors using competition-distorting instruments (such as tax exemptions), and they did not drive the cluster-development process. Instead, the government at all levels in these clusters was careful to support emerging trends set forth by universities and the private sector leadership by providing generous research funding in key areas, helping with some convocation and networking, (later) improving the regulatory environment at the pace set by the private sector, and, in the case of California, creating sophisticated demand as a key customer to early firms.

Samsung Electronics' recent decision to move its cell phone factory from Manaus, a fiscal haven in the Amazon to the high-tech city of

Campinas illustrates the importance of a good workforce and infrastructure over tax subsidies. In turn, Campinas' high-tech region did not emerge from any master industrial strategy but emerged because the University of Campinas (UNICAMP) has been a steady provider of scientific talent. Similarly, the institutional architecture of California's early clusters was shaped by innovations stemming from academic institutions.

A single individual's leadership, that of Frank Telman, had an enormous consequence for the creation of Silicon Valley. It was thanks to his relationship with his students that Hewlett-Packard (HP) was born, which, in turn, spun out many other companies and venture-funding organizations. The creation of an academic-business institute linking research and development (R&D) with commercialization (SRI, then known as Stanford Research Institute, also started by Telman) had tremendous importance for Silicon Valley. San Diego's leadership was more top-down, but the University of California at San Diego (UCSD) was similarly the initiator of business–academic partnerships, as well as the breeding ground for mother firms in San Diego's biotech cluster (e.g., Hybritech).

Knowledge-intensive business leaders also played a key role in starting and growing technology companies by creating new networks of cooperation and defining when to cooperate and when to compete.

One of the most important skills for these academic and business entrepreneurs has been their ability to network by being opportunistic in creating their own "rules of the game" or institutions, as well as being committed to making a good idea happen, regardless of external constraints. There is no exact formula for successful entrepreneurs, as Amar Bhidé, an expert on this subject at Columbia Business School has said, but it involves having a vision and taking strategic actions. "Learning how to learn" becomes a critical skill for success. This could be one useful ongoing framework for aspiring entrepreneurs in academia and business.

This recipe has profound implications for countries including Brazil, where everyone seems to be waiting forever for other people to get things done, or "after *Carnaval*" as the saying goes here. This is the Brazilian mental wall, of waiting for someone else to do something for the country or waiting for a national savior, like the political equivalent of Pelé or

Ronaldinho who would score the saving goal for Brazil in the final minute. *Porto Digital* and Silicon Valley did not wait for the government to create the right institutional environment, financing, networking organizations, and grand economic vision. Pernambucan and Californian entrepreneurs created these situations themselves, creating novel funding mechanisms that were appropriate for them as well as their own institutions ("rules of the game"), such as forums to exchange ideas, deal-making mechanisms, and innovations across the value-chain, from product development to after-sale services.

In Brazil and other developing countries, professors and top university administrators are some of the most underutilized resources in starting knowledge-based environments to create prosperity, as the cases of *Digital Port* and Silicon Valley illustrates. They could, for example,

▶ lead networking efforts with the private sector by creating associations with university–business advisory memberships (including the Federal University of Pernambuco, Stanford, and UCSD);

▶ lead efforts to commercialize scientific innovations into prosperity-generating products and services, working with corporations and the government (consider the SRI model and Recife's *Centro de Estudos e Sistemas Avancados* (CESAR) (Advanced Research and Systems Center);

▶ improve the quality of science curriculum by increasing resource allocations to science programs and improving the quality of its curriculum, resulting in more research opportunities and interaction among faculty and students, as well as supporting their entrepreneurship efforts.

Instead, Brazilian universities are notorious for emphasizing quantity over quality of their students and placing low emphasis on science and technology.

Developing countries will fail to see more Digital Harbors unless academic leaders focus on delivering high-quality instruction in the applied sciences and become a proactive force in creating institutions of prosperity.

The Second Mental Wall

Companies prioritize access to financing and government favors rather than focusing on business strategies to beat the competition. Along with this, wealth is invested in capital markets rather than in productive activities.

Businesses must prioritize learning and applying world-class business strategies (many of them outlined elsewhere in this book) over lobbying activities, avoiding addictive competition-distorting solutions such as subsidies and protection from foreign competition. As Michael Fairbanks put it, one of the most destructive patterns for businesses in the developing world is the subtle change from employing business-upgrading activities to seeking government privileges as a growth "strategy." Brazilian firms have a long history of such addictive behavior.

Reinvest in productive activities rather than in capital markets. It is businesspeople, not the government, who have the ultimate lever to generate employment and socioeconomic prosperity. But wealthy Brazilians have little incentive to invest in productive activities, since returns on even "conservative" investments in financial markets, fueled by a national interest rate of around 20 percent, yield such a superior return. This is combined with cumbersome business regulations and delays, including very rigid labor legislation, that discourage reinvestments in productive activities.

Such a vicious cycle of stagnation should be broken for two reasons. First, diversifying investment with productive activities against different types of shocks makes good business sense. Second, deliberately deciding to invest in distinct productive activities based on innovation and quality-employment generation is one of the most effective ways that wealthy individuals and businesspeople can improve economic and social conditions. By primarily relying on capital markets, these investors put themselves at risk by not diversifying their investments and missing out on exciting knowledge-based investment opportunities led by universities and smart entrepreneurs.

One practical way for wealthy individuals to start is to work proactively with universities to look for such investment opportunities and to form "angel" investment networks. At the very least, this will up the ante for university leaders to act. The shifting of such investment habits by wealthy individuals remains largely an untapped resource in emerging markets.

THE THIRD MENTAL WALL

Focus on reducing poverty rather than on creating prosperity. Focusing on poverty reduction instead of prosperity is more than a matter of semantics. Prosperity creation is not a scheme for making the rich richer but a fundamental starting approach. A mental wall around poverty reduction often inhibits the formation of "economic engines," as illustrated by the bias against tourism and software industries in the opening story. Poverty reduction often focuses on low-cost schemes such as social-solidarity movements, cooperatives, and state-owned enterprises and commodities industries that use workers with low wages without any economic pressure to raise their skill levels. Development professionals—aid-agency leaders, development consultants, policy decision makers, nongovernmental-organization activists, etc.—should prioritize long-term actions that thrust the poor out of poverty, rather than investing one million dollars to obtain a fifty thousand dollar increase in aggregate wage and income improvements. As one country director from the World Bank said privately, "Of course, these [poverty-reduction] programs are having some impact. We are throwing millions of dollars at them! No wonder people are better off." But doing people a little good with a lot of money is bad stewardship of aid and public resources. What is worse, it leaves us with a false sense of security that enough has been done, while trapping workers in low-skill jobs with ever-lowering wages.

Specifically, development professionals should discriminate toward high-impact, higher pay interventions. When faced with a choice on how to use limited resources to help the poor, a well-executed private-sector-oriented solution—such as cluster development, corporate social responsibility, and microfinance—is more effective in terms of impact and sustainability than supporting cooperatives in low-skill industries or community development using solidarity schemes (though these are better than doing nothing).

The Fourth Mental Wall

To maintain political and economic independence, the state assumes a strong role in promoting national industries through industrial policies instead of creating a national-security strategy based on science-and-technology excellence.

National governments have a key supporting role in generating wealth —not as being the master planner but by making strategic investments, such as policies that support science-and-technology infrastructure, as has been the recent cases of India, South Korea, and other Asian Tigers. In the case of Korea, a passion for science was combined with a passion for beating Japan, and embracing competition became a question of national honor. So far, countries such as Brazil have given only a marginal role to technology policy. Brazil could transform its long-term development landscape by creating a national-security strategy for science and technology. This would be a special presidential or interministerial committee to design a national science and technology strategy, including benchmarking with leading industrialized and emerging countries, assessing the role of science in Brazil's economic development, creating demand for applications via knowledge-intensive projects, and coming up with a robust research-funding strategy.

Brazil is significantly behind in scientific innovation rankings not only among other emerging economies but even in its own region. The country has fewer patents per capita than its Latin American rivals such as Argentina and Mexico. As Eugênio Staub, the CEO of Gradiente (one of Brazil's largest firms) told me, Brazil does not spend its substantial R&D resources (1 percent of its gross domestic product) in an efficient manner. It is important to acknowledge that Brazil cannot become a world-class economy if scientific research management remains as second or third priority as it is today.

Three of Brazil's key economic reform priorities today—lowering interest rates, taxes, and relaxing labor regulations—are moving very slowly and are politically difficult to implement. This picture is not much different in many other developing countries. The hopeful news is that, as much as such government actions have an important role in the future welfare of nations, it is time to recognize that the fundamental choice to improve the welfare of developing countries lies not with the government but with leaders in businesses, academia, and others who are willing to rise to the challenge.

I was flying again, this time back to my home in São Paulo. I was weary but glad that my weeks of travel had ended, at least for the moment. I decided to check my e-mail. It included an automatic reply to an e-mail I had sent to Alberto, written both in Portuguese and English: "I am on a business trip to New York. . . . I can be reached at the Brazilian-American Chamber of Commerce at . . ."

He is on the move, I thought; this guy never stops. I opened the newspaper. To my surprise, there was a small headline in the economic section, which read "Import-Substitution Discarded in Industrial Policy." I smiled. There was hope. The battle to win the war on uncompetitive behavior is being fought every day by anonymous warriors, armed with a laptop, a passport, and boarding passes. I ordered some more coconut water. I was getting addicted to this stuff.

29. Deciding What Not to Do

ERIC KACOU

GISENYI, RWANDA

• • •

I T WAS a beautiful spring day in Kigali, Rwanda. Spring is the short rainy season. The light, perpetual rain brings a nice aroma: a distinctly African smell, one I find very calming. As I walked into the Ministry of Trade, I eagerly anticipated my monthly update with the minister. Our meetings focused on necessary trade reforms and the performance of exports, both critical to the country's bid to create prosperity for its citizens. I felt privileged and honored to be part of Rwanda's transformation.

Jean Umukiza,[1] the minister, is a strong reformer committed to change. He had recently joined the cabinet and was a leader with a vision for his country and a desire to act. He made the hard choice to be a leader in a tumultuous time, and I have grown as a professional getting to know him and the challenges he faces each day. As usual, the minister listened intently to my update. However, I noticed that despite his courteous attention, his mind was elsewhere. The minister had just returned from a trade fair in Japan where Rwandan coffee and tea samples had received significant premiums. He smelled an opportunity for Rwanda. He looked me in the eye: "From now on, Rwanda should export instant coffee."

My heart missed a beat. I thought to myself, "There is something wrong here." The minister risked making an uninformed decision that could jeopardize the future of five hundred thousand coffee-growing families.

---

1. Name is a pseudonym.

Exporting a finished product and value addition sound attractive, but they are not panaceas. I was tempted to launch into a discussion, but I lacked the data to make a compelling argument. I owed it to the coffee growers, to the minister, and to myself to approach this situation carefully.

Why was I so disturbed by the minister's proposal? As I pondered, my mind focused on Agnibilikero and Gisenyi, two villages with a personal significance to me. As a self-respecting African, I religiously visit my two villages. As the birthplace of my parents, Agnibilikero is my first village, and I have adopted Gisenyi because it reminds me of Agnibilikero. The memories of my most recent visits are vivid, and the contrast is profound. While Gisenyi is now prospering, Agnibilikero is becoming poorer.

Most instant-cocoa drinkers will never know this: there is a 10 percent probability that their last cup of hot cocoa originated in Agnibilikero, a city of six hundred thousand in eastern Côte d'Ivoire. An industrious people, most Agnis work twelve hours a day every day of the week to produce excellent cocoa (and an average cup of instant coffee). This tradition dates back sixty years, and most Agnis' children today are raised to become *gros planteurs de café-cacao*—big coffee–cocoa farmers.

My uncle Eba is no exception. After his undergraduate studies, Tonton Eba chose to return to Agnibilikero. This was a bold and selfless move, since, in the late 1970s, most educated Ivorians were choosing comfortable civil service jobs in the city. Instead, my uncle chose the hard life of a farmer to support his extended family. For twenty-five years, Tonton Eba has awakened at 4 a.m. to visit his farms. His leadership of the family's three hundred hectares has been outstanding, but he has often questioned his choice of career as the situation of Agni coffee–cocoa farmers has steadily worsened since 1982.

The luster attached with being a *gros planteur de café-cacao* is vanishing. Big farmers who used to be prosperous are now living in misery. Still, my uncle is holding on to his dream. A practical man, he has also invested in tomatoes and chicken as the income from coffee and cocoa dwindled. "You live abroad. Can't you find me somebody to buy my coffee and my cocoa?" Tonton Eba asked me, with his usual bluntness. His intuition that he needed better customers was correct: a root cause of his woes was Côte d'Ivoire's focus on the highly competitive (and least profitable) commercial cocoa and coffee segments. But the real problem originated in the past decisions that Côte d'Ivoire as a country had made.

The year 1987 brought a rude awakening for all Ivorians. Côte d'Ivoire, the "miracle of Africa," went bankrupt. Cocoa, the main engine of growth, stalled because global overproduction created a slump in world prices. In May 1987, Côte d'Ivoire defaulted on a debt of nine million U.S. dollars, and in July 1987, Felix Houphouet-Boigny, Côte d'Ivoire's first president, decided to place an embargo on Ivorian cocoa. All cocoa exports were halted in a bid to strong-arm speculators into increasing prices. The move backfired, and on June 5, 1989, the state halved the price to producers, beginning the cycle of misery that has persisted through today. At the time, I did not have the courage to tell my uncle that his woes were endemic to the industry and difficult to fix.

Little did I know that, a few years later and two thousand kilometers southeast, I would be grappling firsthand with these same issues in Rwanda. To connoisseurs, Rwandan coffee is one of Africa's highest-quality Arabicas. The hills of Gisenyi (on the northern tip of Lake Kivu) host some of Rwanda's finest bourbon Arabica. Emmanuel Rwakaraga, a *gros planteur de café*, is one of Gisenyi's foremost leaders and the head of *Cooperative pour la Promotion des Activites-Café* (COOPAC), now Rwanda's largest coffee cooperative. I first met Emmanuel Rwakaraga in September 2001, during a visit to COOPAC. His work ethic and blunt honesty also impressed me.

A conversation on the beach sealed our personal bond. Emmanuel had returned from Congo after the 1994 genocide to revive his father's coffee plantations. Emmanuel's father had built Rwanda's first coffee-washing station in 1956. Three years later, Emmanuel's family was forced to flee to neighboring Congo when he was a three-year-old toddler. After 1994, he returned, like many other refugees, to rebuild Rwanda. The spark in his eyes reminded me of Tonton Eba. Emmanuel shared Uncle Eba's dream to be a *gros planteur de café*. Emmanuel Rwakaraga has already surpassed his own father. No one less than President Paul Kagame inaugurated COOPAC's new washing station. As we toured the washing station, I asked Emmanuel how he taught his members about quality. He replied, "Farmers with excellent cherries get a premium. Farmers with poor-quality cherries go back with their coffee." Seeing my puzzled look, he said with gravitas, "This is the only way to get people to care about their coffee. Now that farmers understand we are serious, we hardly ever have to reject cherries anymore."

This commitment to quality is essential to Rwanda's coffee turnaround. Coffee has traditionally been Rwanda's foremost cash crop. In 1990, coffee exports reached a record sixty-six million U.S. dollars. In 2001, the sector went through its toughest crisis with exports down to twenty million dollars. Rwanda's coffee sector was trapped in a low-quality/low-quantity loop. Rwanda's coffee sector leaders realized that high-quality Arabica was the only way out of the commodity trap.

Emmanuel has been at the forefront of the transformation of Rwanda's coffee industry. In 2006, COOPAC boasted twenty-five thousand families, up from just two hundred in 2001. Fully washed production is two hundred fifty tons per year, a nonexistent industry in 2001. The farmers are receiving 110 Rwandan francs or twenty cents plus their share of profits, double their 2001 revenues. COOPAC has multiyear contracts with buyers in the United States, France, and Germany. Max Havelaar, the world's largest fair-trade coffee distributor, has agreed to distribute COOPAC coffee. The Rwandan coffee industry has experienced an impressive turnaround following its decision to export Arabica fully washed beans.

Agnibilikero and Gisenyi are at the opposite ends of the spectrum of commodity choices. Côte d'Ivoire is a major player in the mainstream cocoa market, but Rwanda has managed to enter the high-quality Arabica segment, and the industry is flourishing as a result. Thirty washing stations have been opened in the last year alone, and coffee farmers are sending their kids to school again. As I sit in the minister's office, I see the danger that he could make a choice as wrong as that of President Houphouet-Boigny in Côte d'Ivoire twenty years ago and undermine Rwanda's progress.

Building competitiveness is all about making informed choices. As my colleague Michael Fairbanks has written, five preconditions must be present for nations to improve their competitiveness and, therefore, the standards of living of their people. These preconditions for change are leadership, moral purpose, tension, receptivity to change, and new insight. When all five of these conditions are not met, wrong choices are made, and meaningful change is unlikely. Furthermore, prosperity-inducing change remains elusive, and leaders alienate themselves from their industries and political base. If he made the wrong choice, Minister Umukiza could alienate Rwanda's coffee industry as well as American and European customers who buy Rwandan coffee. I began to think about how these preconditions applied to the question facing the minister.

Leadership starts with an individual but is seldom an individual affair. Leadership is paramount for change to permeate a nation. Leaders cannot solve a problem by saying, "It is not my problem." But at the same time, leaders often believe government knows better. They say to themselves, "My industry stakeholders are weak. It is, therefore, my personal (or the government's) responsibility to solve this problem." This mentality breeds over-responsibility, which is a common constraint to meaningful leadership. While Minister Umukiza is a strong personal leader, I was afraid that he might not be willing to include other stakeholders in his decision-making process.

Moral purpose is the compelling aspiration that ignites the desire for change. This is often an ideal that leaders committed to making a difference for their people hold dear to their hearts. Moral purpose is a powerful precondition for change because it has an emotional aspect that compels leaders to persist against all odds. Moral purpose is something Minister Umukiza has in abundance. A refugee most of his life, he has learned to succeed against all odds. With a PhD in economics, Minister Umukiza gave up his deanship at one of Africa's most prestigious universities. The minister is profoundly moved by the suffering of his people and wants a world that is more just for his people.

Tension, or a sense of urgency, refers to triggers making the current situation unbearable. Natural disasters, multifaceted crises, and war often instill the desire for change. In Rwanda, Minister Umukiza has witnessed improvements in the standard of living of coffee farmers, but poverty is still ubiquitous in Rwanda. These improvements are not happening fast enough. Minister Umukiza is reminded of the 1994 genocide, which claimed the lives of one million Rwandans. He knows deep inside that increased prosperity for the average citizen would have prevented such a tragedy and is also the key to maintaining a peaceful country. He, therefore, wants to see economic growth and prosperity happen in his lifetime. The future of his children depends on such prosperity, and the time for that change is now.

Minister Umukiza has the right sense of tension, moral purpose, and leadership. But how does he do on receptivity and insight, the other two preconditions for change?

Receptivity is the willingness to listen to new ideas and embrace change. Receptivity has several dimensions including personal experience, culture, and/or education. Courage or audacity is an often-ignored dimension, which encapsulates the willingness to challenge the status quo. Most accomplished leaders know that audacity is the hallmark of leadership, but it can become a pitfall for leaders when they cling to their opinions. When Minister Umukiza voiced his plans at an informal gathering with some of Rwanda's U.S. coffee customers, their feedback was lost on the minister.

Insight refers to the knowledge required to make informed strategic choices. Developing the right insights requires a careful balance between vision and economic reality. Indeed, an essential part of developing insight is having the discipline to frame choices within three domains: strategy, assets, and operations. Strategic insights inform the choice of an attractive industry and customer segment. Operational insights address the practicality of delivering the chosen product in a profitable way. Last, but not least, insights identify the assets required to succeed.

Creating prosperity and increasing competitiveness require that leaders make the right choices. Choices based on insights make markets work for developing countries. While it is true that leaders' capacities to develop insight may improve gradually with practice, it never becomes an effortless process. The proper development of insights clearly is a complex process, requiring continual adjustment.

Insight and knowledge of the coffee industry were the most important missing pieces in the minister's flawed argument. Entering the instant-coffee market, despite being a finished product, would be a step backward for Rwanda. I had to help him frame the prospects of the coffee industry in a way that clarified the choices he needed to make.

I began by trying to understand the Mental Models he was operating

under. In my experience, decision makers can have outdated beliefs about
how their industries work, some of which often date back to colonial
times. Many of these beliefs started originally as good ideas but lose value
through generalization. They become particularly dangerous when they
gain popularity in leaders' circles or in development conferences.

Value addition has, unfortunately, become one such fad. The thinking goes that many Asian countries developed because they were able to
manufacture and export finished goods. Therefore, manufacturing finished goods in developing countries is the key to creating prosperity.
Unfortunately, value addition is not a strategy; it does not indicate which
product to develop for which customers. In fact, value addition comes
from the ability to develop the product with the right characteristics. Fully
washed Arabica coffee or "engineered" roses are examples of such sophisticated products.

The first step toward true insight is to uncover these hidden belief systems. It requires setting aside personal prejudices, so as to understand the
market accurately and be willing to learn from the experiences of other
countries. It also requires an openess to test hypotheses with customers,
producers, and other relevant industry players. Unfortunately, the energy
to develop data-driven insight is often lacking.

The second issue I needed to drive home is the need to choose your customers in attractive segments to really grow the industry. Industry players
must target specific customers since they simply cannot serve everyone.
This choice may be excruciatingly painful, but it must be made. Indeed, if
one country can satisfy the needs of certain select customer segments, then
this country has accomplished more than most will ever accomplish.

There are no inherently good or bad customer segments. But different
groups have different levels of suitability. Commercial low-grade Arabica
and Robusta dominate the world coffee (with 49 percent and 33 percent
of volume, respectively). Yet both segments are dominated by vertically
integrated multinationals such as Nestlé and would be a poor choice for a
country such as Rwanda.

Instead, Rwanda's coffee industry decided to focus on the highly profitable high-quality Arabica segment. This segment (currently 7 percent of the
world market volume) is growing at over 15 percent per annum. Customers

cherish the product, leading importers to pay more than double the price of ordinary Rwandan Arabica coffee. In addition, Rwanda achieved highly encouraging coffee-tasting results from two major American specialty-coffee roasters. Rwanda has the ideal combination of high altitude, ideal rainfall, and geographical location to grow a high-quality Arabica coffee. Last but not least, most quality coffee importers/roasters are highly interested in testing Rwanda's quality coffee. This analysis confirmed a significant market opportunity.

The Rwandan industry had found an attractive customer segment that was willing to purchase a high-quality bean. The decision as to what coffee to produce had confronted the industry, and it had made an informed choice that was paying dividends already. The industry considered three options in attempting to maximize the value of its high-quality Arabica: fully washed Arabica, roasted Arabica, and freeze-dried instant Arabica. Fully washed coffee emerged as the most economically attractive option because it commands a margin of ninety-one cents per kilo. Besides providing many jobs, this option is cost-effective because of the limited investments required. Roasting offers the first opportunity to create a consumable coffee. Toll roasting commands a smaller margin of seventy-six cents per kilo but might suggest an interesting economic opportunity for the future. The profitability analysis ruled out instant coffee, which has a negative margin of $2.20 per kilo because of high power and logistics costs. Basically, Rwandese investors would lose money for every kilo exported of instant coffee. The choice to go for fully washed, high-quality Arabica made economic and social sense for the country, and the market analysis proved it. We had gone through the insight-gathering process, and investments were under way in terms of infrastructure and knowledge building for Rwanda to execute its coffee strategy. I needed to show the minister that this endogenous process should speak louder than a one-line development epithet around "value addition."

Six weeks after our initial conversation, I have set up a meeting with Minister Umukiza to discuss the choice Rwanda is facing on how to maximize the value of its high-quality Arabica exports. My initial surprise has turned into resolve. I am clear that Rwanda needs to focus on fully washed Arabica. I trust that our insights from this data-driven process will help the minister find his way to an informed decision, a decision that will ensure Gisenyi does not suffer the fate of Agnibilikero.

As I prepare for my meeting with the minister, I know deep inside that being able to structure the discussion with empathy and clarity will influence my ability to be effective. Minister Umukiza is a tremendous leader who has a vision imbued with a moral purpose for his country and a desire to act. He made the hard choice to be a leader in a tumultuous time. Spending time with him has enabled me to look a leader in the eye and inform him that great strategy is, sometimes, deciding what not to do.

Epilogue

• • •

D R. RICK WARREN wrote in *The Purpose Driven Life* that there are concrete steps to finding one's life's purpose: consider your dreams, set some goals, figure out what you are good at, clarify your values, aim high, go for it, be disciplined, involve others, and never give up.

We can say that the contributors to this volume have lived up to this challenge. These writers are either OTF advisors to nations, past or present, or leaders of nations whom we have served. They have worked in scores of nations and, in this volume, have presented insights and experiences from around thirty of them.

We asked all the contributors to give us their experience working in the world's poorest countries and tell us about working on enterprise solutions to poverty. We believe that each contributor, in his or her own way, is an integrator: someone who is generative with the concepts of globalization, who attempted to be deeply introspective; to cope with ambiguity as the writer searched for his or her own vision within it; and to integrate between such domains as politics, commerce, science, and the arts. After all, our challenge is not to just *experience* globalization, everything mixing with everything else, but to accelerate those specific determinants that are in the service of humankind.

Please help us to accelerate our learning with your impressions or by correcting errors you might have discovered and filling in the gaps in our understanding with citations, ideas, and the experiences of others. As we wrote, we can hardly preach the merits of change in the world's poorest countries and not be willing to change ourselves.

Ideas@otfgroup.com

Eric Kacou

Ken Hynes

Managing Directors

List of Contributors

· · ·

Aref Adamali has worked on competitiveness projects in Rwanda, the Caribbean, and Afghanistan. Aref worked in the World Bank's Global ICT Department. He holds a degree in economic and political development from Columbia. He is a citizen of Kenya.

Michael Brennan is an advisor to SEVEN and has led projects in Afghanistan, Eastern Europe, the Caribbean, and Africa. He was a teacher in Africa and a Peace Corps business advisor in Bulgaria. He holds an MBA from the University of Rochester's William Simon School and has led projects at Fidelity, J. P. Morgan and Morgan Stanley.

Sally Christie is a manager in the OTF Group's Caribbean Region, where she currently leads the firm's work in Trinidad and Tobago. She has previously worked in Africa, Asia, and Latin America. She was educated at Wharton School of the University of Pennsylvania and McGill University and is a citizen of Canada.

Marcela Escobari-Rose is executive director of Harvard's Center for International Development. She led the Americas region at OTF Group where she advised heads of state and private sector leaders on export competitiveness, and led investment-banking engagements with J. P. Morgan. Marcela is a graduate of Swarthmore College and the Harvard Kennedy School. She is a citizen of Bolivia.

Diego Garcia Etcheto has advised clients on competitiveness around the world, including leading work with the marble cluster in Afghanistan. He was a U.S. marine in East Timor and holds degrees from Cornell University and the Wharton School of the University of Pennsylvania. He is a citizen of the United States and Venezuela.

Michael Fairbanks is a cofounder of SEVEN and the OTF Group. He was a U.S. Peace Corps teacher in Kenya, and coauthored Harvard Business School's landmark book on business strategy in emerging markets, *Plowing the Sea, Nurturing the Hidden Sources of Growth in Developing Nations*. He has worked closely with the presidents and prime ministers of twenty nations. He is a citizen of the United States, Ireland, and Rwanda.

Malik Fal leads Microsoft's Business Marketing and Operations Group covering forty-nine African countries. He was OTF Group Vice President, Africa region. He is a graduate of the Harvard Kennedy School and is a citizen of France and Senegal.

Ashraf Ghani is chairman of the Institute of State Effectiveness, and former finance minister of the Islamic Republic of Afghanistan. He was an architect of the world's first constitution that integrates Islamic principles with democracy and women's rights.

Robert Henning has lived and advised clients in Rwanda, Afghanistan, and the Caribbean. He was a Peace Corps volunteer in Africa and holds an MBA from Georgetown University.

Elizabeth Hooper is executive director of SEVEN. She is completing her ALM in Anthropology at Harvard. She also writes fiction.

Kenneth Hynes is a managing director of the OTF Group. He leads the firm's work throughout Latin America and the Caribbean. He is a graduate of the Fletcher School at Tufts University and is a citizen of Canada.

Donald Kaberuka is president of the African Development Bank. He was minister of finance of Rwanda for seven years after the genocide and is recognized as an instrumental figure in rebuilding the nation.

Eric Kacou is a managing director of the OTF Group. He leads the firm's work in Africa, including the Rwanda National Innovation and Competitiveness Program and the Pioneers of Prosperity Africa Prize. He has advised leaders throughout Africa and worked in a range of industries. He holds an MBA from the Wharton School of the University of Pennsylvania and is a citizen of Côte d'Ivoire.

H. E. President Paul Kagame is president of the Republic of Rwanda. He was a major general in the Rwanda Defense Forces and led the revolution that ended the genocide. He created a new constitution that favored proportionate representation of ethnic groups and women, created a democracy, and is considered one of the most progressive leaders in Africa.

Kwang W. Kim has worked on promoting cluster competitiveness throughout Latin America and the Caribbean. He was previously with the OTF Group and the World Bank. He is a citizen of Korea and Brazil.

Luis Alberto Moreno is president of the Inter-American Development Bank. He was minister of development of Colombia during the opening of its economy and the ambassador to the United States who helped design and implement Plan Colombia.

Anne Morriss has more than a decade of experience in grassroots development. She has lived and worked extensively in Brazil, Ecuador, Mexico, and the Dominican Republic and is now working on a book about transformative leadership. She holds an MBA from the Harvard Business School.

David Rabkin is a vice president at American Express and was a cofounder of the OTF Group. David has also worked at Price Waterhouse and Procter & Gamble and holds an MBA from the Harvard Business School. He has worked in over a dozen nations, including the Palestinian Authority and Jamaica, where he was a well-known business columnist.

Dr. Rick Warren leads the twenty-eight-thousand-member Saddleback Church and is author of the global best seller *The Purpose Driven Life*. He is widely regarded as one of the world's most influential religious leaders.

Andreas Widmer has helped build start-up companies with cumulative exits valued at over $730 million. He has brought more than one hundred technology products to market in the United States, Europe, Asia, Africa, and Latin America. He cofounded SEVEN, is a citizen of Switzerland and the United States, and was a member of the Swiss Guard protecting Pope John Paul II.

Index

...